PLUM'S PEACHES

Other anthologies by the same author:

TALES FROM THE DRONE'S CLUB
WODEHOUSE ON CRIME

Note on Chronicity

Readers who Notice Things will in the course of reading this book Notice that in one story Prohibition is in effect; in another, the President is Harry Truman; in another, **silent** motion pictures are a comparatively recent phenomenon; and another predates the use of "SOS" as a distress signal, employing instead the **Titanic**-era "CQD." This is not an indication that Mr. Wodehouse had less of a grasp on what happened than most of us, but the inevitable upshot of writing and being published over a period of seventy-five years. If some reference baffles you, check the copyright date on the title page overleaf, and all will probably become clear.

PLUM'S PEACHES

P.G. WODEHOUSE

EDITED AND WITH A PREFACE BY D. R. BENSEN

INTERNATIONAL POLYGONICS, LTD.
NEW YORK CITY

PLUM'S PEACHES

Library of Congress Cataloging-in-Publication Data

Wodehouse, P. G. (Pelham Grenville), 1881-1975.
  Plum's peaches / p. g. Wodehouse
     p. cm.
  ISBN 1-55882-100-7 : $21.95
  1. Women-Fiction. I. Title.
PR6045.053A6   1991b
823'.912—dc20   91-57931 CIP
Library of Congress Card Catalog No. 91-57931
ISBN 1-55882-100-7

Printed and manufactured in the United States of America.
First IPL printing August 1991
10 9 8 7 6 5 4 3 2 1

The Stories (and the Peaches)

Preface: Bring on the Girls*

The cast of characters that appears on the mind's stage when P. G. Wodehouse is thought of is almost exclusively male: Bertie and Jeeves, Lord Emsworth, Uncle Fred, all the industriously idle members of the Drones Club. An anthropophagous aunt or so may foam and snap in the background, but the lads—of whatever chronological age, they all seem to have been halted in mental growth somewhere between twelve and eighteen—are the featured players. When we examine them, though, we find that far more often than not, they are motivated by one force.

Women.

It was said of Freddie Widgeon in a story not included here that if all the girls he had fallen in love with were laid end to end they would reach from Piccadilly Circus to Hyde Park Corner—further, in the opinion of one Drone, as some of them were pretty tall. Freddie Widgeon is the very type of a Wodehouse leading man (or juvenile), with a heart too easily made glad: Bertie Wooster's life is a succession of pursuits of and escapes from women; the golfing stalwarts are as susceptible as operatic tenors; the hot blood of the multitalented Mulliners seethes with ardor; even the imperturbable Jeeves allows himself at least one romantic perturbation. One could say *cherchez la femme* about most Wodehouse stories, except that there's no need to—*la femme* is vividly on stage, giving an award-worthy supporting performance.

*Yes, this title has been used already, for Wodehouse and Guy Bolton's joint recollections of their life in the musical theater. That's why we couldn't call the book that, but it is okay to use it as the title for something else, like a preface. If you called a book *Gone with the Wind*, you would be in a lot of trouble, but nobody would mind if you called your cat that—except the cat.

This collection honors some of the outstanding ladies in Pelham G. ("Plum") Wodehouses' work—the peaches (and a lemon or so) in the garden of love his male characters attempt to cultivate. There is the incomparable Bobbie Wickham, a strong contender for the *belle dame sans merci* prize for the most disastrous girl to get next to; mighty-thewed Agnes Flack, to love whom is to court a broken nose; patrician Aurelia Cammarleigh and her curious tastes in entertainment; cinematerror Minna Nordstrom, who knew when to play hardball; opulent Maudie WIlberforce, gladdener of many evenings at the old Criterion; Sally Preston, whose hobby was getting engaged; and others you may as well wait to meet until you actually buy (or borrow) this book.

We have concentrated, as Wodehouse preferred to, on the young and livelier ladies who people his work. The *gandes dames* such as Lady Constance Keeble are a bit daunting for the light-hearted collection that this aims to be, and they are restricted here to walk-ons or noises off. We do regret, though, the absence of the grandest, at least in bluk, of all Wodehouse's *dames*, the great black Berkshire sow, Empress of Blandings. The Empress has a quiet dignity and disinclination to mix into other people's business that other Wodehouse females, of whatever age or state, would do well to emulate, except that there would go most of the plot complications. She appears in only one short story we know of, and that was used in another recent collection. However, it won't do to have her totally absent from a book on Wodehouse's *femmes vitales*, so she has been given a place on the cover—seen but not read, as it were—lending a touch of majesty much in the manner of a Royal Personage opening a fete and then trotting off, leaving the rest of the participants to get on with it.

The stories are organized thematically, as it was that or

drop them in at random. The first section deals with the perils faced for (or in) love, from a dragonlike aunt to an actual dragon; the second with the problem of overabundance, what happens when boy gets girl and girl gets boys. Relationships between the sexes may be customarily mediated by the affections, but as the third section show, blackmail, conscious or not, can be highly effective. The traditional role of Woman as inspiration and conservator of male talent receives just about the due the concept is worth in the cases of George Mackintosh and Archibald Mulliner presented in the fourth section; another tradition, that of Man as pursuer and Woman as pursued, is drastically reversed in the next, with Man showing excellent form in vanishing over the horizon when faced with the love of a good woman; and the final pair of stories celebrates the embodiment of the Eternal Feminine in even the youngest members of the stronger sex.

Wodehouse himself knew some of the outstanding women of the century—musical stage stars of the twenties, movie queens, and above all his wife Ethel, widely acknowledged as both charming and formidable, often both at once—and appears to have regarded them with a combination of mild alarm and appreciative respect. That seems as well an appropriate attitude to take toward this monstrously entertaining regiment of women he created.

D. R. Bensen
Croton-on-Hudson
June 1991

Dragons and Other Perils

Showing, among other things, that dangers can be relative, and vice versa.

The Indian Summer of an Uncle

Ask anyone at the Drones', and they will tell you that Bertram Wooster is a fellow whom it is dashed difficult to deceive. Old Lynx-Eye is about what it amounts to. I observe and deduce. I weigh the evidence and draw my conclusions. And that is why Uncle George had not been in my midst more than about two minutes before I, so to speak, saw all. To my trained eye the thing stuck out a mile.

And yet it seemed so dashed absurd. Consider the facts, if you know what I mean.

I mean to say, for years, right back to the time when I first went to Eton, this bulging relative had been one of the recognized eyesores of London. He was fat then, and day by day in every way has been getting fatter ever since, till now tailors measure him just for the sake of the exercise. He is what they call a prominent London clubman—one of those birds in tight morning coats and gray toppers whom you see toddling along St. James's Street on fine afternoons, puffing a bit as they make the grade. Slip a ferret into any good club between Piccadilly and Pall Mall, and you would start half a dozen Uncle Georges.

He spends his time lunching and dining at the Buffers' and, between meals, sucking down spots in the smoking room and talking about the lining of his stomach to anyone who will listen. About twice a year his liver lodges a formal protest and he goes off to Harrogate or Carlsbad to get planed down. Then back again and on with the programme. The last bloke in the world, in short, who you would think would ever fall a victim to the divine pash. And yet, if you will believe me, that was absolutely the strength of it.

This old pestilence blew in on me one morning at about the hour of the after-breakfast cigarette.

"Oh, Bertie," he said.

"Hullo?"

"You know those ties you've been wearing. Where did you get them?"

"Blucher's, in the Burlington Arcade."

"Thanks."

He walked across to the mirror and stood in front of it, gazing at himself in an earnest manner.

"Smut on your nose?" I asked courteously.

Then I suddenly perceived that he was wearing a sort of horrible simper, and I confess it chilled the blood to no little extent. Uncle George, with face in repose, is hard enough on the eye. Simpering, he goes right above the odds.

"Ha!" he said.

He heaved a long sigh, and turned away. Not too soon, for the mirror was on the point of cracking.

"I'm not so old," he said, in a musing sort of voice.

"So old as what?"

"Properly considered, I'm in my prime. Besides, what a young and inexperienced girl needs is a man of weight and years to lean on. The sturdy oak, not the sapling."

It was at this point that, as I said above, I saw all.

"Great Scott, Uncle George!" I said. "You aren't thinking of getting married?"

"Who isn't?" he said.

"You aren't," I said.

"Yes, I am. Why not?"

"Oh, well . . ."

"Marriage is an honourable state."

"Oh, absolutely."

"It might make you a better man, Bertie."

"Who says so?"

"I say so. Marriage might turn you from a frivolous young scallywag into—er—a non-scallywag. Yes, confound you, I *am* thinking of getting married, and if Agatha comes sticking her oar in I'll—I'll—well, I shall know what to do about it."

He exited on the big line, and I rang the bell for Jeeves. The situation seemed to me one that called for a cozy talk.

"Jeeves," I said.

"Sir?"

"You know my uncle George?"

"Yes, sir. His lordship has been familiar to me for some years."

"I don't mean do you know my uncle George. I mean do you know what my uncle George is thinking of doing?"

"Contracting a matrimonial alliance, sir."

"Good Lord! Did he tell you?"

"No, sir. Oddly enough, I chance to be acquainted with the other party in the matter."

"The girl?"

"The young person, yes, sir. It was from her aunt, with whom she resides, that I received the information that his lordship was contemplating matrimony."

"Who is she?"

"A Miss Platt, sir. Miss Rhoda Platt. Of Wistaria Lodge, Kitchener Road, East Dulwich."

"Young?"

"Yes, sir."

"The old fathead!"

"Yes, sir. The expression is one which I would, of course, not have ventured to employ myself, but I confess to thinking his lordship somewhat ill advised. One must remem-

ber, however, that it is not unusual to find gentlemen of
a certain age yielding to what might be described as a
'sentimental urge.' They appear to experience what I may
term a sort of 'Indian summer,' a kind of temporarily
renewed youth. The phenomenon is particularly noticeable, I am given to understand, in the United States of
America among the wealthier inhabitants of the city of Pitts-
burgh. It is notorious, I am told, that sooner or later, unless restrained, they always endeavour to marry chorus girls.
Why this should be so, I am at a loss to say, but . . ."

I saw that this was going to take some time. I tuned out.

"From something in Uncle George's manner, Jeeves, as
he referred to my aunt Agatha's probable reception of the
news, I gather that this Miss Platt is not of the *noblesse*."

"No, sir. She is a waitress at his lordship's club."

"My God! The proletariat!"

"The lower middle classes, sir."

"Well, yes, by stretching it a bit, perhaps. Still, you know
what I mean."

"Yes, sir."

"Rummy thing, Jeeves," I said thoughtfully, "this modern
tendency to marry waitresses. If you remember, before he
settled down young Bingo Little was repeatedly trying to
do it."

"Yes, sir."

"Odd!"

"Yes, sir."

"Still, there it is, of course. The point to be considered
now is, What will Aunt Agatha do about this? You know
her, Jeeves. She is not like me. I'm broadminded. If Uncle
George wants to marry waitresses, let him, say I. I hold
that the rank is but the penny stamp—"

"Guinea stamp, sir."

"All right, guinea stamp. Though I don't believe there is such a thing. I shouldn't have thought they came higher than five bob. Well, as I was saying, I maintain that the rank is but the guinea stamp and a girl's a girl for all that."

"'For *a'* that,' sir. The poet Burns wrote in the North British dialect."

"Well, 'a' that,' then, if you prefer it."

"I have no preference in the matter, sir. It is simply that the poet Burns—"

"Never mind about the poet Burns."

"No, sir."

"Forget the poet Burns."

"Very good, sir."

"Expunge the poet Burns from your mind."

"I will do so immediately, sir."

"What we have to consider is not the poet Burns but the aunt Agatha. She will kick, Jeeves."

"Very probably, sir."

"And, what's worse, she will lug me into the mess. There is only one thing to be done. Pack the toothbrush and let us escape while we may, leaving no address."

"Very good, sir."

At this moment the bell rang.

"Ha!" I said. "Someone at the door."

"Yes, sir."

"Probably Uncle George back again. I'll answer it. You go and get ahead with the packing."

"Very good, sir."

I sauntered along the passage, whistling carelessly, and there on the mat was Aunt Agatha. Herself. Not a picture.

A nasty jar.

"Oh, hullo!" I said, it seeming but little good to tell her I was out of town and not expected back for some weeks.

"I wish to speak to you, Bertie," said the Family Curse.
"I am greatly upset."

She legged it into the sitting room and volplaned into a
chair. I followed, thinking wistfully of Jeeves packing in
the bedroom. That suitcase would not be needed now. I
knew what she must have come about.

"I've just seen Uncle George," I said, giving her a lead.

"So have I," said Aunt Agatha, shivering in a marked
manner. "He called on me while I was still in bed to inform
me of his intention of marrying some impossible girl from
South Norwood."

"East Dulwich, the cognoscenti inform me."

"Well, East Dulwich, then. It is the same thing. But who
told you?"

"Jeeves."

"And how, pray, does Jeeves come to know all about it?"

"There are very few things in this world, Aunt Agatha,"
I said gravely, "that Jeeves doesn't know all about. He's met
the girl."

"Who is she?"

"One of the waitresses at the Buffers."

I had expected this to register, and it did. The relative
let out a screech rather like the Cornish Express going
through a junction.

"I take it from your manner, Aunt Agatha," I said, "that
you want this thing stopped."

"Of course it must be stopped."

"Then there is but one policy to pursue. Let me ring for
Jeeves and ask his advice."

Aunt Agatha stiffened visibly. Very much the *grande
dame* of the old regime.

"Are you seriously suggesting that we should discuss this
intimate family matter with your manservant?"

"Absolutely. Jeeves will find the way."

"I have always known that you were an imbecile, Bertie," said the flesh and blood, now down at about three degrees Fahrenheit, "but I did suppose that you had some proper feeling, some pride, some respect for your position."

"Well, you know what the poet Burns says."

She squelched me with a glance.

"Obviously the only thing to do," she said, "is to offer this girl money."

"Money?"

"Certainly. It will not be the first time your uncle has made such a course necessary."

We sat for a bit, brooding. The family always sits brooding when the subject of Uncle George's early romance comes up. I was too young to be actually in on it at the time, but I've had the details frequently from many sources, including Uncle George. Let him get even the slightest bit pickled, and he will tell you the whole story, sometimes twice in an evening. It was a barmaid at the Criterion, just before he came into the title. Her name was Maudie and he loved her dearly, but the family would have none of it. They dug down into the sock and paid her off. Just one of those human-interest stories, if you know what I mean.

I wasn't so sold on this money-offering scheme.

"Well, just as you like, of course," I said, "but you're taking an awful chance. I mean, whenever people do it in novels and plays they always get the dickens of a welt. The girl gets the sympathy of the audience every time. She just draws herself up and looks at them with clear, steady eyes, causing them to feel not a little cheesy. If I were you, I would sit tight and let Nature take its course."

"I don't understand you."

"Well, consider for a moment what Uncle George looks

like. No Greta Garbo, believe me. I should simply let the
girl go on looking at him. Take it from me, Aunt Agatha,
I've studied human nature and I don't believe there's a female in the world who could see Uncle George fairly often
in those waistcoats he wears without feeling that it was due
to her better self to give him the gate. Besides, this girl sees
him at meal times, and Uncle George with his head down
among the foodstuffs is a spectacle which—"

"If it is not troubling you too much, Bertie, I should be
greatly obliged if you would stop drivelling."

"Just as you say. All the same, I think you're going to
find it dashed embarrassing, offering this girl money."

"I am not proposing to do so. *You* will undertake the
negotiations."

"Me?"

"Certainly. I should think a hundred pounds would be
ample. But I will give you a blank check, and you are at
liberty to fill it in for a higher sum if it becomes necessary.
The essential point is that, cost what it may, your uncle
must be released from this entanglement."

"So you're going to shove this off on me?"

"It is quite time you did something for the family."

"And when she draws herself up and looks at me with
clear, steady eyes, what do I do for an encore?"

"There is no need to discuss the matter any further. You
can get down to East Dulwich in half an hour. There is a
frequent service of trains. I will remain here to await your
report."

"But, listen!"

"Bertie, you will go and see this woman immediately."

"Yes, but dash it!"

"Bertie!"

I threw in the towel.

"Oh, right ho, if you say so."

"I do say so."

"Oh well, in that case, right ho."

I don't know if you have ever tooled off to East Dulwich to offer a strange female a hundred smackers to release your Uncle George. In case you haven't, I may tell you that there are plenty of things that are lots better fun. I didn't feel any too good driving to the station. I didn't feel any too good in the train. And I didn't feel any too good as I walked to Kitchener Road. But the moment when I felt least good was when I had actually pressed the front doorbell and a rather grubby-looking maid had let me in and shown me down a passage and into a room with pink paper on the walls, a piano in the corner, and a lot of photographs on the mantelpiece.

Barring a dentist's waiting room, which it rather resembles, there isn't anything that quells the spirit much more than one of these suburban parlours. They are extremely apt to have stuffed birds in glass cases standing about on small tables, and if there is one thing which gives the man of sensibility that sinking feeling it is the cold, accusing eye of a ptarmigan, or whatever it may be that has had its interior organs removed and sawdust substituted.

There were three of these cases in the parlour of Wistaria Lodge, so that, wherever you looked, you were sure to connect. Two were singletons, the third a family group, consisting of a father bullfinch, a mother bullfinch, and little Master Bullfinch, the last named of whom wore an expression that was definitely that of a thug and did more to damp my *joie de vivre* than all the rest of them put together.

I had moved to the window and was examining the aspidistra in order to avoid this creature's gaze, when I heard

the door open and, turning, found myself confronted by
something which, since it could hardly be the girl, I took
to be the aunt.

"Oh, good-morning," I said.

The words came out rather roopily, for I was feeling a
bit on the stunned side. I mean to say, the room being so
small and this exhibit so large, I had got that feeling of wanting air. There are some people who don't seem to be intended to be seen close to, and this aunt was one of them.
Billowy curves, if you know what I mean. I should think
that in her day she must have been a very handsome girl,
though even then on the substantial side. By the time she
came into my life she had taken on a good deal of excess
weight. She looked like a photograph of an opera singer
of the 'eighties. Also the orange hair and the magenta dress.

However, she was a friendly soul. She seemed glad to
see Bertram. She smiled broadly.

"So here you are at last!" she said.

I couldn't make anything of this.

"Eh?"

"But I don't think you had better see my niece just yet.
She's just having a nap."

"Oh, in that case . . ."

"Seems a pity to wake her, doesn't it?"

"Oh, absolutely," I said, relieved.

"When you get the influenza you don't sleep at night, and
then if you doze off in the morning, well, it seems a pity
to wake someone, doesn't it?"

"Miss Platt has influenza?"

"That's what we think it is. But, of course, you'll be able
to say. But we needn't waste time. Since you're here, you
can be taking a look at my knee."

"Your knee?"

I am all for knees at their proper time and, as you might say, in their proper place, but somehow this didn't seem the moment. However, she carried on according to plan.

"What do you think of that knee?" she asked, lifting the seven veils.

Well, of course, one has to be polite.

"Terrific!" I said.

"You wouldn't believe how it hurts me sometimes."

"Really?"

"A sort of shooting pain. It just comes and goes. And I'll tell you a funny thing."

"What's that?" I said, feeling I could do with a good laugh.

"Lately I've been having the same pain just here, at the end of the spine."

"You don't mean it!"

"I do. Like red-hot needles. I wish you'd have a look at it."

"At your spine?"

"Yes."

I shook my head. Nobody is fonder of a bit of fun than myself, and I am all for Bohemian camaraderie and making a party go, and all that. But there is a line, and we Woosters know when to draw it.

"It can't be done," I said austerely. "Not spines. Knees, yes. Spines, no," I said.

She seemed surprised.

"Well," she said, "you're a funny sort of doctor, I must say."

I'm pretty quick, as I said before, and I began to see that something in the nature of a misunderstanding must have arisen.

"Doctor?"

"Well, you call yourself a doctor, don't you?"

"Did you think I was a doctor?"

"Aren't you a doctor?"

"No. Not a doctor."

We had got it straightened out. The scales had fallen from our eyes. We knew where we were.

I had suspected that she was a genial soul. She now endorsed this view. I don't think I have ever heard a woman laugh so heartily.

"Well, that's the best thing!" she said, borrowing my handkerchief to wipe her eyes. "Did you ever! But if you aren't the doctor, who are you?"

"Wooster's the name. I came to see Miss Platt."

"What about?"

This was the moment, of course, when I should have come out with the check and sprung the big effort. But somehow I couldn't make it. You know how it is. Offering people money to release your uncle is a scaly enough job at best, and when the atmosphere's not right the shot simply isn't on the board.

"Oh, just came to see her, you know." I had rather a bright idea. "My uncle heard she was seedy, don't you know, and asked me to look in and make inquiries," I said.

"Your uncle?"

"Lord Yaxley."

"Oh! So you are Lord Yaxley's nephew?"

"That's right. I suppose he's always popping in and out here, what?"

"No. I've never met him."

"You haven't?"

"No. Rhoda talks a lot about him, of course, but for some reason she's never so much as asked him to look in for a cup of tea."

I began to see that this Rhoda knew her business. If I'd been a girl with someone wanting to marry me and knew that there was an exhibit like this aunt hanging around the home, I, too, should have thought twice about inviting him to call until the ceremony was over and he had actually signed on the dotted line. I mean to say, a thoroughly good soul—heart of gold beyond a doubt—but not the sort of thing you wanted to spring on Romeo before the time was ripe.

"I suppose you were all very surprised when you heard about it?" she said.

" 'Surprised' is right."

"Of course, nothing is definitely settled yet."

"You don't mean that? I thought . . ."

"Oh, no. She's thinking it over."

"I see."

"Of course, she feels it's a great compliment. But then sometimes she wonders if he isn't too old."

"My aunt Agatha has rather the same idea."

"Of course, a title *is* a title."

"Yes, there's that. What do you think about it yourself?"

"Oh, it doesn't matter what I think. There's no doing anything with girls these days, is there?"

"Not much."

"What I often say is, I wonder what girls are coming to. Still, there it is."

"Absolutely."

There didn't seem much reason why the conversation shouldn't go on for ever. She had the air of a woman who has settled down for the day. But at this point the maid came in and said the doctor had arrived.

I got up.

"I'll be tooling off, then."

"If you must."

"I think I'd better."

"Well, pip pip."

"Toodle-oo," I said, and out into the fresh air.

Knowing what was waiting for me at home, I would have preferred to go to the club and spend the rest of the day there. But the thing had to be faced.

"Well?" said Aunt Agatha, as I trickled into the sitting room.

"Well, yes and no," I replied

"What do you mean? Did she refuse the money?"

"Not exactly."

"She accepted it?"

"Well, there, again, not precisely."

I explained what had happened. I wasn't expecting her to be any too frightfully pleased, and it's as well that I wasn't, because she wasn't. In fact, as the story unfolded, her comments became fruitier and fruitier, and when I had finished she uttered an exclamation that nearly broke a window. It sounded something like "Gor!"—as if she had started to say "Gor-blimey!" and had remembered her ancient lineage just in time.

"I'm sorry," I said. "And can a man say more? I lost my nerve. The old morale suddenly turned blue on me. It's the sort of thing that might have happened to anyone."

"I never heard of anything so spineless in my life."

I shivered, like a warrior whose old wound hurts him.

"I'd be most awfully obliged, Aunt Agatha," I said, "if you would not use that word 'spine.' It awakens memories."

The door opened. Jeeves appeared.

"Sir?"

"Yes, Jeeves?"

"I thought you called, sir."

"No, Jeeves."

"Very good, sir."

There are moments when, even under the eye of Aunt Agatha, I can take the firm line. And now, seeing Jeeves standing there with the light of intelligence simply fizzing in every feature, I suddenly felt how perfectly footling it was to give this preeminent source of balm and comfort the go-by simply because Aunt Agatha had prejudices against discussing family affairs with the staff. It might make her say "Gor!" again, but I decided to do as we ought to have done right from the start—put the case in his hands.

"Jeeves," I said, "this matter of Uncle George."

"Yes, sir."

"You know the circs."

"Yes, sir."

"You know what we want."

"Yes, sir."

"Then advise us. And make it snappy. Think on your feet."

I heard Aunt Agatha rumble like a volcano just before it starts to set about the neighbours, but I did not wilt. I had seen the sparkle in Jeeves's eye which indicated that an idea was on the way.

"I understand that you have been visiting the young person's home, sir?"

"Just got back."

"Then you no doubt encountered the young person's aunt?"

"Jeeves, I encountered nothing else but."

"Then the suggestion which I am about to make will, I feel sure, appeal to you, sir. I would recommend that you confronted his lordship with this woman. It has always been her intention to continue residing with her niece after the latter's marriage. Should he meet her, this reflection might give his lordship pause. As you are aware, sir, she is a kind-hearted woman, but definitely of the people."

"Jeeves, you are right! Apart from anything else, that orange hair!"

"Exactly, sir."

"Not to mention the magenta dress."

"Precisely, sir."

"I'll ask her to lunch tomorrow, to meet him. You see," I said to Aunt Agatha, who was still fermenting in the background, "a ripe suggestion first crack out of the box. Did I or did I not tell you—"

"That will do, Jeeves," said Aunt Agatha.

"Very good, madam."

For some minutes after he had gone Aunt Agatha strayed from the point a bit, confining her remarks to what she thought of a Wooster who could lower the prestige of the clan by allowing menials to get above themselves. Then she returned to what you might call the "main issue."

"Bertie," she said, "you will go and see this girl again tomorrow, and this time you will do as I told you."

"But, dash it! With this excellent alternative scheme, based firmly on the psychology of the individual—"

"That is quite enough, Bertie. You heard what I said. I am going. Good-bye."

She buzzed off, little knowing of what stuff Bertram Wooster was made. The door had hardly closed before I was shouting for Jeeves.

"Jeeves," I said, "the recent aunt will have none of your excellent alternative scheme, but none the less I propose to go through with it unswervingly. I consider it a ball of fire. Can you get hold of this female and bring her here for lunch tomorrow?"

"Yes, sir."

"Good. Meanwhile, I will be phoning Uncle George. We

will do Aunt Agatha good despite herself. What is it the poet says, Jeeves?"

"The poet Burns, sir?"

"Not the poet Burns. Some other poet. About doing good by stealth."

"These little acts of unremembered kindness, sir?"

"That's it in a nutshell, Jeeves."

I suppose "doing good by stealth" ought to give one a glow, but I can't say I found myself exactly looking forward to the binge in prospect. Uncle George by himself is a mouldy enough luncheon companion, being extremely apt to collar the conversation and confine it to a description of his symptoms, he being one of those birds who can never be brought to believe that the general public isn't agog to hear about the lining of his stomach. Add the aunt, and you have a little gathering which might well dismay the stoutest. The moment I woke I felt conscious of some impending doom, and the cloud, if you know what I mean, grew darker all the morning. By the time Jeeves came in with the cocktails I was feeling pretty low.

"For two pins, Jeeves," I said, "I would turn the whole thing up and leg it to the Drones'."

"I can readily imagine that this will prove something of an ordeal, sir."

"How did you get to know these people, Jeeves?"

"It was through a young fellow of my acquaintance, sir, Colonel Mainwaring-Smith's personal gentleman's gentleman. He and the young person had an understanding at the time, and he desired me to accompany him to Wistaria Lodge and meet her."

"They were engaged?"

"Not precisely engaged, sir. An understanding."

"What did they quarrel about?"

"They did not quarrel, sir. When his lordship began to pay his addresses the young person, naturally flattered, began to waver between love and ambition. But even now she has not formally rescinded the understanding."

"Then, if your scheme works and Uncle George edges out, it will do your pal a bit of good?"

"Yes, sir, Smethurst—his name is Smethurst—would consider it a consummation devoutly to be wished."

An unseen hand without tootled on the bell, and I braced myself to play the host. The binge was on.

"Mrs. Wilberforce, sir," announced Jeeves.

"And how I'm to keep a straight face with you standing behind my chair and saying 'Madam, can I tempt you with a potato?' is more than I know," said the aunt, sailing in, looking larger and pinker and matier than ever. "I know him, you know," she said, jerking a thumb after Jeeves. "He's been round and taken tea with us."

"So he told me."

She gave the sitting room the once-over.

"You've got a nice place here," she said, "though I like more pink about. It's so cheerful. What's that you've got there? Cocktails?"

"Martini with a spot of absinthe," I said, beginning to pour.

She gave a girlish squeal.

"Don't you try to make me drink that stuff! Do you know what would happen if I touched one of those things? I'd be racked with pain. What they do to the lining of your stomach!"

"Oh, I don't know."

"I do. If you had been a barmaid as long as I was you'd know, too."

"Oh—er—were you a barmaid?"

"For years, when I was younger than I am. At the Criterion."

I dropped the shaker.

"There!" she said, pointing the moral. "That's through drinking that stuff. Makes your hand wobble. What I always used to say to the boys was: 'Port, if you like. Port's wholesome. I appreciate a drop of port myself. But these new-fangled messes from America, no.' But they would never listen to me."

I was eyeing her warily. Of course, there must have been thousands of barmaids at the Criterion in its time, but still it gave one a bit of a start. It was years ago that Uncle George's dash at a mesalliance had occurred—long before he came into the title—but the Wooster clan still quivered at the name of the Criterion.

"Er—when you were at the Cri.," I said, "did you ever happen to run into a fellow of my name?"

"I've forgotten what it is. I'm always silly about names."

"Wooster."

"Wooster! When you were there yesterday I thought you said 'Foster.' Wooster! Did I run into a fellow named Wooster? Well!! Why, George Wooster and me—Piggy, I used to call him—were going off to the registrar's, only his family heard of it and interfered. They offered me a lot of money to give him up, and, like a silly girl, I let them persuade me. If I've wondered once what became of him, I've wondered a thousand times. Is he a relation of yours?"

"Excuse me," I said. "I just want a word with Jeeves." I legged it for the pantry.

"Jeeves!"

"Sir?"

"Do you know what's happened?"

"No, sir."

"This female—"

"Sir?"

"She's Uncle George's barmaid!"

"Sir?"

"Oh, dash it, you must have heard of Uncle George's barmaid. You know all the family history. The barmaid he wanted to marry years ago."

"Ah, yes, sir."

"She's the only woman he ever loved. He's told me so a million times. Every time he gets to the second liqueur he always becomes maudlin about this female. What a dashed bit of bad luck! The first thing we know the call of the past will be echoing in his heart. I can feel it, Jeeves. She's just his sort. The first thing she did when she came in was to start talking about the lining of her stomach. You see the hideous significance of that, Jeeves? The lining of his stomach is Uncle George's favourite topic of conversation. It means that he and she are kindred souls. This woman and he will be like . . ."

"Deep calling to deep, sir?"

"Exactly."

"Most disturbing, sir."

"What's to be done?"

"I could not say, sir."

"I'll tell you what I'm going to do—phone him and say the lunch is off."

"Scarcely feasible, sir. I fancy that is his lordship at the door now."

And so it was. Jeeves let him in, and I followed him as he navigated down the passage to the sitting room. There was a stunned silence as he went in, and then a couple of the startled yelps you hear when old buddies get together after long separation.

"Piggy!"

"Maudie!"

"Well, I never!"

"Well, I'm dashed!"

"Did you ever!"

"Well, bless my soul!"

"Fancy you being Lord Yaxley!"

"Came into the title soon after we parted."

"Just to think!"

"You could have knocked me down with a feather!"

I hung about in the offing, now on this leg, now on that. For all the notice they took of me, I might just as well have been the late Bertram Wooster, disembodied.

"Maudie, you don't look a day older, dash it!"

"Nor do you, Piggy."

"How have you been all these years?"

"Pretty well. The lining of my stomach isn't all it should be."

"Good Gad! You don't say so? I have trouble with the lining of *my* stomach."

"It's a sort of heavy feeling after meals. What are you trying for it?"

"I've been taking Perkins' Digestine."

"My dear girl, no use! No use at all. Tried it myself for years, and got no relief. Now, if you really want something that is some good . . ."

I slid away. The last I saw of them, Uncle George was down beside her on the Chesterfield, buzzing hard.

"Jeeves," I said, tottering into the pantry.

"Sir?"

"There will only be two for lunch. Count me out. If they notice I'm not there tell them I was called away by an urgent phone message. The situation has got beyond Bertram,

Jeeves. You will find me at the Drones'."

"Very good, sir."

It was latish in the evening when one of the waiters came to me as I played a distrait game of snooker pool and informed me that Aunt Agatha was on the phone.

"Bertie!"

"Hullo?"

I was amazed to note that her voice was that of an aunt who feels that things are breaking right. It had the birdlike trill.

"Bertie, have you the check I gave you?"

"Yes."

"Then tear it up. It will not be needed."

"Eh?"

"I say it will not be needed. Your uncle has been speaking to me on the telephone. He is not going to marry that girl."

"Not?"

"No. Apparently he has been thinking it over and sees how unsuitable it would have been. But what is astonishing is that he *is* going to be married!"

"He is?"

"Yes, to an old friend of his, a Mrs. Wilberforce. A woman of sensible age, he gave me to understand. I wonder which Wilberforces that would be. There are two main branches of the family—the Essex Wilberforces and the Cumberland Wilberforces. I believe there is also a cadet branch somewhere in Shropshire."

"And one in East Dulwich," I said.

"What did you say?"

"Nothing," I said. "Nothing."

I hung up. Then back to the old flat, feeling a trifle sandbagged.

"Well, Jeeves," I said, and there was censure in the eyes. "So I gather everything is nicely settled?"

"Yes, sir. His lordship formally announced the engagement between the sweets and cheese courses, sir."

"He did, did he?"

"Yes, sir."

I eyed the man sternly.

"You do not appear to be aware of it Jeeves," I said, in a cold, level voice, "but this binge has depreciated your stock very considerably. I have always been accustomed to look upon you as a counsellor without equal. I have, so to speak, hung upon your lips. And now see what you have done. All this is the direct consequence of your scheme, based on the psychology of the individual. I should have thought, Jeeves, that, knowing the woman—meeting her socially, as you might say, over the afternoon cup of tea—you might have ascertained that she was Uncle George's barmaid."

"I did, sir."

"What!"

"I was aware of the fact, sir."

"Then you must have known what would happen if she came to lunch and met him."

"Yes, sir."

"Well, I'm dashed!"

"If I might explain, sir. The young man Smethurst, who is greatly attached to the young person, is an intimate friend of mine. He applied to me some little while back in the hope that I might be able to do something to insure that the young person followed the dictates of her heart and refrained from permitting herself to be lured by gold and the glamour of his lordship's position. There will now be no obstacle to their union."

"I see. Little acts of unremembered kindness, what?"

"Precisely, sir."

"And how about Uncle George? You've landed him pretty nicely in the cart."

"No, sir, if I may take the liberty of opposing your view. I fancy that Mrs. Wilberforce should make an ideal mate for his lordship. If there was a defect in his lordship's mode of life, it was that he was a little unduly attached to the pleasures of the table."

"Ate like a pig, you mean?"

"I would not have ventured to put it in quite that way, sir, but the expression does meet the facts of the case. He was also inclined to drink rather more than his medical adviser would have approved of. Elderly bachelors who are wealthy and without occupation tend somewhat frequently to fall into this error, sir. The future Lady Yaxley will check this. Indeed, I overheard her ladyship saying as much as I brought in the fish. She was commenting on a certain puffiness of the face which had been absent in his lordship's appearance in the earlier days of their acquaintanceship, and she observed that his lordship needed looking after. I fancy, sir, that you will find the union will turn out an extremely satisfactory one."

It was—what's the word I want—it was plausible, of course, but still I shook the onion.

"But, Jeeves!"

"Sir?"

"She *is*, as you remarked not long ago, definitely of the people." He looked at me in a reproachful sort of way.

"Sturdy lower-middle-class stock, sir."

"H'm!"

"Sir?"

"I said 'H'm!' Jeeves."

"Besides, sir, remember what the poet Tennyson said.

Kind hearts are more than coronets."

"And which of us is going to tell Aunt Agatha that?"

"If I might make the suggestion, sir, I would advise that we omit to communicate with Mrs. Spenser Gregson in any way. I have your suitcase practically packed. It would be a matter of but a few minutes to bring the car round from the garage . . ."

"And off over the horizon to where men are men?"

"Precisely, sir."

"Jeeves," I said, "I'm not sure that even now I can altogether see eye to eye with you regarding your recent activities. You think you have scattered light and sweetness on every side. I am not so sure. However, with this latest suggestion you have rung the bell. I examine it narrowly and I find no flaw in it. It is the goods. I'll get the car at once."

"Very good, sir."

"Remember what the poet Shakespeare said, Jeeves."

"What was that, sir?"

" 'Exit hurriedly, pursued by a bear.' You'll find it in one of his plays. I remember drawing a picture of it on the side of the page, when I was at school."

A Slice of Life

The conversation in the bar-parlour of the Anglers' Rest had drifted round to the subject of the Arts: and somebody asked if that film-serial, *The Vicissitudes of Vera*, which they were showing down at the Bijou Dream, was worth seeing.

"It's very good," said Miss Postlethwaite, our courteous and efficient barmaid, who is a prominent first-nighter. "It's about this mad professor who gets this girl into his toils and tries to turn her into a lobster."

"Tries to turn her into a lobster?" echoed we, surprised.

"Yes, sir. Into *a* lobster. It seems he collected thousands and thousands of lobsters and mashed them up and boiled down the juice from their glands and was just going to inject it into this Vera Dalrymple's spinal column when Jack Frobisher broke into the house and stopped him."

"Why did he do that?"

"Because he didn't want the girl he loved to be turned into a lobster."

"What we mean," said we, "is why did the professor want to turn the girl into a lobster?"

"He had a grudge against her."

This seemed plausible, and we thought it over for a while. Then one of the company shook his head disapprovingly.

"I don't like stories like that," he said. "They aren't true to life."

"Pardon me, sir," said a voice. And we were aware of Mr. Mulliner in our midst.

"Excuse me interrupting what may be a private discussion," said Mr. Mulliner, "but I chanced to overhear the recent remarks, and you, sir, have opened up a subject on which I happen to hold strong views—to wit, the question of what is and what is not true to life. How can we, with our limited experience, answer that question? For all we know, at this very moment hundreds of young women all over the country may be in the process of being turned into lobsters. Forgive my warmth, but I have suffered a good deal from this sceptical attitude of mind which is so prevalent nowadays. I have even met people who refused to believe my story about my brother Wilfred, purely because it was a little out of the ordinary run of the average man's experience."

Considerably moved, Mr. Mulliner ordered a hot Scotch with a slice of lemon.

"What happened to your brother Wilfred? Was he turned into a lobster?"

"No," said Mr. Mulliner, fixing his honest blue eyes on the speaker, "he was not. It would be perfectly easy for me to pretend that he was turned into a lobster; but I have always made it a practice—and I always shall make it a practice—to speak nothing but the bare truth. My brother Wilfred simply had rather a curious adventure."

My brother Wilfred (said Mr. Mulliner) is the clever one of the family. Even as a boy he was always messing about with chemicals, and at the University he devoted his time entirely to research. The result was that while still quite a young man he had won an established reputation as the inventor of what are known to the trade as Mulliner's Magic Marvels—a general term embracing the Raven Gipsy Face-Cream, the Snow of the Mountains Lotion, and many other preparations, some designed exclusively for the toilet, others of a curative nature, intended to alleviate the many ills to which the flesh is heir.

Naturally, he was a very busy man: and it is to this absorption in his work that I attribute the fact that, though—like all the Mulliners—a man of striking personal charm, he had reached his thirty-first year without ever having been involved in an affair of the heart. I remember him telling me once that he simply had no time for girls.

But we all fall sooner or later, and these strong concentrated men harder than any. While taking a brief holiday one year at Cannes, he met a Miss Angela Purdue, who was staying at his hotel, and she bowled him over completely.

She was one of these jolly, outdoor girls; and Wilfred had told me that what attracted him first about her was her wholesome, sunburned complexion. In fact, he told Miss Purdue the same thing when, shortly after he had proposed and been accepted, she asked him in her girlish way what it was that had first made him begin to love her.

"It's such a pity," said Miss Purdue, "that sunburn fades so soon. I do wish I knew some way of keeping it."

Even in his moments of holiest emotion Wilfred never forgot that he was a business man.

"You should try Mulliner's Raven Gipsy Face-Cream," he said. "It comes in two sizes—the small (or half-crown) jar and the large jar at seven shillings and sixpence. The large jar contains three and a half times as much as the small jar. It is applied nightly with a small sponge before retiring to rest. Testimonials have been received from numerous members of the aristocracy and may be examined at the office by any bona-fide inquirer."

"Is it really good?"

"I invented it," said Wilfred, simply.

She looked at him adoringly.

"How clever you are! Any girl ought to be proud to marry you."

"Oh, well," said Wilfred, with a modest wave of his hand.

"All the same, my guardian is going to be terribly angry when I tell him we're engaged."

"Why?"

"I inherited the Purdue millions when my uncle died, you see, and my guardian has always wanted me to marry his son, Percy."

Wilfred kissed her fondly, and laughed a defiant laugh.

"Jer mong feesh der selar," he said lightly.

But, some days after his return to London, whither the girl had preceded him, he had occasion to recall her words. As he sat in his study, musing on a preparation to cure the pip in canaries, a card was brought to him.

"Sir Jasper ffinch-ffarrowmere, Bart.," he read. The name was strange to him.

"Show the gentleman in," he said. And presently there entered a very stout man with a broad pink face. It was a face whose natural expression should, Wilfred felt, have been jovial, but at the moment it was grave.

"Sir Jasper Finch-Farrowmere?" said Wilfred.

"ffinch-ffarrowmere," corrected the visitor, his sensitive ear detecting the capital letters.

"Ah, yes. You spell it with two small f's."

"Four small f's."

"And to what do I owe the honour—"

"I am Angela Purdue's guardian."

"How do you do? A whisky-and-soda?"

"I thank you, no. I am a total abstainer. I found that alcohol had a tendency to increase my weight, so I gave it up. I have also given up butter, potatoes, soups of all kinds, and— However," he broke off, the fanatic gleam which comes into the eyes of all fat men who are describing their system of diet fading away, "this is not a social call, and

I must not take up your time with idle talk. I have a message for you, Mr. Mulliner. From Angela."

"Bless her!" said Wilfred. "Sir Jasper, I love that girl with a fervour which increases daily."

"Is that so?" said the baronet. "Well, what I came to say was, it's all off."

"What?"

"All off. She sent me to say that she had thought it over and wanted to break the engagement."

Wilfred's eyes narrowed. He had not forgotten what Angela had said about this man wanting her to marry his son. He gazed piercingly at his visitor, no longer deceived by the superficial geniality of his appearance. He had read too many detective stories where the fat, jolly, red-faced man turns out a fiend in human shape to be a ready victim to appearances.

"Indeed?" he said coldly. "I should prefer to have this information from Miss Purdue's own lips."

"She won't see you. But, anticipating this attitude on your part, I brought a letter from her. You recognise the writing?"

Wilfred took the letter. Certainly, the hand was Angela's, and the meaning of the words he read unmistakable. Nevertheless, as he handed the missive back, there was a hard smile on his face.

"There is such a thing as writing a letter under compulsion," he said.

The baronet's pink face turned mauve.

"What do you mean, sir?"

"What I say."

"Are you insinuating—"

"Yes, I am."

"Pooh, sir!"

"Pooh to you!" said Wilfred. "And, if you want to know

what I think, you poor ffish, I believe your name is spelled with a capital F, like anybody else's."

Stung to the quick, the baronet turned on his heel and left the room without another word.

Although he had given up his life to chemical research, Wilfred Mulliner was no mere dreamer. He could be the man of action when necessity demanded. Scarcely had his visitor left when he was on his way to the Senior Test-Tubes, the famous chemists' club in St. James's. There, consulting Kelly's *County Families*, he learnt that Sir Jasper's address was ffinch Hall in Yorkshire. He had found out all he wanted to know. It was at ffinch Hall, he decided, that Angela must now be immured.

For that she was being immured somewhere he had no doubt. That letter, he was positive, had been written by her under stress of threats. The writing was Angela's but he declined to believe that she was responsible for the phraseology and sentiments. He remembered reading a story where the heroine was forced into courses which she would not otherwise have contemplated by the fact that somebody was standing over her with a flask of vitriol. Possibly this was what that bounder of a baronet had done to Angela.

Considering this possibility, he did not blame her for what she had said about him, Wilfred, in the second paragraph of her note. Nor did he reproach her for signing herself "Yrs truly, A. Purdue." Naturally, when baronets are threatening to pour vitriol down her neck, a refined and sensitive young girl cannot pick her words. This sort of thing must of necessity interfere with the selection of the *mot juste.*

That afternoon, Wilfred was in a train on his way to Yorkshire. That evening, he was in the ffinch Arms in the village of which Sir Jasper was the squire. That night, he was in the gardens of ffinch Hall, prowling softly round the house, listening.

And presently, as he prowled, there came to his ears from an upper window a sound that made him stiffen like a statue and clench his hands till the knuckles stood out white under the strain.

It was the sound of a woman sobbing.

Wilfred spent a sleepless night, but by morning he had formed his plan of action. I will not weary you with a description of the slow and tedious steps by which he first made the acquaintance of Sir Jasper's valet, who was an habitue of the village inn, and then by careful stages won the man's confidence with friendly words and beer. Suffice it to say that, about a week later, Wilfred had induced this man with bribes to leave suddenly on the plea of an aunt's illness, supplying—so as to cause his employer no inconvenience—a cousin to take his place.

This cousin, as you will have guessed, was Wilfred himself. But a very different Wilfred from the dark-haired, clean-cut young scientist who had revolutionised the world of chemistry a few months before by proving that $H_2O + b3g4z7 - m9z8 = g6f5p3x$. Before leaving London on what he knew would be a dark and dangerous enterprise, Wilfred had taken the precaution of calling in at a well-known costumier's and buying a red wig. He had also purchased a pair of blue spectacles: but for the *role* which he had now undertaken these were, of course, useless. A blue-spectacled valet could not but have aroused suspicion in the most guileless baronet. All that Wilfred did, therefore, in the way of preparation, was to don the wig, shave off his moustache, and treat his face to a light coating of the Raven Gipsy Face-Cream. This done, he set out for ffinch Hall.

Externally, ffinch Hall was one of those gloomy, sombre country-houses which seem to exist only for the purpose of having horrid crimes committed in them. Even in his brief visit to the grounds, Wilfred had noticed fully half a dozen places which seemed incomplete without a cross indicating spot where body was found by the police. It was the sort of house where ravens croak in the front garden just before the death of the heir, and shrieks ring out from behind barred windows in the night.

Nor was its interior more cheerful. And, as for the personnel of the domestic staff, that was less exhilarating than anything else about the place. It consisted of an aged cook who, as she bent over her cauldrons, looked like something out of a travelling company of *Macbeth*, touring the smaller towns of the North, and Murgatroyd, the butler, a huge, sinister man with a cast in one eye and an evil light in the other.

Many men, under these conditions, would have been daunted. But not Wilfred Mulliner. Apart from the fact that, like all the Mulliners, he was as brave as a lion, he had come expecting something of this nature. He settled down to his duties and kept his eyes open, and before long his vigilance was rewarded.

One day, as he lurked about the dim-lit passage-ways, he saw Sir Jasper coming up the stairs with a laden tray in his hands. It contained a toast-rack, a half bot. of white wine, pepper, salt, veg., and in a covered dish something which Wilfred, sniffing cautiously, decided was a cutlet.

Lurking in the shadows, he followed the baronet to the top of the house. Sir Jasper paused at a door on the second floor. He knocked. The door opened, a hand was stretched forth, the tray vanished, the door closed, and the baronet moved away.

So did Wilfred. He had seen what he had wanted to see, discovered what he had wanted to discover. He returned to the servants' hall, and under the gloomy eyes of Murgatroyd began to shape his plans.

"Where have you been?" demanded the butler, suspiciously.

"Oh, hither and thither," said Wilfred, with a well-assumed airiness.

Murgatroyd directed a menacing glance at him.

"You'd better stay where you belong," he said, in his thick growling voice. "There's things in this house that don't want seeing."

"Ah!" agreed the cook, dropping an onion in the cauldron.

Wilfred could not repress a shudder.

But even as he shuddered, he was conscious of a certain relief. At least, he reflected, they were not starving his darling. That cutlet had smelt uncommonly good: and, if the bill of fare was always maintained at this level, she had nothing to complain of in the catering.

But his relief was short-lived. What, after all, he asked himself, are cutlets to a girl who is imprisoned in a locked room of a sinister country-house and is being forced to marry a man she does not love? Practically nothing. When the heart is sick, cutlets merely alleviate, they do not cure. Fiercely Wilfred told himself that, come what might, few days should pass before he found the key to that locked door and bore away his love to freedom and happiness.

The only obstacle in the way of this scheme was that it was plainly going to be a matter of the greatest difficulty to find the key. That night, when his employer dined, Wilfred searched his room thoroughly. He found nothing. The key, he was forced to conclude, was kept on the baronet's person.

Then how to secure it?

It is not too much to say that Wilfred Mulliner was non-plussed. The brain which had electrified the world of Science by discovering that if you mixed a stiffish oxygen and potassium and added a splash of trinitrotoluol and a spot of old brandy you got something that could be sold in America as champagne at a hundred and fifty dollars the case, had to confess itself baffled.

To attempt to analyse the young man's emotions, as the next week dragged itself by, would be merely morbid. Life cannot, of course, be all sunshine: and in relating a story like this, which is a slice of life, one must pay as much attention to shade as to light: nevertheless, it would be tedious were I to describe to you in detail the soul-torments which afflicted Wilfred Mulliner as day followed day and no solution to the problem presented itself. You are all intelligent men, and you can picture to yourselves how a high-spirited young fellow, deeply in love, must have felt; knowing that the girl he loved was languishing in what practically amounted to a dungeon, though situated on an upper floor, and chafing at his inability to set her free.

His eyes became sunken. His cheek-bones stood out. He lost weight. And so noticeable was this change in his physique that Sir Jasper ffinch-ffarrowmere commented on it one evening in tones of unconcealed envy.

"How the devil, Straker," he said—for this was the pseudonym under which Wilfred was passing, "do you manage to keep so thin? Judging by the weekly books, you eat like a starving Esquimau, and yet you don't put on weight. Now I, in addition to knocking off butter and potatoes, have started drinking hot unsweetened lemon-juice each night before retiring: and yet, damme," he said—for, like all baronets, he was careless in his language, "I weighed myself this morning, and I was up another six ounces. What's the explanation?"

"Yes, Sir Jasper," said Wilfred, mechanically.

"What the devil do you mean, Yes, Sir Jasper?"

"No, Sir Jasper."

The baronet wheezed plaintively.

"I've been studying this matter closely," he said, "and it's one of the seven wonders of the world. Have you ever seen a fat valet? Of course not. Nor has anybody else. There is no such thing as a fat valet. And yet there is scarcely a moment during the day when a valet is not eating. He rises at six-thirty, and at seven is having coffee and buttered toast. At eight, he breakfasts off porridge, cream, eggs, bacon, jam, bread, butter, more eggs, more bacon, more jam, more tea, and more butter, finishing up with a slice of cold ham and a sardine. At eleven o'clock he has his 'elevenses,' consisting of coffee, cream, more bread and more butter. At one, luncheon—a hearty meal, replete with every form of starchy food and lots of beer. If he can get at the port, he has port. At three, a snack. At four, another snack. At five, tea and buttered toast. At seven—dinner, probably with floury potatoes, and certainly with lots more beer. At nine, another snack. And at ten-thirty he retires to bed, taking with him a glass of milk and a plate of biscuits to keep himself from getting hungry in the night. And yet he remains as slender as a string-bean, while I, who have been dieting for years, tip the beam at two hundred and seventeen pounds, and am growing a third and supplementary chin. These are mysteries, Straker."

"Yes, Sir Jasper."

"Well, I'll tell you one thing," said the baronet, "I'm getting down one of those indoor Turkish Bath cabinet-affairs from London; and if that doesn't do the trick, I give up the struggle."

The indoor Turkish Bath duly arrived and was unpacked; and it was some three nights later that Wilfred, brooding in the servants' hall, was aroused from his reverie by Murgatroyd.

"Here," said Murgatroyd, "wake up. Sir Jasper's calling you."

"Calling me what?" asked Wilfred, coming to himself with a start.

"Calling you very loud," growled the butler.

It was indeed so. From the upper regions of the house there was proceeding a series of sharp yelps, evidently those of a man in mortal stress. Wilfred was reluctant to interfere in any way if, as seemed probable, his employer was dying in agony; but he was a conscientious man, and it was his duty, while in the sinister house, to perform the work for which he was paid. He hurried up the stairs; and, entering Sir Jasper's bedroom, perceived the baronet's crimson face protruding from the top of the indoor Turkish Bath.

"So you've come at last!" cried Sir Jasper. "Look here, when you put me into this infernal contrivance just now, what did you do to the dashed thing?"

"Nothing beyond what was indicated in the printed pamphlet accompanying the machine, Sir Jasper. Following the instructions, I slid Rod A into Groove B, fastening with Catch C—"

"Well, you must have made a mess of it, somehow. The thing's stuck. I can't get out."

"You can't?" cried Wilfred.

"No. And the bally apparatus is getting considerably hotter than the hinges of the Inferno." I must apologise for Sir Jasper's language, but you know what baronets are. "I'm being cooked to a crisp."

A sudden flash of light seemed to blaze upon Wilfred Mulliner.

"I will release you, Sir Jasper—"

"Well, hurry up, then."

"On one condition." Wilfred fixed him with a piercing gaze. "First, I must have the key."

"There isn't a key, you idiot. It doesn't lock. It just clicks when you slide Gadget D into Thingummybob E."

"The key I require is that of the room in which you are holding Angela Purdue a prisoner."

"What the devil do you mean? Ouch!"

"I will tell you what I mean, Sir Jasper ffinch-ffarrowmere. I am Wilfred Mulliner!"

"Don't be an ass. Wilfred Mulliner has black hair. Yours is red. You must be thinking of someone else."

"This is a wig," said Wilfred. "By Clarkson." He shook a menacing finger at the baronet. "You little thought, Sir Jasper ffinch-ffarrowmere, when you embarked on this dastardly scheme, that Wilfred Mulliner was watching your every move. I guessed your plans from the start. And now is the moment when I checkmate them. Give me that key, you Fiend."

"ffiend," corrected Sir Jasper, automatically.

"I am going to release my darling, to take her away from this dreadful house, to marry her by special licence as soon as it can legally be done."

In spite of his sufferings, a ghastly laugh escaped Sir Jasper's lips.

"You are, are you!"

"I am."

"Yes, you are!"

"Give me the key."

"I haven't got it, you chump. It's in the door."

"Ha, ha!"

"It's no good saying 'Ha, ha!' It is in the door. On Angela's side of the door."

"A likely story! But I cannot stay here wasting time. If you will not give me the key, I shall go up and break in the door."

"Do!" Once more the baronet laughed like a tortured soul. "And see what she'll say."

Wilfred could make nothing of this last remark. He could, he thought, imagine very clearly what Angela would say. He could picture her sobbing on his chest, murmuring that she knew he would come, that she had never doubted him for an instant. He leapt for the door.

"Here! Hi! Aren't you going to let me out?"

"Presently," said Wilfred. "Keep cool." He raced up the stairs.

"Angela," he cried, pressing his lips against the panel. "Angela!"

"Who's that?" answered a well-remembered voice from within.

"It is I—Wilfred. I am going to burst open the door. Stand clear of the gates."

He drew back a few paces, and hurled himself at the woodwork. There was a grinding crash, as the lock gave. And Wilfred, staggering on, found himself in a room so dark that he could see nothing.

"Angela, where are you?"

"I'm here. And I'd like to know why you are, after that letter I wrote you. Some men," continued the strangely cold voice, "do not seem to know how to take a hint."

Wilfred staggered, and would have fallen had he not clutched at his forehead.

"That letter?" he stammered. "You surely didn't mean what you wrote in that letter?"

"I meant every word and I wish I had put in more."

"But—but—but— But don't you love me, Angela?"

A hard, mocking laugh rang through the room.

"Love you? Love the man who recommended me to try Mulliner's Raven Gipsy Face-Cream!"

"What do you mean?"

"I will tell you what I mean. Wilfred Mulliner, look on your handiwork!"

The room became suddenly flooded with light. And there, standing with her hand on the switch, stood Angela—a queenly, lovely figure, in whose radiant beauty the sternest critic would have noted but one flaw—the fact that she was piebald.

Wilfred gazed at her with adoring eyes. Her face was partly brown and partly white, and on her snowy neck were patches of sepia that looked like the thumb-prints you find on the pages of books in the Free Library: but he thought her the most beautiful creature he had ever seen. He longed to fold her in his arms: and but for the fact that her eyes told him that she would undoubtedly land an upper-cut on him if he tried it he would have done so.

"Yes," she went on, "this is what you have made of me, Wilfred Mulliner—you and that awful stuff you call the Raven Gipsy Face-Cream. This is the skin you loved to touch! I took your advice and bought one of the large jars at seven and six, and see the result! Barely twenty-four hours after the first application, I could have walked into any circus and named my own terms as the Spotted Princess of the Fiji Islands. I fled here to my childhood home, to hide myself. And the first thing that happened"—her voice broke—"was that my favourite hunter shied at me and tried to bite pieces out of his manger: while Ponto, my little dog, whom I have reared from a puppy, caught one sight of my face and is now in the hands of the vet. and unlikely to recover. And it was you, Wilfred Mulliner, who brought this curse upon me."

Many men would have wilted beneath these searing words, but Wilfred Mulliner merely smiled with infinite compassion and understanding.

"It is quite all right," he said. "I should have warned you, sweetheart, that this occasionally happens in cases where the skin is exceptionally delicate and finely-textured. It can be speedily remedied by an application of the Mulliner Snow of the Mountains Lotion, four shillings the medium-sized bottle."

"Wilfred! Is this true?"

"Perfectly true, dearest. And is this all that stands between us?"

"No!" shouted a voice of thunder.

Wilfred wheeled sharply. In the doorway stood Sir Jasper ffinch-ffarrowmere. He was swathed in a bath-towel, what was visible of his person being a bright crimson. Behind him, toying with a horse-whip, stood Murgatroyd, the butler.

"You didn't expect to see me, did you?"

"I certainly," replied Wilfred, severely, "did not expect to see you in a lady's presence in a costume like that."

"Never mind my costume." Sir Jasper turned.

"Murgatroyd, do your duty!"

The butler, scowling horribly, advanced into the room.

"Stop!" screamed Angela.

"I haven't begun yet, miss," said the butler, deferentially.

"You sha'n't touch Wilfred. I love him."

"What!" cried Sir Jasper. "After all that has happened?"

"Yes. He has explained everything."

A grim frown appeared on the baronet's vermilion face.

"I'll bet he hasn't explained why he left me to be cooked in that infernal Turkish Bath. I was beginning to throw out clouds of smoke when Murgatroyd, faithful fellow, heard my cries and came and released me."

"Though not my work," added the butler.

Wilfred eyed him steadily.

"If," he said, "you used Mulliner's Reduc-o, the recognised specific for obesity, whether in the tabloid form at three shillings the tin, or as a liquid at five and six the flask, you would have no need to stew in Turkish Baths. Mulliner's Reduc-o, which contains no injurious chemicals, but is compounded purely of health-giving herbs, is guaranteed to remove excess weight, steadily and without weakening after-effects, at the rate of two pounds a week. As used by the nobility."

The glare of hatred faded from the baronet's eyes.

"Is that a fact?" he whispered.

"It is."

"You guarantee it?"

"All the Mulliner preparations are fully guaranteed."

"My boy!" cried the baronet. He shook Wilfred by the hand. "Take her," he said, brokenly. "And with her my b-blessing."

A discreet cough sounded in the background.

"You haven't anything, by any chance, sir," asked Murgatroyd, "that's good for lumbago?"

"Mulliner's Ease-o will cure the most stubborn case in six days."

"Bless you, sir, bless you," sobbed Murgatroyd. "Where

can I get it?"

"At all chemists."

"It catches me in the small of the back principally, sir."

"It need catch you no longer," said Wilfred.

There is little to add. Murgatroyd is now the most lissom butler in Yorkshire. Sir Jasper's weight is down under the fifteen stone and he is thinking of taking up hunting again. Wilfred and Angela are man and wife; and never, I am informed, have the wedding-bells of the old church at ffinch village rung out a blither peal than they did on that June morning when Angela, raising to her love a face on which the brown was as evenly distributed as on an antique walnut table, replied to the clergyman's question, "Wilt thou, Angela, take this Wilfred?" with a shy, "I will." They now have two bonny bairns—the small, or Percival, at a preparatory school in Sussex, and the large, or Ferdinand, at Eton.

Here Mr. Mulliner, having finished his hot Scotch, bade us farewell and took his departure.

A silence followed his exit. The company seemed plunged in deep thought. Then somebody rose.

"Well, good-night all," he said.

It seemed to sum up the situation.

Sir Agravaine
A Tale of King Arthur's Round Table

Some time ago, when spending a delightful week-end at the ancestral castle of my dear old friend, the Duke of Weatherstonhope (pronounced Wop), I came across an old black-letter MS. It is on this that the story which follows is based.

I have found it necessary to touch the thing up a little here and there, for writers in those days were weak in construction. Their idea of telling a story was to take a long breath and start droning away without any stops or dialogue till the thing was over.

I have condensed the title. In the original it ran, " 'How it came about that ye good Knight Sir Agravaine ye Dolorous of ye Table Round did fare forth to succor a damsel in distress and after divers journeyings and perils by flood and by field did win her for his bride and right happily did they twain live ever afterwards,' by Ambrose ye monk."

It was a pretty snappy title for those times, but we have such a high standard in titles nowadays that I have felt compelled to omit a few yards of it.

We may now proceed to the story.

The great tournament was in full swing. All through the afternoon boiler-plated knights on mettlesome chargers had hurled themselves on each other's spears, to the vast contentment of all. Bright eyes shone; handkerchiefs fluttered; musical voices urged chosen champions to knock the cover off their brawny adversaries. The cheap seats had long since become hoarse with emotion. All round the arena rose the cries of itinerant merchants: "Iced malvoisie," "Score-cards;

ye cannot tell the jousters without a score-card." All was revelry and excitement.

A hush fell on the throng. From either end of the arena a mounted knight in armour had entered.

The herald raised his hand.

"Ladeez'n gemmen! Battling Galahad and Agravaine the Dolorous. Galahad on my right, Agravaine on my left. Squires out of the ring. Time!"

A speculator among the crowd offered six to one on Galahad, but found no takers. Nor was the public's caution without reason.

A moment later the two had met in a cloud of dust, and Agravaine, shooting over his horse's crupper, had fallen with a metallic clang.

He picked himself up, and limped slowly from the arena. He was not unused to this sort of thing. Indeed, nothing else had happened to him in his whole jousting career.

The truth was that Sir Agravaine the Dolorous was out of his element at King Arthur's court, and he knew it. It was this knowledge that had given him that settled air of melancholy from which he derived his title.

Until I came upon this black-letter MS. I had been under the impression, like, I presume, everybody else, that every Knight of the Round Table was a model of physical strength and beauty. Malory says nothing to suggest the contrary. Nor does Tennyson. But apparently there were exceptions, of whom Sir Agravaine the Dolorous must have been the chief.

There was, it seems, nothing to mitigate this unfortunate man's physical deficiencies. There is a place in the world for the strong, ugly man, and there is a place for the weak, handsome man. But to fall short both in features and in muscle is to stake your all on brain. And in the days of King

Arthur you did not find the populace turning out to do homage to brain. It was a drug in the market. Agravaine was a good deal better equipped than his contemporaries with grey matter, but his height in his socks was but five feet four; and his muscles, though he had taken three correspondence courses in physical culture, remained distressingly flaccid. His eyes were pale and mild, his nose snub, and his chin receded sharply from his lower lip, as if Nature, designing him, had had to leave off in a hurry and finish the job anyhow. The upper teeth, protruding, completed the resemblance to a nervous rabbit.

Handicapped in this manner, it is no wonder that he should feel sad and lonely in King Arthur's court. At heart he ached for romance; but romance passed him by. The ladies of the court ignored his existence, while, as for those wandering damsels who came periodically to Camelot to complain of the behaviour of dragons, giants, and the like, and to ask permission of the king to take a knight back with them to fight their cause (just as, nowadays, one goes out and calls a policeman), he simply had no chance. The choice always fell on Lancelot or some other popular favourite.

The tournament was followed by a feast. In those brave days almost everything was followed by a feast. The scene was gay and animated. Fair ladies, brave knights, churls, varlets, squires, scurvy knaves, men-at-arms, malapert rogues—all were merry. All save Agravaine. He sat silent and moody. To the jests of Dagonet he turned a deaf ear. And when his neighbour, Sir Kay, arguing with Sir Percivale on current form, appealed to him to back up his statement that Sir Gawain, though a workman-like middle-weight, lacked the punch, he did not answer, though the subject was one on which he held strong views. He sat on, brooding.

As he sat there, a man-at-arms entered the hall.

"Your majesty," he cried, "a damsel in distress waits without."

There was a murmur of excitement and interest.

"Show her in," said the king, beaming.

The man-at-arms retired. Around the table the knights were struggling into an upright position in their seats and twirling their moustaches. Agravaine alone made no movement. He had been through this sort of thing so often. What were distressed damsels to him? His whole demeanour said, as plainly as if he had spoken the words, "What's the use?"

The crowd at the door parted, and through the opening came a figure at the sight of whom the expectant faces of the knights turned pale with consternation. For the newcomer was quite the plainest girl those stately halls had ever seen. Possibly the only plain girl they had ever seen, for no instance is recorded in our authorities of the existence at that period of any such.

The knights gazed at her blankly. Those were the grand old days of chivalry, when a thousand swords would leap from their scabbards to protect defenceless woman, if she were beautiful. The present seemed something in the nature of a special case, and nobody was quite certain as to the correct procedure.

An awkward silence was broken by the king.

"Er—yes?" he said.

The damsel halted.

"Your majesty," she cried "I am in distress. I crave help!"

"Just so," said the king, uneasily, flashing an apprehensive glance at the rows of perturbed faces before him. "Just so. What—er—what is the exact nature of the—ah—trouble? Any assistance these gallant knights can render will,

I am sure, be—ah—eagerly rendered."

He looked imploringly at the silent warriors. As a rule, this speech was the signal for roars of applause. But now there was not even a murmur.

"I may say enthusiastically," he added.

Not a sound.

"Precisely," said the king, ever tactful. "And now—you were saying?"

"I am Yvonne, the daughter of Earl Dorm of the Hills," said the damsel, "and my father has sent me to ask protection from a gallant knight against a fiery dragon that ravages the countryside."

"A dragon, gentlemen," said the king, aside. It was usually a safe draw. Nothing pleased the knight of that time more than a brisk bout with a dragon. But now the tempting word was received in silence.

"Fiery," said the king.

Some more silence.

The king had recourse to the direct appeal. "Sir Gawain, this court would be greatly indebted to you if—"

Sir Gawain said he had strained a muscle at the last tournament.

"Sir Pelleas."

The king's voice was growing flat with consternation. The situation was unprecedented.

Sir Pelleas said he had an ingrowing toe-nail.

The king's eye rolled in anguish around the table. Suddenly it stopped. It brightened. His look of dismay changed to one of relief.

A knight had risen to his feet. It was Agravaine.

"Ah!" said the king, drawing a deep breath.

Sir Agravaine gulped. He was feeling more nervous than he had ever felt in his life. Never before had he risen to volunteer his services in a matter of this kind, and his state of mind was that of a small boy about to recite his first piece of poetry.

It was not only the consciousness that every eye, except one of Sir Balin's which had been closed in the tournament that afternoon, was upon him. What made him feel like a mild gentleman in a post-office who has asked the lady assistant if she will have time to attend to him soon and has caught her eye, was the fact that he thought he had observed the damsel Yvonne frown as he rose. He groaned in spirit. This damsel, he felt, wanted the proper goods or none at all. She might not be able to get Sir Lancelot or Sir Galahad; but she was not going to be satisfied with a half-portion.

The fact was that Sir Agravaine had fallen in love at first sight. The moment he had caught a glimpse of the damsel Yvonne, he loved her devotedly. To others she seemed plain and unattractive. To him she was a Queen of Beauty. He was amazed at the inexplicable attitude of the knights around him. He had expected them to rise in a body to clamour for the chance of assisting this radiant vision. He could hardly believe, even now, that he was positively the only starter.

"This is Sir Agravaine the Dolorous," said the king to the damsel. "Will you take him as your champion?"

Agravaine held his breath. But all was well. The damsel bowed.

"Then, Sir Agravaine," said the king, "perhaps you had better have your charger sent round at once. I imagine that the matter is pressing—time and—er—dragons wait for no man."

Ten minutes later Agravaine, still dazed, was jogging along to the hills, with the damsel by his side.

It was some time before either of them spoke. The damsel seemed preoccupied, and Agravaine's mind was a welter of confused thoughts, the most prominent of which and the one to which he kept returning being the startling reflection that he, who had pined for romance so long, had got it now in full measure.

A dragon! Fiery withal. Was he absolutely certain that he was capable of handling an argument with a fiery dragon? He would have given much for a little previous experience of this sort of thing. It was too late now, but he wished he had had the forethought to get Merlin to put up a magic prescription for him, rendering him immune to dragon-bites. But did dragons bite? Or did they whack at you with their tails? Or just blow fire?

There were a dozen such points that he would have liked to have settled before starting. It was silly to start out on a venture of this sort without special knowledge. He had half a mind to plead a forgotten engagement and go straight back.

Then he looked at the damsel, and his mind was made up. What did death matter if he could serve her?

He coughed. She came out of her reverie with a start.

"This dragon, now?" said Agravaine.

For a moment the damsel did not reply. "A fearsome worm, Sir Knight," she said at length. "It raveneth by day and by night. It breathes fire from its nostrils."

"Does it!" said Agravaine. "*Does* it! You couldn't give some idea what it looks like, what kind of *size* it is?"

"Its body is as thick as ten stout trees, and its head touches the clouds."

"Does it!" said Agravaine thoughtfully. "*Does* it!"

"Oh, Sir Knight, I pray you have a care."

"I will," said Agravaine. And he had seldom said anything more fervently. The future looked about as bad as it could be. Any hopes he may have entertained that this dragon might turn out to be comparatively small and inoffensive were dissipated. This was plainly no debilitated wreck of a dragon, its growth stunted by excessive firebreathing. A body as thick as ten stout trees! He would not even have the melancholy satisfaction of giving the creature indigestion. For all the impression he was likely to make on that vast interior, he might as well be a salted almond.

As they were speaking, a dim mass on the skyline began to take shape.

"Behold!" said the damsel. "My father's castle." And presently they were riding across the drawbridge and through the great gate, which shut behind them with a clang.

As they dismounted a man came out through a door at the further end of the courtyard.

"Father," said Yvonne, "this is the gallant knight Sir Agravaine, who has come to—" it seemed to Agravaine that she hesitated for a moment.

"To tackle our dragon?" said the father. "Excellent. Come right in."

Earl Dorm of the Hills was a small, elderly man, with what Agravaine considered a distinctly furtive air about him. His eyes were too close together, and he was overlavish with a weak, cunning smile. Even Agravaine, who was in the mood to like the whole family, if possible, for Yvonne's sake, could not help feeling that appearances were against this particular exhibit. He might have a heart of gold beneath the outward aspect of a confidence-trick expert whose hobby was dog-stealing, but there was no doubt that his exterior did not inspire a genial glow of confidence.

"Very good of you to come," said the earl.

"It's a pleasure," said Agravaine. "I have been hearing

all about the dragon."

"A great scourge," agreed his host. "We must have a long talk about it after dinner."

It was the custom in those days in the stately homes of England for the whole strength of the company to take their meals together. The guests sat at the upper table, the ladies in a gallery above them, while the usual drove of men-at-arms, archers, malapert rogues, varlets, scurvy knaves, scullions, and plug-uglies, attached to all medieval households, squashed in near the door, wherever they could find room.

The retinue of Earl Dorm was not strong numerically—the household being, to judge from appearances, one that had seen better days; but it struck Agravaine that what it lacked in numbers it made up in toughness. Among all those at the bottom of the room there was not one whom it would have been agreeable to meet alone in a dark alley. Of all those foreheads not one achieved a height of more than one point nought four inches. A sinister collection, indeed, and one which, Agravaine felt, should have been capable of handling without his assistance any dragon that ever came into the world to stimulate the asbestos industry.

He was roused from his reflections by the voice of his host.

"I hope you are not tired after your journey, Sir Agravaine? My little girl did not bore you, I trust? We are very quiet folk here. Country mice. But we must try to make your visit interesting."

Agravaine felt that the dragon might be counted upon to do that. He said as much.

"Ah, yes, the dragon," said Earl Dorm, "I was forgetting the dragon. I want to have a long talk with you about that dragon. Not now. Later on."

His eye caught Agravaine's, and he smiled that weak, cunning smile of his. And for the first time the knight was conscious of a curious feeling that all was not square and aboveboard in this castle. A conviction began to steal over him that in some way he was being played with, that some game was afoot which he did not understand, that—in a word—there was dirty work at the cross-roads.

There was a touch of mystery in the atmosphere which made him vaguely uneasy. When a fiery dragon is ravaging the countryside to such an extent that the C.Q.D. call has been sent out to the Round Table, a knight has a right to expect the monster to be the main theme of conversation. The tendency on his host's part was apparently to avoid touching on the subject at all. He was vague and elusive; and the one topic on which an honest man is not vague and elusive is that of fiery dragons. It was not right. It was as if one should 'phone for the police and engage them, on arrival, in a discussion on the day's football results.

A wave of distrust swept over Agravaine. He had heard stories of robber chiefs who lured strangers into their strongholds and then held them prisoners while the public nervously dodged their anxious friends who had formed subscription lists to make up the ransom. Could this be such a case? The man certainly had an evasive manner and a smile which would have justified any jury in returning a verdict without leaving the box. On the other hand, there was Yvonne. His reason revolted against the idea of that sweet girl being a party to any such conspiracy.

No, probably it was only the Earl's unfortunate manner. Perhaps he suffered from some muscular weakness of the face which made him smile like that.

Nevertheless, he certainly wished that he had not allowed himself to be deprived of his sword and armour. At the time it had seemed to him that the Earl's remark that the latter needed polishing and the former stropping betrayed only a kindly consideration for his guest's well-being. Now, it had the aspect of being part of a carefully-constructed plot.

On the other hand—here philosophy came to his rescue—if anybody did mean to start anything, his sword and armour might just as well not be there. Any one of those mammoth low-brows at the door could eat him, armour and all.

He resumed his meal, uneasy but resigned.

Dinner at Earl Dorm's was no lunch-counter scuffle. It started early and finished late. It was not till an advanced hour that Agravaine was conducted to his room.

The room which had been allotted to him was high up in the eastern tower. It was a nice room, but to one in Agravaine's state of supressed suspicion a trifle too solidly upholstered. The door was of the thickest oak, studded with iron nails. Iron bars formed a neat pattern across the only window.

Hardly had Agravaine observed these things when the door opened, and before him stood the damsel Yvonne, pale of face and panting for breath.

She leaned against the doorpost and gulped.

"Fly!" she whispered.

Reader, if you had come to spend the night in the lonely castle of a perfect stranger with a shifty eye and a rogues' gallery smile, and on retiring to your room had found the door kick-proof and the window barred, and if, immediately after your discovery of these phenomena, a white-faced young lady had plunged in upon you and urged you to immediate flight, wouldn't that jar you?

It jarred Agravaine.

"Eh?" he cried.

"Fly! Fly, Sir Knight."

Another footstep sounded in the passage. The damsel gave a startled look over her shoulder.

"And what's all this?"

Earl Dorm appeared in the dim-lit corridor. His voice had a nasty tinkle in it.

"Your—your daughter," said Agravaine, hurriedly, "was just telling me that breakfast would—"

The sentence remained unfinished. A sudden movement of the earl's hand, and the great door banged in his face. There came the sound of a bolt shooting into its socket. A key turned in the lock. He was trapped.

Outside, the earl had seized his daughter by the wrist and was administering a paternal cross-examination.

"What were you saying to him?"

Yvonne did not flinch.

"I was bidding him fly."

"If he wants to leave this castle," said the earl, grimly, "he'll have to."

"Father," said Yvonne, "I can't."

"Can't what?"

"I can't."

His grip on her wrist tightened. From the other side of the door came the muffled sound of blows on the solid oak.

"Oh?" said Earl Dorm. "You can't, eh? Well, listen to me. You've got to. Do you understand? I admit he might be better-looking, but—"

"Father, I love him."

He released her wrist, and stared at her in the uncertain light.

"You love him!"

"Yes."

"Then what—? Why? Well, I never did understand women," he said at last, and stumped off down the passage.

While this cryptic conversation was in progress, Agravaine, his worst apprehensions realized, was trying to batter down the door. After a few moments, however, he realized the futility of his efforts, and sat down on the bed to think.

At the risk of forfeiting the reader's respect, it must be admitted that his first emotion was one of profound relief. If he was locked up like this, it must mean that that dragon story was fictitious, and that all danger was at an end of having to pit his inexperience against a ravening monster who had spent a lifetime devouring knights. He had never liked the prospect, though he had been prepared to go through with it, and to feel that it was definitely cancelled made up for a good deal.

His mind next turned to his immediate future. What were they going to do with him? On this point he felt tolerably comfortable. This imprisonment could mean nothing more than that he would be compelled to disgorge a ransom. This did not trouble him. He was rich, and, now that the situation had been switched to a purely business basis, he felt that he could handle it.

In any case, there was nothing to be gained by sitting up, so he went to bed, like a good philosopher.

The sun was pouring through the barred window when he was awoke by the entrance of a gigantic figure bearing food and drink.

He recognized him as one of the scurvy knaves who had dined at the bottom of the room the night before—a vast, beetle-browed fellow with a squint, a mop of red hair, and a genius for silence. To Agravaine's attempts to engage him in conversation he replied only with grunts, and in a short time left the room, closing and locking the door behind him.

He was succeeded at dusk by another of about the same

size and ugliness, and with even less conversational *elan*. This one did not even grunt.

Small-talk, it seemed, was not an art cultivated in any great measure by the lower orders in the employment of Earl Dorm.

The next day passed without incident. In the morning the strabismic plug-ugly with the red hair brought him food and drink, while in the evening the non-grunter did the honours. It was a peaceful life, but tending towards monotony, and Agravaine was soon in the frame of mind which welcomes any break in the daily round.

He was fortunate enough to get it.

He had composed himself for sleep that night, and was just dropping comfortably off, when from the other side of the door he heard the sound of angry voices.

It was enough to arouse him. On the previous night silence had reigned. Evidently something out of the ordinary was taking place.

He listened intently and distinguished words.

"Who was it I did see thee coming down the road with?"

"Who was it thou didst see me coming down the road with?"

"Aye, who was it I did see thee coming down the road with?"

"Who dost thou think thou art?"

"Who do I think that I am?"

"Aye, who dost thou think thou art?"

Agravaine could make nothing of it. As a matter of fact, he was hearing the first genuine cross-talk that had ever occurred in those dim, pre-music-hall days. In years to come dialogue on these lines was to be popular throughout the length and breadth of Great Britain. But till then it had been unknown.

The voices grew angrier. To an initiated listener it would have been plain that in a short while words would be found inadequate and the dagger, that medieval forerunner of the slap-stick, brought into play. But to Agravaine, all inexperienced, it came as a surprise when suddenly with a muffled thud two bodies fell against the door. There was a scuffling noise, some groans, and then silence.

And then with amazement he heard the bolt shoot back and a key grate in the keyhole.

The door swung open. It was dark outside, but Agravaine could distinguish a female form, and, beyond, a shapeless mass which he took correctly to be the remains of the two plug-uglies.

"It is I, Yvonne," said a voice.

"What is it? What has been happening?"

"It was I. I set them against each other. They both loved one of the kitchen-maids. I made them jealous. I told Walt privily that she had favoured Dickon, and Dickon privily that she loved Walt. And now—"

She glanced at the shapeless heap, and shuddered. Agravaine nodded.

"No wedding-bells for her," he said, reverently.

"And I don't care. I did it to save you. But come! We are wasting time. Come! I will help you to escape."

A man who has been shut up for two days in a small room is seldom slow off the mark when a chance presents itself of taking exercise. Agravaine followed without a word, and together they crept down the dark staircase until they had reached the main hall. From somewhere in the distance came the rhythmic snores of scurvy knaves getting their eight hours.

Softly Yvonne unbolted a small door, and, passing through it, Agravaine found himself looking up at the stars, while the great walls of the castle towered above him.

"Good-bye," said Yvonne.

There was a pause. For the first time Agravaine found himself examining the exact position of affairs. After his sojourn in the guarded room, freedom looked very good to him. But freedom meant parting from Yvonne.

He looked at the sky and he looked at the castle walls, and he took a step back towards the door.

"I'm not so sure I want to go," he said.

"Oh, fly! Fly, Sir Knight!" she cried.

"You don't understand," said Agravaine. "I don't want to seem to be saying anything that might be interpreted as in the least derogatory to your father in any way whatever, but without prejudice, surely he is just a plain, ordinary brigand? I mean it's only a question of a ransom? And I don't in the least object—"

"No, no, no." Her voice trembled. "He would ask no ransom."

"Don't tell me he kidnaps people just as a hobby!"

"You don't understand. He—No, I cannot tell you. Fly!"

"What don't I understand?"

She was silent. Then she began to speak rapidly. "Very well. I will tell you. Listen. My father had six children, all daughters. We were poor. We had to stay buried in this out-of-the-way spot. We saw no one. It seemed impossible that any of us should ever marry. My father was in despair. Then he said, 'If we cannot get to town, the town must come to us.' So he sent my sister Yseult to Camelot to ask the king to let us have a knight to protect us against a giant with three heads. There was no giant, but she got the knight. It was Sir Sagramore. Perhaps you knew him?"

Agravaine nodded. He began to see daylight.

"My sister Yseult was very beautiful. After the first day

Sir Sagramore forgot all about the giant, and seemed to want to do nothing else except have Yseult show him how to play cat's cradle. They were married two months later, and my father sent my sister Elaine to Camelot to ask for a knight to protect us against a wild unicorn."

"And who bit?" asked Agravaine, deeply interested.

"Sir Malibran of Devon. They were married within three weeks, and my father—I can't go on. You understand now."

"I understand the main idea," said Agravaine. "But in my case—"

"You were to marry me," said Yvonne. Her voice was quiet and cold, but she was quivering.

Agravaine was conscious of a dull, heavy weight pressing on his heart. He had known his love was hopeless, but even hoplessness is the better for being indefinite. He understood now.

"And you naturally want to get rid of me before it can happen," he said. "I don't wonder. I'm not vain. . . .Well, I'll go. I knew I had no chance. Good-bye."

He turned. She stopped him with a sharp cry.

"What do you mean? You cannot wish to stay now? I am saving you."

"Saving me! I have loved you since the moment you entered the Hall at Camelot," said Agravaine.

She drew in her breath.

"You—you love me!"

They looked at each other in the starlight. She held out her hands.

"Agravaine!"

She drooped towards him, and he gathered her into his arms. For a novice, he did it uncommonly well.

It was about six months later that Agravaine, having ridden into the forest, called upon a Wise Man at his cell.

In those days almost anyone who was not a perfect bone-head could set up as a Wise Man and get away with it. All you had to do was live in a forest and grow a white beard. This particular Wise Man, for a wonder, had a certain amount of rude sagacity. He listened carefully to what the knight had to say.

"It has puzzled me to such an extent," said Agravaine, "that I felt that I must consult a specialist. You see me. Take a good look at me. What do you think of my personal appearance? You needn't hesitate. It's worse than that. I am the ugliest man in England."

"Would you go so far as that?" said the Wise Man, politely.

"Farther. And everybody else thinks so. Everybody except my wife. She tells me that I am a model of manly beauty. You know Lancelot? Well, she says I have Lancelot whipped to a custard. What do you think of that? And here's another thing. It is perfectly obvious to me that my wife is one of the most beautiful creatures in existence. I have seen them all, and I tell you that she stands alone. She is literally marooned in Class A, all by herself. Yet she insists that she is plain. What do you make of it?"

The Wise Man stroked his beard.

"My son," he said, "the matter is simple. True love takes no account of looks."

"No?" said Agravaine.

"You two are affinities. Therefore, to you the outward aspect is nothing. Put it like this. Love is a thingummybob who what-d'you-call-its."

"I'm beginning to see," said Agravaine.

"What I meant was this. Love is a wizard greater than Merlin. He plays odd tricks with the eyesight."

"Yes," said Agravaine.

"Or, put it another way. Love is a sculptor greater than Praxiteles. He takes an unsightly piece of clay and moulds it into a thing divine."

"I get you," said Agravaine.

The Wise Man began to warm to his work.

"Or shall we say—?"

"I think I must be going," said Agravaine. "I promised my wife I would be back early."

"We might put it—" began the Wise Man perseveringly.

"I understand," said Agravaine, hurriedly. "I quite see now. Good-bye."

The Wise Man sighed resignedly.

"Good-bye, Sir Knight," he said. "Good-bye. Pay at ye desk."

And Agravaine rode on his way marvelling.

Redundant Loves

Another area in which more is not always better.

Feet of Clay

With the coming of dusk the blizzard which had been blowing all the afternoon had gained in force, and the trees outside the club-house swayed beneath it. The falling snow rendered the visibility poor, but the Oldest Member, standing at the smoking-room window, was able to recognize the familiar gleam of Cyril Jukes's heather-mixture plus-fours as he crossed the icebound terrace from the direction of the caddy shed, and he gave a little nod of approval. No fair weather golfer himself when still a player, he liked to see the younger generation doing its round in the teeth of November gales.

On Cyril Jukes's normally cheerful face, as he entered the room some moments later, there was the sort of look which might have been worn by a survivor of the last days of Pompeii. What had been happening to Cyril Jukes in the recent past it was impossible to say, but the dullest eye could discern that it had been plenty, and the Oldest Member regarded him sympathetically.

"Something on your mind, my boy?"

"A slight tiff with the helpmeet."

"I am sorry. What caused it?"

"Well, you know her little brother, and you will agree with me, I think, that his long game wants polishing up."

"Quite."

"This can be done only by means of unremitting practice."

"Very true."

"So I took him out for a couple of rounds after lunch. We've just got back. We found the little woman waiting for us. She seemed rather stirred. Directing my attention to the fact that the child was bright blue and that icicles had formed on him, she said that if he expired his blood would be on my head. She then took him off to thaw him out with hot-water bottles. Life can be very difficult."

"Very."

"I suppose there *was* a sort of nip in the air, though I hadn't noticed it myself, but I had meant so well. Do you think that when a man's wife calls him a fatheaded sadist, she implies that married happiness is dead and the home in the melting pot?"

The Sage patted him on the shoulder.

"Courage," he said. "She may be a little annoyed for the moment, but the mood will pass and she will understand and forgive. Your wife is a golfer and, when calmer, cannot fail to realize how lucky she is to have married a man with the true golfing spirit. For that is what matters in this life.That is what counts. I mean the spirit that animated Horace Bewstridge, causing him to spank his loved one's mother on the eighteenth green when she interfered with his putting; the inner fire that drove Rollo Podmarsh on to finish his round, though he thought he had been poisoned, because he had a chance of breaking a hundred for the first time; the spirit which saved Agnes Flack and Sidney McMurdo, bringing them at last to peace and happiness. I think I may have mentioned Agnes Flack and Sidney McMurdo to you before. They were engaged to be married."

"She was a large girl, wasn't she?"

"Very large. And Sidney was large, also. That was what made the thing so satisfactory to their friends and well-wishers. Too often in this world you find the six-foot-three man teaming up with the four-foot-ten girl and five-foot-eleven girl linking her lot with something which she would seem to have dug out of Singer's troupe of midgets: but in the union of Agnes Flack and Sidney McMurdo there was none of this discrepancy. Sidney weighed two hundred pounds and was all muscle, and Agnes weighed a hundred and sixty pounds and was all muscle, too. And, more important still, both had been assiduous golfers since childhood. Theirs was a love based on mutual respect. Sidney's habit of always getting two hundred and fifty yards from the tee fascinated Agnes, and he in his turn was enthralled by her short game, which was exceptionally accurate."

It was in warmer weather than this (the Sage proceeded, having accepted his companion's offer of a hot toddy) that the story began which I am about to relate. The month was August, and from a cloudless sky the sun blazed down on the popular sea-shore resort of East Bampton, illuminating with its rays the beach, the pier, the boardwalk, the ice-cream stands, the hot doggeries and the shimmering ocean. In the last-named, about fifty yards from shore, Agnes Flack was taking her customary cooler after the day's golf and thinking how much she loved Sidney McMurdo.

Sidney himself was not present. He was still in the city, working for the insurance company which had bespoken his services, counting the days to his vacation and thinking how much he loved Agnes Flack.

When girls are floating in warm water, dreaming of the man they adore, it sometimes happens that there comes to them a sort of exaltation of the soul which demands physical expression. It came now to Agnes Flack. God, the way she looked at it, was in His heaven and all right with the world, and it seemed to her that something ought to be done about it. And as practically the only thing you can do in the way of physical expression in the water is to splash, she splashed. With arms and feet she churned up great fountains of foam, at the same time singing a wordless song of ecstasy.

The trouble about doing that sort of thing when swimming is that people are apt to be misled. Agnes Flack's was one of those penetrating voices which sound like the down express letting off steam at a level crossing, and in the number which she had selected for rendition there occurred a series of high notes which she held with determination and vigour. It is not surprising, therefore, that a passing stranger who was cleaving the waves in her vicinity should have got his facts twisted.

A moment later Agnes, in the middle of a high note, was surprised to find herself gripped firmly beneath the arms and towed rapidly shorewards.

Her annoyance was extreme, and it increased during the trip, most of which was made with her head under water. By the time she arrived at the beach, she had swallowed perhaps a pint and a half, and her initial impulse was to tell her assailant what she thought of his officiousness. But just as she was about to do so friendly hands, seizing her from behind, pulled her backwards and started rolling her over a barrel. And when she fought herself free the man had vanished.

Her mood was still ruffled and resentful when she stepped out of the elevator that night on her way down to dinner, for the feeling that she was full of salt water had not wholly disappeared. And it was as she was crossing the lounge with a moody frown on her brow that a voice at her side said "Oh, hullo, there you are, what?" and she turned to see a tall, slender, willowy man with keen blue eyes and a sun-tanned face.

"Feeling all right again?" asked the handsome stranger.

Agnes, who had been about to draw herself to her full

height and say "Sir!" suddenly divined who this must be.

"Was it you—" she began.

He raised a deprecating hand.

"Don't thank me, dear lady, don't thank me. I'm always saving people's lives, and they will try to thank me. It was nothing, nothing. Different, of course, if there had been sharks."

Anges was staring like a child at a saucer of ice cream. She had revised her intention of telling this man what she thought of him. His eyes, his clean-cut face, his perfect figure and his clothes had made a profound and instantaneous impression on her, giving her the sort of sensation which she had experienced on the occasion when she had done the short third at Squashy Hollow in one, a sort of dizzying feeling that life had nothing more to offer.

"Sharks get in the way and hamper a man. The time I saved the Princess della Raviogli in the Indian Ocean there were half a dozen of them, horsing about and behaving as if the place belonged to them. I had to teach one or two of them a sharp lesson with my Boy Scout pocket knife. The curse of the average shark is that if you give it the slightest encouragement it gets above itself and starts putting on airs."

Agnes felt that she must speak, but there seemed so little that she could say.

"You're English, aren't you?" she asked.

He raised a deprecating hand.

"Call me rather a cosmopolite, dear lady. I was born in the old country and have resided there from time to time and even served my sovereign in various positions of trust such as Deputy Master of the Royal Buckhounds, but all my life I have been a rover. I flit. I move to and fro. They say of me: 'Last week he was in Pernambuco, but goodness knows where he is now. China, possibly, or Africa or the North Pole.' Until recently I was in Hollywood. They were doing a film of life in the jungle, where might is right and the strong man comes into his own, and they roped me in as adviser. By the way, introduce myself, what? Fosdyke is the name. Captain Jack Fosdyke."

Agnes's emotion was now such that she was unable for a moment to recall hers. Then it came back to her.

"Mine is Flack," she said, and the statement seemed to interest her companion.

"No, really? I've just been spending the week-end with an old boy named Flack, down at Sands Point."

"Josiah Flack?"

"That's right. Amazing place he has. Absolute palace. They tell me he's one of the richest men in America. Rather pathetic. This lonely old man, rolling in the stuff, but with no chick or child."

"He is my uncle. How was he?"

"Very frail. Very, very frail. Not long for this world, it seemed to me." A sharp tremor ran through Captain Jack Fosdyke. It was as if for the first time her words had penetrated to his consciousness. "Your *uncle*, did you say?"

"Yes."

"Are you his only niece?"

"Yes."

"God bless my soul!" cried Captain Jack Fosdyke with extraordinary animation. "Here, come and have a cocktail. Come and have some dinner. Well, well, well, well, well!"

At the dinner table the spell which her companion was casting on Agnes Flack deepened in intensity. There seemed no limits to the power of this wonder man. He met the head waiter's eye and made him wilt. He spoke with polished knowledge of food and wine, comparing the hospitality of princes of his acquaintance with that of African chiefs he had known. Between the courses he danced like something dark and slithery from the Argentine. Little wonder that ere long he had Agnes Flack fanning herself with her napkin.

A girl who could, had she seen good reason to do so, have felled an ox with a single blow, in the presence of Captain Jack Fosdyke she felt timid and fluttering. He was turning on the charm as if through the nozzle of a hose-pipe, and it was going all over her and she liked it. She was conscious of a dreamlike sensation, as if she were floating on a pink cloud over an ocean of joy. For the first time in weeks the image of Sidney McMurdo had passed completely from her mind. There was still, presumably, a McMurdo, Sidney, in the telephone book, but in the thoughts of Agnes Flack, no.

The conversation turned to sports and athleticism.

"You swim wonderfully," she said, for that salt water had long since ceased to rankle.

"Yes, I've always been a pretty decent swimmer. I learned in the lake at Wapshott."

"Wapshott?"

"Wapshott Castle, Wapshott-on-the-Wap, Hants., the family seat. I don't go there often nowadays—too busy—but when I do I have a good time. Plenty of ridin', shootin', fishin' and all that."

"Are you fond of riding?"

"I like steeplechasin'. The spice of danger, don't you know, what? Ever seen the Grand National?"

"Not yet."

"I won it a couple of times. I remember on the second occasion Lady Astor saying to me that I ought to saw off a leg and give the other fellows a chance. Lord Beaverbrook, who overheard the remark, was much amused."

"You seem to be marvellous at everything."

"I am."

"Do you play golf?"

"Oh, rather. Scratch."

"We might have a game to-morrow."

"Not to-morrow. Lunching in Washington. A bore, but I can't get out of it. Harry insisted."

"Harry?"

"Truman. We'll have a game when I get back. I may be able to give you a pointer or two. Bobby Jones said to me once that he would never have won the British and American Amateur and Open, if he hadn't studied my swing."

Agnes gasped.

"You don't know Bobby Jones?"

"We're like brothers."

"I once got his autograph."

"Say the word, dear lady, and I'll get you a signed photograph."

Agnes clutched at the table. She had thought for a moment that she was going to faint. And so the long evening wore on.

Mark you, I do not altogether blame Agnes Flack. Hers had been a sheltered life, and nothing like Captain Jack Fosdyke had ever happened to her before. Here was a man who, while looking like something out of a full page coloured advertisement in a slick paper magazine, seemed to have been everywhere and to know everybody.

When he took her out in the moonlight and spoke nonchalantly of Lady Astor, Lord Beaverbrook, Borneo head hunters, Mervyn Le Roy and the brothers Shubert one can appreciate her attitude and understand how inevitable it was that Sidney McMurdo should have gone right back in the betting. In accepting the addresses of Sidney McMurdo, she realized that she had fallen into the error of making her selection before walking the length of the counter.

In short, to hurry on this painful part of my story, when Sidney McMurdo eventually arrived with his suitcase and bag of clubs and was about to clasp Agnes Flack to his forty-four-inch bosom, he was surprised and distressed to observe her step back and raise a deprecating hand. A moment later she was informing him that she had made a mistake and that the photograph on her dressing-table at even date was not his but that of Captain Jack Fosdyke, to whom she was now betrothed.

This, of course, was a nice bit of news for a devoted *fiance* to get after a four-hour journey on a hot day in a train without a dining-car, and it is not too much to say that for an instant Sidney McMurdo tottered beneath it like a preliminary bout heavy-weight who has been incautious enough to place his jaw *en rapport* with the fist of a fellow member of the Truck Drivers' Union. Dimly he heard Agnes Flack saying that she would be a sister to him, and this threat, for he was a man already loaded up with sisters almost beyond capacity, brought him out of what had promised to be a lasting coma.

His eyes flashed, his torso swelled, the muscles leaped about all over him under his pullover, and with a muttered "Is zat so?" he turned on his heel and left her, but not before he had asked for and obtained his supplanter's address. It was his intention to visit the latter and begin by picking him up by the scruff of the neck and shaking him like a rat. After that he would carry on as the inspiration of the moment dictated.

My efforts up to the present having been directed towards limning the personalities of Agnes Flack and Captain Jack

Fosdyke, I have not yet given you anything in the nature of a comprehensive character study of Sidney McMurdo. I should now reveal that he was as fiercely jealous a man as ever swung an aluminium putter. Othello might have had a slight edge on him in that respect, but it would have been a very near thing. Rob him of the girl he loved, and you roused the lion in Sidney McMurdo.

He was flexing his muscles and snorting ominously when he reached the cosy bungalow which Captain Jack Fosdyke had rented for the summer season. The Captain, who was humming one of the song hits from last year's war dance of the 'Mgubo-Mgompis and cleaning an elephant gun, looked up inquiringly as he entered, and Sidney glowered down at him, his muscles still doing the shimmy.

"Captain Fosdyke?"

"The same."

"Pleased to meet you."

"Naturally."

"Could I have a word with you?"

"A thousand."

"It is with reference to your sneaking my girl."

"Oh, that?" Are you this McMurdo bird of whom I have heard Agnes speak?"

"I am."

"You were engaged, I understand, till I came along?"

"We were."

"Too bad. Well, that's how it goes. Will you be seeing her shortly?"

"I may decide to confront her again."

"Then you might tell her I've found that elephant gun I mentioned to her. She was anxious to see the notches on it."

Sidney, who had been about to call his companion a

sneaking, slinking serpent and bid him rise and put his hands up, decided that later on would do. He did not at all like this talk of notches and elephant guns.

"Are there notches on your elephant gun?"

"There are notches on all my guns. I use them in rotation. This is the one I shot the chief of the 'Mgobo-Mgumpis with."

The chill which had begun to creep over Sidney McMurdo from the feet upwards became more marked. His clenched fists relaxed, and his muscles paused in their rhythmic dance.

"You shot him?"

"Quite."

"Er—do you often do that sort of thing?"

"Invariably, when chaps smirch the honour of the Fosdykes. If a bally bounder smirches the honour of the Fosdykes, I shoot him like a dog."

"Like a dog?"

"Like a dog."

"What sort of dog?"

"Any sort of dog."

"I see."

There was a pause.

"Would you consider that being plugged in the eye, smirched the honour of the Fosdykes?"

"Unquestionably. I was once plugged in the eye by the chief of the 'Mgeebo-Mgoopies. And when they buried him the little port had seldom seen a costlier funeral."

"I see," said Sidney McMurdo thoughtfully. "I see. Well, good-bye. It's been nice meeting you."

"It always is," said Captain Jack Fosdyke. "Drop in again. I'll show you my tommy gun."

Sidney McMurdo had not much forehead, being one of

those rugged men whose front hair finishes a scant inch or so above the eyebrows, but there was just room on it for a ruminative frown, and he was wearing this as he left the bungalow and set out for a walk along the shore. He was fully alive to the fact that in the recent interview he had cut a poorish figure, failing entirely to express himself and fulfil himself.

But how else, he asked himself, could he have acted? His was a simple nature, easily baffled by the unusual, and he frankly did not see how he could have coped with a rival who appeared to be a combination of mass murderer and United States Armoury. His customary routine of picking rivals up by the scruff of the neck and shaking them like rats plainly would not have answered here.

He walked on, brooding, and so distrait was he that anyone watching him would have given attractive odds that before long he would bump into something. This occurred after he had proceeded some hundred yards, the object into which he bumped being a slender, streamlined, serpentine female who looked like one of those intense young women who used to wreck good men's lives in the silent films but seem rather to have died out since the talkies came in. She was dark and subtle and exotic, and she appeared to be weeping.

Sidney, however, who was a close observer, saw that the trouble was that she had got a fly in her eye, and to whip out his pocket handkerchief and tilt her head back and apply first aid was with him the work of an instant. She thanked him brokenly, blinking as she did so. Then, for the first time seeming to see him steadily and see him whole, she gave a little gasp, and said:

"You!"

Her eyes, which were large and dark and lustrous, like

those of some inscrutable priestess of a strange old religion, focused themselves on him, as she spoke, and seemed to go through him in much the same way as a couple of red hot bullets would go through a pound of butter. He rocked back on his heels, feeling as if someone had stirred up his interior organs with an egg beater.

"I have been waiting for you—oh, so long."

"I'm sorry," said Sidney. "Am I late?"

"My man!"

"I beg your pardon?"

"I love you," explained the beautiful unknown. "Kiss me."

If she had studied for weeks, she could not have found a better approach to Sidney McMurdo and one more calculated to overcome any customer's sales resistance which might have been lurking in him. Something along these lines from a woman something along her lines was exactly what he had been feeling he could do with. A lover who has just got off a stuffy train to find himself discarded like a worn out glove by the girl he has worshipped and trusted is ripe for treatment of this kind.

His bruised spirit began to heal. He kissed her, as directed, and there started to burgeon within him the thought that Agnes Flack wasn't everybody and that it would do her no harm to have this demonstrated to her. A heartening picture flitted through his mind of himself ambling up to Agnes Flack with this spectacular number on his arm, saying to her: "If you don't want me, it would appear that there are others who do."

"Nice day," he said, to help the conversation along.

"Divine. Hark to the wavelets, plashing on the shore. How they seem to fill one with a sense of the inexpressibly ineffable."

"That's right. They do, don't they?"

"Are they singing us songs of old Greece, of Triton blowing on his wreathed horn and the sunlit loves of gods and
goddesses?"

"I'm afraid I couldn't tell you," said Sidney McMurdo.
"I'm a stranger in these parts myself."

She sighed.

"I, too. But it is my fate to be a stranger everywhere. I
live a life apart; alone, aloof, solitary, separate; wrapped
up in my dreams and visions. 'Tis ever so with the artist."

"You're a painter?"

"In ink, not in oils. I depict the souls of men and wom-
en. I am Cora McGuffy Spottsworth."

The name was new to Sidney, who seldom got much beyond the golf weeklies and the house organ of the firm for
which he worked, but he gathered that she must be a writer
of sorts and made a mental note to wire Brentano's for her
complete output and bone it up without delay.

They walked along in silence. At the next ice cream stand
he bought her a nut sundae, and she ate it with a sort of
restrained emotion which suggested the presence of banked-
up fires, one hand wielding the spoon, the other nestling
in his like a white orchid.

Sidney McMurdo was now right under the ether. As he
sipped his sarsaparilla, his soul seemed to heave and bub-
ble like a Welsh rabbit coming to the boil. From regarding
this woman merely as a sort of stooge, to be exhibited to
Agnes Flack as evidence that McMurdo Preferred, even if
she had seen fit to unload her holdings, was far from being
a drug in the market, he had come to look upon her as a
strong man's mate. So that when, having disposed of the
last spoonful, she said she hoped he had not thought her
abrupt just now in saying that she loved him, he replied
"Not at all, not at all," adding that it was precisely the sort

of thing he liked to hear. It amazed him that he could ever have considered a mere number-three-iron-swinging robot like Agnes Flack as a life partner.

"It needs but a glance, don't you think, to recognize one's mate?"

"Oh, sure."

"Especially if you have met and loved before. You remember those old days in Egypt?"

"Egypt?" Sidney was a little bewildered. The town she mentioned was, he knew, in Illinois, but he had never been there.

"In Egypt, Antony."

"The name is Sidney. McMurdo, Sidney George."

"In your present incarnation, possibly. But once, long ago, you were Marc Antony and I was Cleopatra."

"Of course, yes," said Sidney. "It all comes back to me."

"What times those were. That night on the Nile!"

"Some party."

"I drew Revell Carstairs in my Furnace of Sin from my memories of you in the old days. He was tall and broad and strong, but with the heart of a child. All these years I have been seeking for you, and now that I have found you, would you have had me hold back and mask my love from respect for outworn fetishes of convention?"

"You betcher. I mean, you betcher not."

"What have we to do with conventions? The world would say that I have known you for a mere half-hour—"

"Twenty-five minutes," said Sidney, who was rather a stickler for accuracy, consulting his wrist-watch.

"Or twenty-five minutes. In Egypt I was in your arms in forty seconds."

"Quick service."

"That was ever my way, direct and sudden and impulsive. I remember saying once to Mr. Spottsworth—"

Sidney McMurdo was conscious of a quick chill, similar to that which had affected him when Captain Jack Fosdyke had spoken of elephant guns and notches. His moral code, improving after a rocky start in his Marc Antony days, had become rigid and would never allow him to be a breaker-up of homes. Besides, there was his insurance company to be considered. A scandal might mean the loss of his second vice-presidency.

"Mr. Spottsworth?" he echoed, his jaw falling a little. "Is there a Mr. Spottsworth?"

"Not now. He has left me."

"The low hound."

"He had no option. Double pneumonia. By now, no doubt, he has been reincarnated, but probably only as a jellyfish. A jellyfish need not come between us."

"Certainly not," said Sidney McMurdo, speaking warmly, for he had once been stung by one, and they resumed their saunter.

Agnes Flack, meanwhile, though basking in the rays of Captain Jack Fosdyke, had by no means forgotten Sidney McMurdo. In the days that followed their painful interview, in the intervals of brushing up her fifty yards from the pin game in preparation for the Women's Singles contest which was shortly to take place, she found her thoughts dwelling on him quite a good deal. A girl who has loved, even if mistakenly, can never be indifferent to the fortunes of the man whom she once regarded as the lode star of her life. She kept wondering how he was making out, and hoped that his vacation was not being spoiled by a broken heart.

The first time she saw him, accordingly, she should have been relieved and pleased. He was escorting Cora McGuffy

Spottsworth along the boardwalk, and it was abundantly obvious even from a casual glance that if his heart had ever been broken, there had been some adroit work done in the repair shop. Clark Gable could have improved his technique by watching the way he bent over Cora McGuffy Spottsworth and stroked her slender arm. He also, while bending and stroking, whispered into her shell-like ear, and you could see that what he was saying was good stuff. His whole attitude was that of a man who, recognizing that he was on a good thing, was determined to push it along.

But Agnes Flack was not relieved and pleased; she was disturbed and concerned. She was perhaps a hard judge, but Cora McGuffy Spottsworth looked to her like the sort of woman who goes about stealing the plans of forts—or, at the best, leaning back negligently on a settee and saying "Prince, my fan." The impression Agnes formed was of something that might be all right stepping out of a pie at a bachelor party, but not the type you could take home to meet mother.

Her first move, therefore, on encountering Sidney at the golf club one morning, was to institute a probe.

"Who," she demanded, not beating about the bush, "was that lady I saw you walking down the street with?"

Her tone, in which he seemed to detect the note of criticism, offended Sidney.

"That," he replied with a touch of hauteur, "was no lady, that was my *fiancee.*"

Agnes reeled. She had noticed that he was wearing a new tie and that his hair had been treated with Sticko, the pomade that satisfies, but she had not dreamed that matters had proceeded as far as this.

"You are engaged?"

"And how!"

"Oh, Sidney!"

He stiffened.

"That will be all of that 'Oh, Sidney!' stuff," he retorted with spirit. "I don't see what you have to beef about. You were offered the opportunity of a merger, and when you failed to take up your option I was free, I presume, to open negotiations elsewhere. As might have been foreseen, I was snapped up the moment it got about that I was in the market."

Agnes Flack bridled.

"I'm not jealous."

"Then what's your kick?"

"It's just that I want to see you happy."

"I am."

"How can you be happy with a woman who looks like a snake with hips?"

"She has every right to look like a snake with hips. In a former incarnation she used to be Cleopatra. I," said Sidney McMurdo, straightening his tie, "was Antony."

"Who told you that?"

"She did. She has all the facts."

"She must be crazy."

"Not at all. I admit that for a while at our first meeting some such thought did cross my mind, but the matter is readily explained. She is a novelist. You may have heard of Cora McGuffy Spottsworth?"

Agnes uttered a cry.

"What? Oh, she can't be."

"She has documents to prove it."

"But, Sidney, she's awful. At my school two girls were expelled because they were found with her books under their pillows. Her publisher's slogan is 'Spottsworth for Blushes.' You can't intend to marry a woman who notoriously has to write her love scenes on asbestos."

"Well, what price your intending to marry a prominent international plug-ugly who thinks nothing of shooting people with elephant guns?"

"Only African chiefs."

"African chiefs are also God's creatures."

"Not when under the influence of trade gin, Jack says. He says you have to shoot them with elephant guns then. It means nothing more, he says, than if you drew their attention to some ruling by Emily Post. Besides, he knows Bobby Jones."

"So does Bobby Jones's grocer. Does he play golf himself? That's the point."

"He plays beautifully."

"So does Cora. She expects to win the Women's Singles."

Agnes drew herself up haughtily. She was expecting to win the Women's Singles herself.

"She does, does she?"

"Yes, she does."

"Over my dead body."

"That would be a mashie niblick shot," said Sidney McMurdo thoughtfully. "She's wonderful with her mashie niblick."

With a powerful effort Agnes Flack choked down her choler.

"Well, I hope it will be all right," she said.

"Of course it will be all right. I'm the luckiest man alive."

"In any case, it's fortunate that we found out our mistake in time."

"I'll say so. A nice thing it would have been, if all this had happened after we were married. We should have had one of those situations authors have to use a row of dots for."

"Yes. Even if we had been married, I should have flown
to Jack."

"And I should have flown to Cora."

"He once killed a lion with a sardine opener."

"Cora once danced with the Duke of Windsor," said Sidney McMurdo, and with a proud tilt of the chin, went off
to give his betrothed lunch.

As a close student of the game of golf in all its phases
over a considerable number of years, I should say that
Women's Singles at fashionable seashore resorts nearly always follow the same general lines. The participants with
a reasonable hope of bringing home the bacon seldom number more than three or four, the rest being the mere dregs
of the golfing world who enter for the hell of the thing or
because they know they look well in sports clothes. The
preliminary rounds, accordingly, are never worth watching or describing. The rabbits eliminate each other with merry laughs and pretty squeals, and the tigresses massacre the
surviving rabbits, till by the time the semi-final is reached,
only grim-faced experts are left in.

It was so with the tourney this year at East Bampton.
Agnes had no difficulty in murdering the four long handicap fluffies with whom she was confronted in the early
stages, and entered the semi-final with the feeling that the
competition proper was now about to begin.

Watching, when opportunity offered, the play of the future Mrs. Sidney McMurdo, who also had won through to
the penultimate round, she found herself feeling a little easier
in her mind. Cora McGuffy Spottsworth still looked to her
like one of those women who lure men's souls to the shoals
of sin, but there was no question that, as far as knowing
what to do with a number four iron when you put it into

her hands was concerned, she would make a good wife. Her apprehensions regarding Sidney's future were to a certain extent relieved.

It might be that his bride at some future date would put arsenic in his coffee or elope with the leader of a band, but before she did so, she would in all essential respects be a worthy mate. He would never have to suffer that greatest of all spiritual agonies, the misery of the husband whose wife insists on his playing with her daily because the doctor thinks she ought to have fresh air and exercise. Cora McGuffy Spottsworth might, and probably would, recline on tiger skins in the nude and expect Sidney to drink champagne out of her shoe, but she would never wear high heels on the links or say Tee-hee when she missed a putt. On the previous day, while eliminating her most recent opponent, she had done the long hole in four, and Agnes, who had just taken a rather smelly six, was impressed.

The afternoon of the semi-final was one of those heavy, baking afternoons which cause people to crawl about saying that it is not the heat they mind, but the humidity. After weeks of sunshine the weather was about to break. Thunder was in the air, and once sprightly caddies seemed to droop beneath the weight of their bags. To Agnes, who was impervious to weather conditions, this testing warmth was welcome. It might, she felt, affect her adversary's game.

Cora McGuffy Spottsworth and her antagonist drove off first, and once again Agnes was impressed by the lissom fluidity of the other's swing. Sidney, who was hovering lovingly in the offing, watched her effort with obvious approval.

"You won't want that one back, old girl," he said, and a curious pang shot through Agnes, as if she had bitten into a bad oyster. How often had she heard him say the same

thing to her! For an instant she was aware of a sorrowful
sense of loss. Then her eye fell on Captain Jack Fosdyke,
smoking a debonair cigarette, and the anguish abated. If
Captain Jack Fosdyke was not a king among men, she told
herself, she didn't know a king among men when she saw
one.

When the couple ahead were out of distance, she drove
off and achieved her usual faultless shot. Captain Jack Fosdyke said it reminded him of one he had made when playing a friendly round with Harry Hopkins, and they moved
off.

From the moment when her adversary had driven off the
first tee, Agnes Flack had realized that she had no easy task
before her, but one that would test her skill to the utmost.
The woman in question looked like a schoolmistress, and
she hit her ball as if it had been a refractory pupil. And
to increase the severity of Agnes's ordeal, she seldom failed
to hit it straight.

Agnes, too, being at the top of her form, the result was
that for ten holes the struggle proceeded with but slight advantage to either. At the sixth, Agnes, putting superbly,
contrived to be one up, only to lose her lead on the seventh,
where the schoolmistress holed out an iron shot for a bir-
die. They were all square at the turn, and still all square
on the eleventh tee. It was as Agnes was addressing her ball
here that there came a roll of thunder, and the rain which
had been threatening all the afternoon began to descend in
liberal streams.

It seemed to Agnes Flack that Providence was at last in-
tervening on behalf of a good woman. She was always at
her best in dirty weather. Give her a tropical deluge accompanied by thunderbolts and other Acts of God, and she took
on a new vigour. And she just had begun to be filled with

a stern joy, the joy of an earnest golfer who after a grueling struggle feels that the thing is in the bag, when she was chagrined to observe that her adversary appeared to be of precisely the same mind. So far from being discouraged by the warring elements, the schoolmistress plainly welcomed the new conditions. Taking in the rain at every pore with obvious relish, she smote her ball as if it had been writing rude things about her on the blackboard, and it was as much as Agnes could do to halve the eleventh and twelfth.

All this while Captain Fosdyke had been striding round with them, chatting between the strokes of cannibals he had met and lions which had regretted meeting him, but during these last two holes a strange silence had fallen upon him. And it was as Agnes uncoiled herself on the thirteenth tee after another of her powerful drives that she was aware of him at her elbow, endeavouring to secure her attention. His coat collar was turned up, and he looked moist and unhappy.

"I say," he said, "what about this?"

"What?"

"This bally rain."

"Just a Scotch mist."

"Don't you think you had better chuck it?"

Agnes stared.

"Are you suggesting that I give up the match?"

"That's the idea."

Agnes stared again.

"Give up my chance of getting into the final just because of a drop of rain?"

"Well, we're getting dashed wet, what? And golf's only a game, I mean, if you know what I mean."

Agnes's eyes flashed like the lightning which had just struck a tree not far off.

"I would not dream of forfeiting the match," she cried. "And if you leave me now, I'll never speak to you again."

"Oh, right ho," said Captain Jack Fosdyke. "Merely a suggestion."

He turned his collar up a little higher, and the game proceeded.

Agnes was rudely shaken. Those frightful words about golf being only a game kept ringing in her head. This thing had come upon her like one of the thunderbolts which she liked to have around her when playing an important match. In the brief period of time during which she had known him, Captain Jack Fosdyke's game had appealed to her depths. He had shown himself a skilful and meritorious performer, at times brilliant. But what is golfing skill, if the golfing spirit is absent?

Then a healing thought came to her. He had but jested. In the circles in which he moved, the gay world of African chiefs and English dukes in which he had so long had his being, light-hearted badinage of this kind was no doubt *de rigueur*. To hold his place in that world, a man had to be a merry kidder, a light josher and a mad wag. It was probably because he thought she needed cheering up that he had exercised his flashing wit.

Her doubts vanished. Her faith in him was once more firm. It was as if a heavy load had rolled off her heart. Playing her second, a brassie shot, she uncorked such a snorter that a few moments later she found herself one up again.

As for Captain Jack Fosdyke, he was fully occupied trying to keep the rain from going down the back of his neck and reminding himself that Agnes was the only niece of Josiah Flack, a man who had a deep sense of family obligations, more money than you could shake a stick at and one foot in the grave.

Whether or not Agnes's opponent was actually a school-mistress, I do not know. But if she was, the juvenile education of this country is in good hands. In a crisis where a weaker woman might have wilted—one down and five to play—she remained firm and undaunted. Her hat was a frightful object, but it was still in the ring. She fought Agnes, hole after hole, with indomitable tenacity. The fourteenth and fifteenth she halved, but at the sixteenth she produced another of those inspired iron shots and the match was squared. And, going from strength to strength, she won the seventeenth with a twenty-foot putt.

"Dormy," she said, speaking for the first time.

It is always a mistake to chatter on the links. It disturbs the concentration. To this burst of speech I attribute the fact that the schoolmistress's tee shot at the eighteenth was so markedly inferior to its predecessors. The eighteenth was a short hole ending just outside the club-house and even rabbits seldom failed to make the green. But she fell short by some yards, and Agnes, judging the distance perfectly, was on and near the pin. The schoolmistress chipped so successfully with her second that it seemed for an instant that she was about to hole out. But the ball stopped a few inches from its destination, and Agnes, with a three-foot putt for a two, felt her heart leap up like that of the poet Wordsworth when he saw a rainbow. She had not missed more than one three-foot putt a year since her kindergarten days.

It was at this moment that there emerged from the club-house where it had been having a saucer of tea and a slice of cake, a Pekinese dog of hard-boiled aspect. It strolled on to the green, and approaching Agnes's ball subjected it to a pop-eyed scrutiny.

There is a vein of eccentricity in all Pekes. Here, one

would have said, was a ball with little about it to arrest the attention of a thoughtful dog. It was just a regulation blue dot, slightly battered. Yet it was obvious immediately that it had touched a chord. The animal sniffed at it with every evidence of interest and pleasure. It patted it with its paw. It smelled it. Then, lying down, it took it in its mouth and began to chew meditatively.

To Agnes the mere spectacle of a dog on a green had been a thing of horror. Brought up from childhood to reverence the rules of Greens Committees, she had shuddered violently from head to foot. Recovering herself with a powerful effort, she advanced and said "Shoo!" The Peke rolled its eyes sideways, inspected her, dismissed her as of no importance or entertainment value, and resumed its fletcherizing. Agnes advanced another step, and the schoolmistress for the second time broke her Trappist vows.

"You can't move that dog," she said. "It's a hazard."

"Nonsense."

"I beg your pardon, it is. If you get into casual water, you don't mop it up with a brush and pail, do you? Certainly you don't. You play out of it. Same thing when you get into a casual dog."

They train these schoolmistresses to reason clearly. Agnes halted, baffled. Then her eye fell on Captain Jack Fosdyke, and she saw the way out.

"There's nothing in the rules to prevent a spectator, meeting a dog on the course, from picking it up and fondling it."

It was the schoolmistress' turn to be baffled. She bit her lip in chagrined silence.

"Jack, dear," said Agnes, "pick up that dog and fondle it. And," she added, for she was a quick-thinking girl, "when doing so, hold its head over the hole."

It was a behest which one might have supposed that any

knight, eager to win his lady's favour, would have leaped to fulfil. But Captain Jack Fosdyke did not leap. There was a dubious look on his handsome face, and he scratched his chin pensively.

"Just a moment," he said. "This is a thing you want to look at from every angle. Pekes are awfully nippy, you know. They make sudden darts at your ankles."

"Well, you like a spice of danger."

"Within reason, dear lady, within reason."

"You once killed a lion with a sardine opener."

"Ah, but I first quelled him with the power of the human eye. The trouble with Pekes is, they're so shortsighted, they can't see the human eye, so you can't quell them with it."

"You could if you put your face right down close."

"If," said Captain Jack Fosdyke thoughtfully.

Agnes gasped. Already this afternoon she had had occasion to stare at this man. She now stared again.

"Are you afraid of a dog?"

He gave a light laugh.

"Afraid of dogs? That would amuse the boys at Buckingham Palace, if they could hear it. They know what a daredevil I was in the old days when I was Deputy Master of the Royal Buckhounds. I remember one morning coming down to the kennels with my whistle and my bag of dog biscuits and finding one of the personnel in rather an edgey mood. I spoke to it soothingly—'Fido, Fido, good boy, Fido!'—but it merely bared its teeth and snarled, and I saw that it was about to spring. There wasn't a moment to lose. By a bit of luck the Bluemantle Pursuivant at Arms had happened to leave his blue mantle hanging over the back of a chair. I snatched it up and flung it over the animal's head, after which it was a simple task to secure it with stout cords and put on its muzzle. There was a good deal of comment on my adroitness. Lord Slythe and Sayle, who was present, I remember, said to Lord Knubble of Knopp, who was also present, that he hadn't seen anything so resourceful since the day when the Chancellor of the Duchy of Lancaster rang in a bad half-crown on the First Gold Stick in Waiting."

It was the sort of story which in happier days had held Agnes Flack enthralled, but now it merely added to her depression and disillusionment. She made a last attempt to appeal to his better feelings.

"But, Jack, if you don't shift this beastly little object, I shall lose the match."

"Well, what does that matter, dear child? A mere tiddly seaside competition."

Agnes had heard enough. Her eyes were stony.

"You refuse? Then our engagement is at an end."

"Oh, don't say that."

"I do say that."

It was plain that a struggle was proceeding in Captain Jack Fosdyke's soul, or what one may loosely call his soul. He was thinking how rich Josiah Flack was, how fond of his niece, and how frail. On the other hand, the Peke, now suspecting a plot against its well-being, had bared a small but serviceable tooth at the corner of its mouth. The whole situation was very difficult.

As he stood there at a man's cross-roads, there came out of the club-house, smoking a cigarette in a sixteen-inch holder, an expensively upholstered girl with platinum hair and vermilion finger-nails. She bent and picked the Peke up.

"My little angel would appear to be interfering with your hockey-knocking," she said. "Why, hello, Captain Fosdyke. You here? Come along in and give me a cocktail."

She kissed the Peke lovingly on the top of its head and

carried it into the clubhouse. The ball went with them.

"She's gone into the bar," said the schoolmistress. "You'll have to chip out from there. Difficult shot. I'd use a niblick."

Captain Jack Fosdyke was gazing after the girl, a puzzled wrinkle on his forehead.

"I've met her before somewhere, but I can't place her. Who is she?"

"One of the idle rich," said the schoolmistress, sniffing. Her views were Socialistic.

Captain Jack Fosdyke started.

"Idle *rich?*"

"That's Lulabelle Sprockett, the Sprockett's Superfine Sardine heiress. She's worth a hundred million in her own right."

"In her own right? You mean she's actually got the stuff in the bank, where she can lay hands on it whenever she feels disposed? Good God!" cried Captain Jack Fosdyke. "Bless my soul! Well, well, well, well, well!" He turned to Agnes. "Did I hear you mention something about breaking our engagement? Right ho, dear lady, right ho. Just as you say. Nice to have known you. I shall watch your future career with considerable interest. Excuse me," said Captain Jack Fosdyke.

There was a whirring sound, and he disappeared into the club-house.

"I concede the match," said Agnes dully.'

"Might just as well," said the schoolmistress.

Agnes Flack stood on the eighteenth green, contemplating the ruin of her life. It was not the loss of Captain Jack Fosdyke that was making her mourn, for the scales had fallen from her eyes. He had shown himself totally lacking in the golfing spirit, and infatuation was dead. What did

jar her was that she had lost Sidney McMurdo. In this dark
hour all the old love had come sweeping back into her soul
like a tidal wave.

Had she been mad to sever their relations?

The answer to that was "Certainly."

Had she, like a child breaking up a Noah's Ark with a
tack-hammer, deliberately sabotaged her hopes and happiness?

The reply to that was "Quite."

Would she ever see him again?

In the space allotted to this question she could pencil in
the word "Undoubtedly," for he was even now coming out
of the locker-room entrance.

"Sidney!" she cried.

He seemed depressed. His colossal shoulders were drooping, and his eyes were those of a man who has drunk the
wine of life to the lees.

"Oh, hello," he said.

There was a silence.

"How did Mrs. Spottsworth come out?" asked Agnes.

"Eh? Oh, she won."

Agnes's depression hit a new low. There was another
silence.

"She has broken the engagement," said Sidney.

The rain was still sluicing down with undiminished intensity, but it seemed to Agnes Flack, as she heard these
words, that a blaze of golden sunshine had suddenly lit up
the East Bampton golf course.

"She wanted to quit because of the rain," went on Sidney, in a low, toneless voice. "I took her by the ear and
led her round, standing over her with upraised hand as she
made her shots, ready to let her have a juicy one if she
faltered. On one or two occasions I was obliged to do so.

By these means I steered her through to victory, but she didn't like it. Having holed out on the eighteenth for a nice three, which gave her the match, she told me that I had completely changed since those days on the Nile and that she never wished to see or speak to me again in this or any other incarnation."

Agnes was gulping like on of those peculiar fish you catch down in Florida.

"Then you are free?"

"And glad of it. What I ever saw in the woman beats me. But what good is that, when I have lost you?"

"But you haven't."

"Pardon me. What about your Fosdyke?"

"I've just broken my engagement, too. Oh, Sidney, let's go right off and get married under an arch of niblicks before we make any more of these unfortunate mistakes. Let me tell you how that Fosdyke false alarm behaved."

In molten words she began to relate her story, but she had not proceeded far when she was obliged to stop, for Sidney McMurdo's strong arms were about her and he was crushing her to his bosom. And when Sidney McMurdo crushed girls to his bosom, they had to save their breath for breathing purposes, inhaling and exhaling when and if they could.

Something to Worry About

A girl stood on the shingle that fringes Millbourne Bay, gazing at the red roofs of the little village across the water. She was a pretty girl, small and trim. Just now some secret sorrow seemed to be troubling her, for on her forehead were wrinkles and in her eyes a look of wistfulness. She had, in fact, all the distinguishing marks of one who is thinking of her sailor lover.

But she was not. She had no sailor lover. What she was thinking of was that at about this time they would be lighting up the shop-windows in London, and that of all the deadly, depressing spots she had ever visited this village of Millbourne was the deadliest.

The evening shadows deepened. The incoming tide glistened oilily as it rolled over the mud flats. She rose and shivered.

"Goo! What a hole!" she said, eyeing the unconscious village morosely. "*What* a hole!"

This was Sally Preston's first evening in Millbourne. She had arrived by the afternoon train from London—not of her own free will. Left to herself, she would not have come within sixty miles of the place. London supplied all that she demanded from life. She had been born in London; she had lived there ever since—she hoped to die there. She liked fogs, motor-buses, noise, policemen, paper-boys, shops, taxi-cabs, artificial light, stone pavements, houses in long, grey rows, mud, banana-skins, and moving-picture exhibitions. Especially moving-picture exhibitions. It was, indeed, her taste for these that had caused her banishment to Millbourne.

The great public is not yet unanimous on the subject of moving-picture exhibitions. Sally, as I have said, approved of them. Her father, on the other hand, did not. An austere ex-butler, who let lodgings in Ebury Street and preached on Sundays in Hyde Park, he looked askance at the "movies." It was his boast that he had never been inside a theatre in his life, and he classed cinema palaces with theatres as wiles of the devil. Sally, suddenly unmasked as an habitual frequenter of these abandoned places, sprang with one bound into prominence as the Bad Girl of the Family. Instant removal from the range of temptation being the only possible plan, it seemed to Mr. Preston that a trip to the country was indicated.

He selected Millbourne because he had been butler at the Hall there, and because his sister Jane, who had been a parlourmaid at the Rectory, was now married and living in the village.

Certainly he could not have chosen a more promising reformatory for Sally. Here, if anywhere, might she forget the heady joys of the cinema. Tucked away in the corner of its little bay, which an acommodating island converts into a still lagoon, Millbourne lies dozing. In all sleepy Hampshire there is no sleepier spot. It is a place of calm-eyed men and drowsy dogs. Things crumble away and are not replaced. Tradesmen book orders, and then lose interest and forget to deliver the goods. Only centenarians die, and nobody worries about anything—or did not until Sally came and gave them something to worry about.

Next door to Sally's Aunt Jane, in a cosy little cottage with a wonderful little garden, lived Thomas Kitchener, a large, grave, self-sufficing young man, who, by sheer application to work, had become already, though only twenty-five, second gardener at the Hall. Gardening absorbed him. When he was not working at the Hall he was working at home. On the morning following Sally's arrival, it being a Thursday and his day off, he was crouching in a constrained attitude in his garden, every fibre of his being concentrated on the interment of a plump young bulb. Consequently, when a chunk of mud came sailing over the fence, he did not notice it.

A second, however, compelled attention by bursting like a shell on the back of his neck. He looked up, startled. Nobody was in sight. He was puzzled. It could hardly be raining mud. Yet the alternative theory, that someone in the next garden was throwing it, was hardly less bizarre. The nature of his friendship with Sally's Aunt Jane and old Mr. Williams, her husband, was comfortable rather than rollicking. It was inconceivable that they should be flinging clods at him.

As he stood wondering whether he should go to the fence and look over, or simply accept the phenomenon as one of those things which no fellow can understand, there popped up before him the head and shoulders of a girl. Poised in her right hand was a third clod, which, seeing that there was now no need for its services, she allowed to fall to the ground.

"Halloa!" she said. "Good morning."

She was a pretty girl, small and trim. Tom was by way of being the strong, silent man with a career to think of and no time for bothering about girls, but he saw that. There was, moreover, a certain alertness in her expression rarely found in the feminine population of Millbourne, who were apt to be slightly bovine.

"What do you think *you're* messing about at?" she said, affably.

Tom was a slow-minded young man, who liked to have his thoughts well under control before he spoke. He was not one of your gay rattlers. Besides, there was something about this girl which confused him to an extraordinary extent. He was conscious of new and strange emotions. He stood staring silently.

"What's your name, anyway?"

He could answer that. He did so.

"Oh! Mine's Sally Preston. Mrs. Williams is my aunt. I've come from London."

Tom had no remarks to make about London.

"Have you lived here all your life?"

"Yes," said Tom.

"My goodness! Don't you ever feel fed up? Don't you want a change?

Tom considered the point.

"No," he said.

"Well, *I* do. I want one now."

"It's a nice place," hazarded Tom.

"It's nothing of the sort. It's the beastliest hole in existence. It's absolutely chronic. Perhaps you wonder why I'm here. Don't think I *wanted* to come here. Not me! I was sent. It was like this." She gave him a rapid summary of her troubles. "There! Don't you call it a bit thick?" she concluded.

Tom considered this point, too.

"You must make the best of it," he said, at length.

"I won't! I'll make father take me back."

Tom considered this point also. Rarely, if ever, had he been given so many things to think about in one morning.

"How?" he inquired, at length.

"I don't know. I'll find some way. You see if I don't. I'll get away from here jolly quick, I give you *my* word."

Tom bent low over a rose-bush. His face was hidden, but the brown of his neck seemed to take on a richer hue, and his ears were undeniably crimson. His feet moved restlessly, and from his unseen mouth there proceeded the first gallant speech his lips had ever framed. Merely considered as a speech, it was, perhaps, nothing wonderful; but from Tom it was a miracle of chivalry and polish.

What he said was: "I hope not."

And instinct telling him that he had made his supreme effort, and that anything further must be bathos, he turned abruptly and stalked into his cottage, where he drank tea and ate bacon and thought chaotic thoughts. And when his appetite declined to carry him more than half-way through the third rasher, he understood. He was in love.

These strong, silent men who mean to be head-gardeners before they are thirty, and eliminate woman from their lives as a dangerous obstacle to the successful career, pay a heavy penalty when they do fall in love. The average irresponsible young man who has hung about North Street on Saturday nights, walked through the meadows and round by the mill and back home past the creek on Sunday afternoons, taken his seat in the brake for the annual outing, shuffled his way through the polka at the tradesmen's ball, and generally seized all legitimate opportunities for sporting with Amaryllis in the shade, has a hundred advantages which your successful careerer lacks. There was hardly a moment during the days which followed when Tom did not regret his neglected education.

For he was not Sally's only victim in Millbourne. That was the trouble. Her beauty was not of that elusive type which steals imperceptibly into the vision of the rare connoisseur. It was sudden and compelling. It hit you. Bright brown eyes beneath a mass of fair hair, a determined little chin, a slim figure—these are disturbing things; and the youths of peaceful Millbourne sat up and took notice as one youth. Throw your mind back to the last musical comedy you saw. Recall the leading lady's song with chorus of young men, all proffering devotion simultaneously in a neat row? Well, that was how the lads of the village comported themselves towards Sally.

Mr. and Mrs. Williams, till then a highly-esteemed but little-frequented couple, were astonished at the sudden influx of visitors. The cottage became practically a *salon*. There was not an evening when the little sitting-room looking out on the garden was not packed. It is true that the conversation lacked some of the sparkle generally found in the better class of *salon*. To be absolutely accurate, there was hardly any conversation. The youths of Millbourne were sturdy and honest. They were the backbone of England. England, in her hour of need, could have called upon them with the comfortable certainty that, unless they happened to be otherwise engaged, they would leap to her aid.

But they did not shine at small-talk. Conversationally they were a spent force after they had asked Mr. Williams how his rheumatism was. Thereafter they contented themselves with sitting massively about in corners, glowering at each other. Still, it was all very jolly and sociable, and helped to pass the long evenings. And, as Mrs. Williams pointed out, in reply to some rather strong remarks from Mr. Williams on the subject of packs of young fools who made it impossible for a man to get a quiet smoke in his own home, it kept them out of the public-houses.

Tom Kitchener, meanwhile, observed the invasion with growing dismay. Shyness barred him from the evening gatherings, and what was going on in that house, with young bloods like Ted Pringle, Albert Parsons, Arthur

Brown, and Joe Blossom (to name four of the most assiduous) exercising their fascinations at close range, he did not
like to think. Again and again he strove to brace himself
up to join the feasts of reason and flows of soul which he
knew were taking place nightly around the object of his de-
votions, but every time he failed. Habit is a terrible thing;
it shackles the strongest, and Tom had fallen into the habit
of inquiring after Mr. Williams' rheumatism over the garden
fence first thing in the morning.

It was a civil, neighbourly thing to do, but it annihilated
the only excuse he could think of for looking in at night.
He could not help himself. It was like some frightful
scourge—the morphine habit, or something of that sort. Every morning he swore to himself that nothing would induce
him to mention the subject of rheumatism, but no sooner
had the stricken old gentleman's head appeared above the
fence than out it came.

"Morning, Mr. Williams."

"Morning, Tom."

Pause, indicative of a strong man struggling with himself; then:—

"How's the rheumatism, Mr. Williams?"

"Better, thank'ee, Tom."

And there he was, with his guns spiked.

However, he did not give up. He brought to his wooing
the same determination which had made him second
gardener at the Hall at twenty-five. He was a novice at the
game, but instinct told him that a good line of action was
to shower gifts. He did so. All he had to shower was vegetables, and he showered them in a way that would have
caused the goddess Ceres to be talked about. His garden
became a perfect crater, erupting vegetables. Why vegetables? I think I hear some heckler cry. Why not flowers—

fresh, fair, fragrant flowers? You can do a lot with flowers. Girls love them. There is poetry in them. And, what
is more, there is a recognised language of flowers. Shoot
in a rose, or a calceolaria, or an herbaceous border, or something, I gather, and you have made a formal proposal of
marriage without any of the trouble of rehearsing a long
speech and practising appropriate gestures in front of your
bedroom looking-glass. Why, then, did not Thomas Kitchener give Sally Preston flowers? Well, you see, unfortunately, it was now late autumn, and there were no flowers.
Nature had temporarily exhausted her floral blessings, and
was jogging along with potatoes and artichokes and things.
Love is like that. It invariably comes just at the wrong time.
A few months before there had been enough roses in Tom
Kitchener's garden to win the hearts of a dozen girls. Now
there were only vegetables. 'Twas ever thus.

It was not to be expected that a devotion so practically
displayed should escape comment. This was supplied by that
shrewd observer, old Mr. Williams. He spoke seriously to
Tom across the fence on the subject of his passion.

"Young Tom," he said, "drop it."

Tom muttered unintelligibly. Mr. Williams adjusted the
top-hat without which he never stirred abroad, even into
his garden. He blinked benevolently at Tom.

"You're making up to that young gal of Jane's," he
proceeded. "You can't deceive *me*. All these p'taties, and
what not. *I* seen your game fast enough. Just you drop it,
young Tom."

"Why?" muttered Tom, rebelliously. A sudden distaste
for old Mr. Williams blazed within him.

"Why? 'Cos you'll only burn your fingers if you don't,
that's why. I been watching this young gal of Jane's, and
I seen what sort of a young gal she be. She's a flipperty piece,

that's what she be. You marry that young gal, Tom, and you'll never have no more quiet and happiness. She'd just take and turn the place upsy-down on you. The man as marries that young gal has got to be master in his own home. He's got to show her what's what. Now, you ain't got the devil in you to do that, Tom. You're what I might call a sort of a sheep. I admires it in you, Tom. I like to see a young man steady and quiet, same as what you be. So that's how it is, you see. Just you drop this foolishness, young Tom, and leave that young gal be, else you'll burn your fingers, same as what I say."

And, giving his top-hat a rakish tilt, the old gentleman ambled indoors, satisfied that he had dropped a guarded hint in a pleasant and tactful manner.

It is to be supposed that this interview stung Tom to swift action. Otherwise, one cannot explain why he should not have been just as reticent on the subject nearest his heart when bestowing on Sally the twenty-seventh cabbage as he had been when administering the hundred and sixtieth potato. At any rate, the fact remains that, as that fateful vegetable changed hands across the fence, something resembling a proposal of marriage did actually proceed from him. As a sustained piece of emotional prose it fell short of the highest standard. Most of it was lost at the back of his throat, and what did emerge was mainly inaudible. However, as she distinctly caught the word "love" twice, and as Tom was shuffling his feet and streaming with perspiration, and looking everywhere at once except at her, Sally grasped the situation. Whereupon, without any visible emotion, she accepted him.

Tom had to ask her to repeat her remark. He could not believe his luck. It is singular how diffident a normally self-confident man can become, once he is in love. When Colonel

Milvery, of the Hall, had informed him of his promotion
to the post of second gardener, Tom had demanded no *encore*. He knew his worth. He was perfectly aware that he
was a good gardener, and official recognition of the fact
left him gratified, but unperturbed. But this affair of Sally
was quite another matter. It had revolutionised his stan-
dards of value—forced him to consider himself as a man,
entirely apart from his skill as a gardener. And until this
moment he had had grave doubt as to whether, apart from
his skill as a gardener, he amounted to much.

He was overwhelmed. He kissed Sally across the fence
humbly. Sally, for her part, seemed very unconcerned about
it all. A more critical man than Thomas Kitchener might
have said that, to all appearances, the thing rather bored
Sally.

"Don't tell anybody just yet," she stipulated.
Tom would have given much to be allowed to announce
his triumph defiantly to old Mr. Williams, to say nothing
of making a considerable noise about it in the village; but
her wish was law, and he reluctantly agreed.

There are moments in a man's life when, however en-
thusiastic a gardener he may be, his soul soars above vegetables. Tom's shot with a jerk into the animal kingdom. The
first present he gave Sally in his capacity of fiance was a dog.

It was a half-grown puppy with long legs and a long tail,
belonging to no one species, but generously distributing itself among about six. Sally loved it, and took it with her
wherever she went. And on one of these rambles down
swooped Constable Cobb, the village policeman, pointing
out that, contrary to regulations, the puppy had no collar.

It is possible that a judicious meekness on Sally's part
might have averted disaster. Mr. Cobb was human, and

Sally was looking particularly attractive that morning.
Meekness, however, did not come easily to Sally. In a
speech which began as argument and ended (Mr. Cobb
proving solid and unyielding) as pure cheek, she utterly
routed the constable. But her victory was only a moral one,
for as she turned to go Mr. Cobb, dull red and puffing
slightly, was already entering particulars of the affair in his
note-book, and Sally knew that the last word was with him.

On her way back she met Tom Kitchener. He was looking very tough and strong, and at the sight of him a half-
formed idea, which she had regretfully dismissed as imprac-
ticable, of assaulting Constable Cobb, returned to her in
an amended form. Tom did not know it, but the reason why
she smiled so radiantly upon him at that moment was that
she had just elected him to the post of hired assassin. While
she did not want Constable Cobb actually assassinated, she
earnestly desired him to have his helmet smashed down over
his eyes; and it seemed to her that Tom was the man to do it.

She poured out her grievance to him and suggested her
scheme. She even elaborated it.

"Why shouldn't you wait for him one night and throw
him into the creek? It isn't deep, and it's jolly muddy."

"Um!" said Tom, doubtfully.

"It would just teach him," she pointed out.

But the prospect of undertaking the higher education of
the police did not seem to appeal to Tom. In his heart he
rather sympathised with Constable Cobb. He saw the policeman's point of view. It is all very well to talk, but when
you are stationed in a sleepy village where no one ever
murders, or robs, or commits arson, or even gets drunk and
disorderly in the street, a puppy without a collar is simply
a godsend. A man must look out for himself.

He tried to make this side of the question clear to Sally,

but failed signally. She took a deplorable view of his attitude.

"I might have known you'd have been afraid," she said, with a contemptuous jerk of her chin. "Good morning."

Tom flushed. He knew he had never been afraid of anything in his life, except her; but nevertheless the accusation stung. And as he was still afraid of her he stammered as he began to deny the charge.

"Oh, leave off!" said Sally, irritably. "Suck a lozenge."

"I'm not afraid," said Tom, condensing his remarks to their minimum as his only chance of being intelligible.

"You are."

"I'm not. It's just that I—"

A nasty gleam came into Sally's eyes. Her manner was haughty.

"It doesn't matter." She paused. "I've no doubt Ted Pringle will do what I want."

For all her contempt, she could not keep a touch of uneasiness from her eyes as she prepared to make her next remark. There was a look about Tom's set jaw which made her hesitate. But her temper had run away with her, and she went on.

"I am sure he will," she said. "When we became engaged he said that he would do anything for me."

There are some speeches that are such conversational knock-out blows that one can hardly believe that life will ever pick itself up and go on again after them. Yet it does. The dramatist brings down the curtain on such speeches. The novelist blocks his reader's path with a zareba of stars. But in life there are no curtains, no stars, nothing final and definite—only ragged pauses and discomfort. There was such a pause now.

"What do you mean?" said Tom at last. "You promised

to marry me."

"I know I did—and I promised to marry Ted Pringle!"

That touch of panic which she could not wholly repress, the panic that comes to everyone when a situation has run away with them like a strange, unmanageable machine, infused a shade too much of the defiant into Sally's manner. She had wished to be cool, even casual, but she was beginning to be afraid. Why, she could not have said. Certainly she did not anticipate violence on Tom's part. Perhaps that was it. Perhaps it was just because he was so quiet that she was afraid. She had always looked on him contemptuously as an amiable, transparent lout, and now he was puzzling her. She got an impression of something formidable behind his stolidity, something that made her feel mean and insignificant.

She fought against the feeling, but it gripped her; and, in spite of herself, she found her voice growing shrill and out of control.

"I promised to marry Ted Pringle, and I promised to marry Joe Blossom, and I promised to marry Albert Parsons. And I was going to promise to marry Arthur Brown and anybody else who asked me. So now you know! I told you I'd make father take me back to London. Well, when he hears that I've promised to marry four different men, I bet he'll have me home by the first train."

She stopped. She had more to say, but she could not say it. She stood looking at him. And he looked at her. His face was grey and his mouth oddly twisted. Silence seemed to fall on the whole universe.

Sally was really afraid now, and she knew it. She was feeling very small and defenceless in an extremely alarming world. She could not have said what it was that had happened to her. She only knew that life had become of a sudden very vivid, and that her ideas as to what was amusing had undergone a striking change. A man's development is a slow and steady process of the years—a woman's a thing of an instant. In the silence which followed her words Sally had grown up.

Tom broke the silence.

"Is that true?" he said.

His voice made her start. He had spoken quietly, but there was a new note in it, strange to her. Just as she could not have said what it was that had happened to her, so now she could not have said what had happened to Tom. He, too, had changed, but how she did not know. Yet the explanation was simple. He also had, in a sense, grown up. He was no longer afraid of her.

He stood thinking. Hours seemed to pass.

"Come along!" he said, at last, and he began to move off down the road.

Sally followed. The possibility of refusing did not enter her mind.

"Where are you going?" she asked. It was unbearable, this silence.

He did not answer.

In this fashion, he leading, she following, they went down the road into a lane, and through a gate into a field. They passed into a second field, and as they did so Sally's heart gave a leap. Ted Pringle was there.

Ted Pringle was a big young man, bigger even than Tom Kitchener, and, like Tom, he was of silent habit. He eyed the little procession inquiringly, but spoke no word. There was a pause.

"Ted," said Tom, "there's been a mistake."

He stepped quickly to Sally's side, and the next moment he had swung her off her feet and kissed her.

To the type of mind that Millbourne breeds actions speak louder than words, and Ted Pringle, who had gaped, gaped no more. He sprang forward, and Tom, pushing Sally aside, turned to meet him.

I cannot help feeling a little sorry for Ted Pringle. In the light of what happened, I could wish that it were possible to portray him as a hulking brute of evil appearance and worse morals—the sort of person concerning whom one could reflect comfortably that he deserved all he got. I should like to make him an unsympathetic character, over whose downfall the reader would gloat. But honesty compels me to own that Ted was a thoroughly decent young man in every way. He was a good citizen, a dutiful son, and would certainly have made an excellent husband. Furthermore, in the dispute on hand he had right on his side fully as much as Tom. The whole affair was one of those elemental clashings of man and man where the historian cannot sympathise with either side at the expense of the other, but must confine himself to a mere statement of what occurred. And, briefly, what occurred was that Tom, bringing to the fray a pent-up fury which his adversary had had no time to generate, fought Ted to a complete standstill in the space of two minutes and a half.

Sally had watched the proceedings, sick and horrified. She had never seen men fight before, and the terror of it overwhelmed her. Her vanity received no pleasant stimulation from the thought that it was for her sake that this storm had been let loose. For the moment her vanity was dead, stunned by collision with the realities. She found herself watching in a dream. She saw Ted fall, rise, fall again, and lie where he had fallen; and then she was aware that Tom was speaking.

"Come along!"

She hung back. Ted was lying very still. Gruesome ideas presented themselves. She had just accepted them as truth when Ted wriggled. He wriggled again. Then he sat up suddenly, looked at her with unseeing eyes, and said something in a thick voice. She gave a little sob of relief. It was ghastly, but not so ghastly as what she had been imagining.

Somebody touched her arm. Tom was by her side, grim and formidable. He was wiping blood from his face.

"Come along!"

She followed him without a word. And presently, behold, in another field, whistling meditatively and regardless of impending ill, Albert Parsons.

In everything that he did Tom was a man of method. He did not depart from his chosen formula.

"Albert," he said, "there's been a mistake."

And Albert gaped, as Ted had gaped.

Tom kissed Sally with the gravity of one performing a ritual.

The uglinesses of life, as we grow accustomed to them, lose their power to shock, and there is no doubt that Sally looked with a different eye upon this second struggle. She was conscious of a thrill of excitement, very different from the shrinking horror which had seized her before. Her stunned vanity began to tingle into life again. The fight was raging furiously over the trampled turf, and quite suddenly, as she watched, she was aware that her heart was with Tom.

It was no longer two strange brutes fighting in a field. It was her man battling for her sake.

She desired overwhelmingly that he should win, that he should not be hurt, that he should sweep triumphantly over Albert Parsons as he had swept over Ted Pringle.

Unfortunately, it was evident, even to her, that he was

being hurt, and that he was very far from sweeping triumphantly over Albert Parsons. He had not allowed himself
time to recover from his first battle, and his blows were slow
and weary. Albert, moreover, was made of sterner stuff
than Ted. Though now a peaceful tender of cows, there had
been a time in his hot youth when, travelling with a circus,
he had fought, week in, week out, relays of just such rustic
warriors as Tom. He knew their methods—their headlong
rushes, their swinging blows. They were the merest com-
monplaces of life to him. He slipped Tom, he side-stepped
Tom, he jabbed Tom; he did everything to Tom that a
trained boxer can do to a reckless novice, except knock the
fight out of him, until presently, through the sheer labour
of hitting, he, too, grew weary.

Now, in the days when Albert Parsons had fought whole
families of Toms in an evening, he had fought in rounds,
with the boss holding the watch, and half-minute rests, and
water to refresh him, and all orderly and proper. To-day
there were no rounds, no rests, no water, and the peaceful
tending of cows had caused flesh to grow where there had
been only muscle. Tom's headlong rushes became less easy
to side-step, his swinging blows more swift than the scientific counter that shot out to check them. As he tired Tom
seemed to regain strength. The tide of the battle began to
ebb. He clinched, and Tom threw him off. He feinted, and
while he was feinting Tom was on him. It was the climax
of the battle—the last rally. Down went Albert, and stayed
down. Physically, he was not finished; but in his mind a
question had framed itself—the question, "Was it worth
it?"—and he was answering, "No." There were other girls
in the world. No girl was worth all this trouble.

He did not rise.

"Come along!" said Tom.

He spoke thickly. His breath was coming in gasps. He was a terrible spectacle, but Sally was past the weaker emotions. She was back in the Stone Age, and her only feeling was one of passionate pride. She tried to speak, she struggled to put all she felt into words, but something kept her dumb, and she followed him in silence.

In the lane outside his cottage, down by the creek, Joe Blossom was clipping a hedge. The sound of footsteps made him turn.

He did not recognise Tom till he spoke.

"Joe, there's been a mistake," said Tom.

"Been a gunpowder explosion, more like," said Joe, a simple, practical man. "What you been doin' to your face?"

"She's going to marry me, Joe."

Joe eyed Sally inquiringly.

"Eh? You promised to marry *me*."

"She promised to marry all of us. You, me, Ted Pringle, and Albert Parsons."

"Promised—to—marry—all—of—us!"

"That's where the mistake was. She's only going to marry me. I—I've arranged it with Ted and Albert, and now I've come to explain to you, Joe."

"You promised to marry—"

The colossal nature of Sally's deceit was plainly troubling Joe Blossom. He expelled his breath in a long note of amazement. Then he summed up.

"Why, you're nothing more nor less than a Joshua!"

The years that had passed since Joe had attended the village Sunday-school had weakened his once easy familiarity with the characters of the Old Testament. It is possible that he had somebody else in mind.

Tom stuck doggedly to his point.

"You can't marry her, Joe."

Joe Blossom raised his shears and clipped a protruding branch. The point under discussion seemed to have ceased to interest him.

"Who wants to?" he said. "Good riddance!"

They went down the lane. Silence still brooded over them. The words she wanted continued to evade her.

They came to a grassy bank. Tom sat down. He was feeling unutterably tired.

"Tom!"

He looked up. His mind was working dizzily.

"You're going to marry me," he muttered.

She sat down beside him.

"I know," she said. "Tom, dear, lay your head on my lap and go to sleep."

If this story proves anything (beyond the advantage of being in good training when you fight), it proves that you cannot get away from the moving pictures even in a place like Millbourne; for as Sally sat there, nursing Tom, it suddenly struck her that this was the very situation with which that *Romance of the Middle Ages* film ended. You know the one I mean. Sir Percival Ye Something (which has slipped my memory for the moment) goes out after the Holy Grail; meets damsel in distress; overcomes her persecutors; rescues her; gets wounded, and is nursed back to life in her arms. Sally had seen it a dozen times. And every time she had reflected that the days of romance are dead, and that that sort of thing can't happen nowadays.

Guilt Is Good for You

When compassion and caring won't do the job, stark fear is a good bet.

The Rise of Minna Nordstrom

They had been showing the latest Minna Nordstrom picture at the Bijou Dream in the High Street, and Miss Postlethwaite, our sensitive barmaid, who had attended the
premiere, was still deeply affected. She snuffled audibly as
she polished the glasses.

"It's really good, is it?" we asked, for in the bar-parlour
of the Anglers' Rest we lean heavily on Miss Postlethwaite's
opinion where the silver screen is concerned. Her verdict
can make or mar.

" 'Swonderful," she assured us, "It lays bare for all to view
the soul of a woman who dared everything for love. A poignant and uplifting drama of life as it is lived to-day, purify-
ing the emotions with pity and terror."

A Rum and Milk said that if it was as good as all that
he didn't know but what he might not risk ninepence on
it. A Sherry and Bitters wondered what thy paid a woman
like Minna Nordstrom. A Port from the Wood, raising the
conversation from the rather sordid plane to which it threatened to sink, speculated on how motion-picture stars became stars.

"What I mean," said the Port from the Wood, "does a
studio deliberately set out to create a star? Or does it suddenly say to itself 'Hullo, here's a star. What ho!'?"

One of those cynical Dry Martinis who always know
everything said that it was all a question of influence.

"If you looked into it, you would find this Nordstrom
girl was married to one of the bosses."

Mr. Mulliner, who had been sipping his hot Scotch and
lemon in a rather distrait way, glanced up.

"Did I hear you mention the name Minna Nordstrom?"

"We were arguing about how she became a star. I was saying that she must have had a pull of some kind."

"In a sense," said Mr. Mulliner, "you are right. She did have a pull. But it was one due solely to her own initiative and resource. I have relatives and connections in Hollywood, as you know, and I learn much of the inner history of the studio world through these channels. I happen to know that Minna Nordstrom raised herself to her present eminence by sheer enterprise and determination. If Miss Postlethwaite will mix me another hot Scotch and lemon, this time stressing the Scotch a little more vigorously, I shall be delighted to tell you the whole story."

When people talk with bated breath in Hollywood—and it is a place where there is always a certain amount of breath-bating going on—you will generally find, said Mr. Mulliner, that the subject of their conversation is Jacob Z. Schnellen-hamer, the popular president of the Perfecto-Zizzbaum Corporation. For few names are more widely revered than that of this Napoleonic man.

Ask for an instance of his financial acumen, and his admirers will point to the great merger for which he was responsible—that merger by means of which he combined his own company, the Colossal-Exquisite, with those two other vast concerns, the Perfecto-Fishbein and the Zizzbaum Celluloid. Demand proof of his artistic genius, his *flair* for recognizing talent in the raw, and it is given immediately. He was the man who discovered Minna Nordstrom.

To-day when interviewers bring up the name of the world-famous star in Mr. Schnellenhamer's presence, he smiles quietly.

"I had long had my eye on the little lady," he says, "but

for one reason and another I did not consider the time ripe for her *debut*. Then I brought about what you are good enough to call the epoch-making merger, and I was enabled to take the decisive step. My colleagues questioned the wisdom of elevating a totally unknown girl to stardom, but I was firm. I saw that it was the only thing to be done."

"You had vision?"

"I had vision."

All that Mr. Schnellenhamer had, however, on the evening when this story begins was a headache. As he returned from the day's work at the studio and sank wearily into an arm-chair in the sitting-room of his luxurious home in Beverly Hills, he was feeling that the life of the president of a motion-picture corporation was one that he would hesitate to force on any dog of which he was fond.

A morbid meditation, of course, but not wholly unjustified. The great drawback to being the man in control of a large studio is that everybody you meet starts acting at you. Hollywood is entirely populated by those who want to get into the pictures, and they naturally feel that the best way of accomplishing their object is to catch the boss's eye and do their stuff.

Since leaving home that morning Mr. Schnellenhamer had been acted at practically incessantly. First, it was the studio watchman who, having opened the gate to admit his car, proceeded to play a little scene designed to show what he could do in a heavy role. Then came his secretary, two book agents, the waitress who brought him his lunch, a life insurance man, a representative of a film weekly, and a barber. And, on leaving at the end of the day, he got the watchman again, this time in whimsical comedy.

Little wonder, then, that by the time he reached home the magnate was conscious of a throbbing sensation about the temples and an urgent desire for a restorative.

As a preliminary to obtaining the latter, he rang the bell and Vera Prebble, his parlourmaid, entered. For a moment he was surprised not to see his butler. Then he recalled that he had dismissed him just after breakfast for reciting "Gunga Din" in a meaning way while bringing the eggs and bacon.

"You rang, sir?"

"I want a drink."

"Very good, sir."

The girl withdrew, to return a few moments later with a decanter and siphon. The sight caused Mr. Schnellenhamer's gloom to lighten a little. He was justly proud of his cellar, and he knew that the decanter contained liquid balm. In a sudden gush of tenderness he eyed its bearer appreciatively, thinking what a nice girl she looked.

Until now he had never studied Vera Prebble's appearance to any great extent or thought about her much in any way. When she had entered his employment a few days before, he had noticed, of course, that she had a sort of ethereal beauty; but then every girl you see in Hollywood has either ethereal beauty or roguish gaminerie or a dark, slumberous face that hints at hidden passion.

"Put it down there on the small table," said Mr. Schnellenhamer, passing his tongue over his lips.

The girl did so. Then, straightening herself, she suddenly threw her head back and clutched the sides of it in an ecstasy of hopeless anguish.

"Oh! Oh! Oh!" she cried.

"Eh?" said Mr. Schnellenhamer.

"Ah! Ah! Ah!"

"I don't get you at all," said Mr. Schnellenhamer.

She gazed at him with wide, despairing eyes.

"If you knew how sick and tired I am of it all!

Tired...Tired...Tired. The lights...the glitter...the gaiety...It is so hollow, so fruitless. I want to get away from it all, ha-ha-ha-ha-ha!"

Mr. Schnellenhamer retreated behind the Chesterfield. That laugh had had an unbalanced ring. He had not liked it. He was about to continue his backward progress in the direction of the door, when the girl, who had closed her eyes and was rocking to and fro as if suffering from some internal pain, became calmer.

"Just a little thing I knocked together with a view to showing myself in a dramatic role," she said. "Watch! I'm going to register."

She smiled.

"Joy."

She closed her mouth.

"Grief."

She wiggled her ears.

"Horror."

She raised her eyebrows.

"Hate."

Then, taking a parcel from the tray:

"Here," she said, "if you would care to glance at them, are a few stills of myself. This shows my face in repose. I call it 'Reverie.' This is me in a bathing suit...riding...walking...happy among my books...being kind to the dog. Here is one of which my friends have been good enough to speak in terms of praise—as Cleopatra, the warrior-queen of Egypt, at the Pasadena Gas-Fitters' Ball. It brings out what is generally considered my most effective feature—the nose, seen sideways."

During the course of these remarks Mr. Schnellenhamer had been standing breathing heavily. For a while the discovery that this parlourmaid, of whom he had just been thinking so benevolently, was simply another snake in the grass had rendered him incapable of speech. Now his aphasia left him.

"Get out!" he said.

"Pardon?" said the girl.

"Get out this minute. You're fired."

There was a silence. Vera Prebble closed her mouth, wiggled her ears, and raised her eyebrows. It was plain that she was grieved, horror-stricken, and in the grip of a growing hate.

"What," she demanded passionately at length, "is the matter with all you movie magnates? Have you no hearts? Have you no compassion? No sympathy? No understanding? Do the ambitions of the struggling mean nothing to you?"

"No," replied Mr. Schnellenhamer in answer to all five questions.

Vera Prebble laughed bitterly.

"No is right!" she said. "For months I besieged the doors of the casting directors. They refused to cast me. Then I thought that if I could find a way into your homes I might succeed where I had failed before. I secured the post of parlourmaid to Mr. Fishbein of the Perfecto-Fishbein. Halfway through Rudyard Kipling's 'Boots' he brutally bade me begone. I obtained a similar position with Mr. Zizzbaum of the Zizzbaum-Celluloid. The opening lines of 'The Wreck of the *Hesperus*' had hardly passed my lips when he was upstairs helping me pack my trunk. And now you crush my hopes. It is cruel...cruel...Oh, ha-ha-ha-ha-ha!"

She rocked to and fro in an agony of grief. Then an idea seemed to strike her.

"I wonder if you would care to see me in light comedy?...No?...Oh, very well."

With a quick droop of the eyelids and a twitch of the muscles of the cheeks she registered resignation.

"Just as you please," she said. Then her nostrils quivered and she bared the left canine tooth to indicate Menace. "But one last word. Wait!"

"How do you mean, wait?"

"Just wait. That's all."

For an instant Mr. Schnellenhamer was conscious of a twinge of uneasiness. Like all motion-picture magnates, he had about forty-seven guilty secrets, many of them recorded on paper. Was it possible that...

Then he breathed again. All his private documents were secure in a safe-deposit box. It was absurd to imagine that this girl could have anything on him.

Relieved, he lay down on the Chesterfield and gave himself up to day-dreams. And soon, as he remembered that that morning he had put through a deal which would enable him to trim the stuffing out of two hundred and seventy-three exhibitors, his lips curved in a contented smile and Vera Prebble was forgotten.

One of the advantages of life in Hollywood is that the Servant Problem is not a difficult one. Supply more than equals demand. Ten minutes after you have thrown a butler out of the back door his successor is bowling up in his sports-model car. And the same applies to parlourmaids. By the following afternoon all was well once more with the Schnellenhamer domestic machine. A new butler was cleaning the silver: a new parlourmaid was doing whatever parlourmaids do, which is very little. Peace reigned in the home.

But on the second evening, as Mr. Schnellenhamer, the day's tasks over, entered his sitting-room with nothing in his mind but bright thoughts of dinner, he was met by what

had all the appearance of a human whirlwind. This was Mrs.
Schnellenhamer. A graduate of the silent films, Mrs.
Schnellenhamer had been known in her day as the Queen
of Stormy Emotion, and she occasionally saw to it that her
husband was reminded of this.

"Now see what!" cried Mrs. Schnellenhamer.

Mr. Schnellenhamer was perturbed.

"Is something wrong?" he asked nervously.

"Why did you fire that girl, Vera Prebble?"

"She went ha-ha-ha-ha-ha at me."

"Well, do you know what she has done? She has laid information with the police that we are harbouring alcoholic
liquor on our premises, contrary to law, and this afternoon
they came in a truck and took it all away."

Mr. Schnellenhamer reeled. The shock was severe. The
good man loves his cellar.

"Not all?" he cried, almost pleadingly.

"All."

"The Scotch?"

"Every bottle."

"The gin?"

"Every drop."

Mr. Schnellenhamer supported himself against the
Chesterfield.

"Not the champagne?" he whispered.

"Every case. And here we are, with a hundred and fifty
people coming to-night, including the Duke."

Her allusion was to the Duke of Wigan, who, as so many
British dukes do, was at this time passing slowly through
Hollywood.

"And you know how touchy dukes are," proceeded Mrs.
Schnellenhamer. "I'm told that the Lulubelle Mahaffys invited the Duke of Kircudbrightshire for the week-end last

year, and after he had been there two months he suddenly left in a huff because there was no brown sherry."

A motion-picture magnate has to be a quick thinker. Where a lesser man would have wasted time referring to the recent Miss Prebble as a serpent whom he had to all intents and purposes nurtured in his bosom, Mr. Schnellenhamer directed the whole force of his great brain on the vital problem of how to undo the evil she had wrought.

"Listen," he said. "It's all right. I'll get the bootlegger on the 'phone, and he'll have us stocked up again in no time."

But he had overlooked the something in the air of Hollywood which urges its every inhabitant irresistibly into the pictures. When he got his bootlegger's number, it was only to discover that that life-saving tradesman was away from home. They were shooting a scene in *Sundered Hearts* on the Outstanding Screen-Favourites lot, and the bootlegger was hard at work there, playing the role of an Anglican bishop. His secretary said he could not be disturbed, as it got him all upset to be interrupted when he was working.

Mr. Schnellenhamer tried another bootlegger, then another. They were out on location.

And it was just as he had begun to despair that he bethought him of his old friend, Isadore Fishbein; and into his darkness there shot a gleam of hope. By the greatest good fortune it so happened that he and the president of the Perfecto-Fishbein were at the moment on excellent terms, neither having slipped anything over on the other for several weeks. Mr. Fishbein, moreover, possessed as well-stocked a cellar as any man in California. It would be a simple matter to go round and borrow from him all he needed.

Patting Mrs. Schnellenhamer's hand and telling her that there were still blue-birds singing in the sunshine, he ran to his car and leaped into it.

The residence of Isadore Fishbein was only a few hundred
yards away, and Mr. Schnellenhamer was soon whizzing
in through the door. He found his friend beating his head
against the wall of the sitting-room and moaning to himself in a quiet undertone.

"Is something the matter?" he asked, surprised.

"There is," said Mr. Fishbein, selecting a fresh spot on
the tapestried wall and starting to beat his head against that.
"The police came round this afternoon and took away
everything I had."

"Everything?"

"Well, not Mrs. Fishbein," said the other, with a touch
of regret in his voice. "She's up in the bedroom with eight
cubes of ice on her forehead in a linen bag. But they took
every drop of everything else. A serpent, that's what she is."

"Mrs. Fishbein?"

"Not Mrs. Fishbein. That parlourmaid. That Vera Prebble. Just because I stopped her when she got to 'boots, boots,
boots, boots, marching over Africa' she ups and informs
the police on me. And Mrs. Fishbein with a hundred and
eighty people coming to-night, including the ex-King of
Ruritania!"

And, crossing the room, the speaker began to bang his
head against a statue of Genius Inspiring the Motion-Picture
Industry.

A good man is always appalled when he is forced to con-
template the depths to which human nature can sink, and
Mr. Schnellenhamer's initial reaction on hearing of this fresh
outrage on the part of his late parlourmaid was a sort of
sick horror. Then the brain which had built up the Colossal-
Exquisite began to work once more.

"Well, the only for us to do," he said, "is to go round

to Ben Zizzbaum and borrow some of his stock. How do you stand with Ben?"

"I stand fine with Ben," said Mr. Fishbein, cheering up. "I heard something about him last week which I'll bet he wouldn't care to have known."

"Where does he live?"

"Camden Drive."

"Then tally-ho!" said Mr. Schnellenhamer, who had once produced a drama in eight reels of two strong men battling for a woman's love in the English hunting district.

They were soon at Mr. Zizzbaum's address. Entering the sitting-room, they were shocked to observe a form rolling in circles round the floor with its head between its hands. It was travelling quickly, but not so quickly that they were unable to recognize it as that of the chief executive of the Zizzbaum-Celluloid Corporation. Stopped as he was completing his eleventh lap and pressed for an explanation, Mr. Zizzbaum revealed that a recent parlourmaid of his, Vera Prebble by name, piqued at having been dismissed for deliberate and calculated reciting of the works of Mrs. Hemans, had informed the police of his stock of wines and spirits and that the latter had gone off with the whole collection not half an hour since.

"And don't you speak so loud," added the stricken man, "or you'll wake Mrs. Zizzbaum. She's in bed with ice on her head."

"How many cubes?" asked Mr. Fishbein.

"Six."

"Mrs. Fishbein needed eight," said that lady's husband a little proudly.

The situation was one that might well have unmanned the stoutest motion-picture executive, and there were few

motion-picture executives stouter than Jacob Schnellenhamer. But it was characteristic of this man that the tight-
est corner was always the one to bring out the full force
of his intellect. He thought of Mrs. Schnellenhamer waiting for him at home, and it was as if an electric shock of
high voltage had passed through him.

"I've got it," he said. "We must go to Glutz of the Medulla-
Oblongata. He's never been a real friend of mine, but if you
loan him Stella Svelte and I loan him Orlando Byng and
Fishbein loans him Oscar the Wonder-Poodle on his own
terms, I think he'll consent to give us enough to see us
through to-night. I'll get him on the 'phone."

It was some moments before Mr. Schnellenhamer
returned from the telephone booth. When he did so, his as-
sociates were surprised to observe in his eyes a happy gleam.

"Boys," he said, "Glutz is away with his family over the
week-end. The butler and the rest of the help are out joy-
riding. There's only a parlourmaid in the house. I've been
talking to her. So there won't be any need for us to give
him those stars, after all. We'll just run across in the car
with a few axes and help ourselves. It won't cost us above
a hundred dollars to square this girl. She can tell him she
was upstairs when the burglars broke in and didn't hear anything. And there we'll be, with all the stuff we need and
not a cent to pay outside of overhead connected with the
maid."

There was an awed silence.

"Mrs. Fishbein will be pleased."

"Mrs. Zizzbaum will be pleased."

"And Mrs. Schnellenhamer will be pleased," said the leader of the expedition. "Where do you keep your axes,
Zizzbaum?"

"In the cellar."

"Fetch 'em!" said Mr. Schnellenhamer in the voice a Crusader might have used in giving the signal to start against the Paynim.

In the ornate residence of Sigismund Glutz, meanwhile, Vera Prebble, who had entered the service of the head of the Medulla-Oblongata that morning and was already under sentence of dismissal for having informed him with appropriate gestures that a bunch of the boys were whooping it up in the Malemute saloon, was engaged in writing on a sheet of paper a short list of names, one of which she proposed as a *nom de theatre* as soon as her screen career should begin.

For this girl was essentially an optimist, and not even all the rebuffs which she had suffered had been sufficient to quench the fire of ambition in her.

Wiggling her tongue as she shaped the letters, she wrote:

> *Ursuline Delmaine*
> *Theodora Trix*
> *Uvula Gladwyn*

None of them seemed to her quite what she wanted. She pondered. Possibly something a little more foreign and exotic...

> *Greta Garbo*

No, that had been used...

And then suddenly inspiration descended upon her and, trembling a little with emotion, she inscribed on the paper the one name that was absolutely and indubitably right.

Minna Nordstrom

The more she looked at it, the better she liked it. And she was still regarding it proudly when there came the sound of a car stopping at the door and a few moments later in walked Mr. Schnellenhamer, Mr. Zizzbaum and Mr. Fishbein. They all wore Homburg hats and carried axes.

Vera Prebbledrew herself up.

"All goods must be delivered in the rear," she had begun haughtily, when she recognized her former employers and paused, surprised.

The recognition was mutual. Mr. Fishbein started. So did Mr. Zizzbaum.

"Serpent!" said Mr. Fishbein.

"Viper!" said Mr. Zizzbaum.

Mr. Schnellenhamer was more diplomatic. Though as deeply moved as his colleagues by the sight of this traitress, he realized that this was no time for invective.

"Well, well, well," he said, with a geniality which he strove to render frank and winning, "I never dreamed it was you on the 'phone, my dear. Well, this certainly makes everything nice and smooth—us all being, as you might say, old friends."

"Friends?" retorted Vera Prebble. "Let me tell you..."

"I know, I know. Quite, quite. But listen. I've got to have some liquor to-night..."

"What do you mean, *you* have?" said Mr. Fishbein.

"It's all right, it's all right," said Mr. Schnellenhamer soothingly. "I was coming to that. I wasn't forgetting you. We're all in this together. The good old spirit of co-operation. You see, my dear," he went on, "that little joke you played on us...oh, I'm not blaming you. Nobody laughed more heartily than myself..."

"Yes, they did," said Mr. Fishbein, alive now to the fact that this girl before him must be conciliated. "I did."

"So did I," said Mr. Zizzbaum.

"We all laughed very heartily," said Mr. Schnellenhamer. "You should have heard us. A girl of spirit, we said to ourselves. Still, the little pleasantry has left us in something of a difficulty, and it will be worth a hundred dollars to you, my dear, to go upstairs and put cotton-wool in your ears while we get at Mr. Glutz's cellar door with our axes."

Vera Prebble raised her eyebrows.

"What do you want to break down the cellar door for? I know the combination of the lock."

"You do?" said Mr. Schnellenhamer joyfully.

"I withdraw that expression 'Serpent,' " said Mr. Fishbein.

"When I used the term 'Viper,' " said Mr. Zizzbaum, "I was speaking thoughtlessly."

"And I will tell it you," said Vera Prebble, "at a price."

She drew back her head and extended an arm, twiddling the fingers at the end of it. She was plainly registering something, but they could not discern what it was.

"There is only one condition on which I will tell you the combination of Mr. Glutz's cellar, and that is this. One of you has got to give me a starring contract for five years."

The magnates started.

"Listen," said Mr. Zizzbaum, "you don't want to star."

"You wouldn't like it," said Mr. Fishbein.

"Of course you wouldn't," said Mr. Schnellenhamer. "You would look silly starring—an inexperienced girl like you. Now, if you had said a nice small part..."

"Star."

"Or featured..."

"Star."

The three men drew back a pace or two and put their

heads together.

"She means it," said Mr. Fishbein.

"Her eyes," said Mr. Zizzbaum. "Like stones."

"A dozen times I could have dropped something heavy on that girl's head from an upper landing, and I didn't do it," said Mr. Schnellenhamer remorsefully.

Mr. Fishbein threw up his hands.

"It's no use. I keep seeing that vision of Mrs. Fishbein floating before me with eight cubes of ice on her head. I'm going to star this girl."

"*You* are?" said Mr. Zizzbaum. "And get the stuff? And leave me to go home and tell Mrs. Zizzbaum there won't be anything to drink at her party to-night for a hundred and eleven guests including the Vice-President of Switzerland? No, sir! *I* am going to star her."

"I'll outbid you."

"You won't outbid *me*. Not till they bring me word that Mrs. Zizzbaum has lost the use of her vocal cords."

"Listen," said the other tensely. "When it comes to using vocal cords, Mrs. Fishbein begins where Mrs. Zizzbaum leaves off."

Mr. Schnellenhamer, that cool head, saw the peril that loomed.

"Boys," he said, "if we once start bidding against one another, there'll be no limit. There's only one thing to be done. We must merge."

His powerful personality carried the day. It was the President of the newly-formed Perfecto-Zizzbaum Corporation who a few moments later stepped forward and approached the girl.

"We agree."

And, as he spoke, there came the sound of some heavy vehicle stopping in the road outside. Vera Prebble uttered a stricken exclamation.

"Well, of all the silly girls!" she cried distractedly. "I've just remembered that an hour ago I telephoned the police, informing them of Mr. Glutz's cellar. And here they are!"

Mr. Fishbein uttered a cry, and began to look round for something to bang his head against. Mr. Zizzbaum gave a short, sharp moan, and started to lower himself to the floor. But Mr. Schnellenhamer was made of sterner stuff.

"Pull yourselves together, boys," he begged them. "Leave all this to me. Everything is going to be all right. Things have come to a pretty pass," he said, with a dignity as impressive as it was simple, "if a free-born American citizen cannot bribe the police of his native country."

"True," said Mr. Fishbein, arresting his head when within an inch and a quarter of a handsome Oriental vase.

"True, true," said Mr. Zizzbaum, getting up and dusting his knees.

"Just let me handle the whole affair," said Mr. Schnellenhamer. "Ah, boys!" he went on, genially.

Three policemen had entered the room—a sergeant, a patrolman, and another patrolman. Their faces wore a wooden, hard-boiled look.

"Mr. Glutz?" said the sergeant.

"Mr. Schnellenhamer," corrected the great man. "But Jacob to you, old friend."

The sergeant seemed in no wise mollified by this amiability.

"Prebble, Vera?" he asked, addressing the girl.

"Nordstrom, Minna," she replied.

"Got the name wrong, then. Anyway, it was you who 'phoned us that there was alcoholic liquor on the premises?"

Mr. Schnellenhamer laughed amusedly.

"You mustn't believe everything that girl tells you, sergeant. She's a great kidder. Always was. If she said that, it was just one of her little jokes. I know Glutz. I know his views. And many is the time I have heard him say that the laws of his country are good enough for him and that he would scorn not to obey them. You will find nothing here, sergeant."

"Well, we'll try," said the other. "Show us the way to the cellar," he added, turning to Vera Prebble.

Mr. Schnellenhamer smiled a winning smile.

"Now, listen," he said. "I've just remembered I'm wrong. Silly mistake to make, and I don't know how I made it. There *is* a certain amount of the stuff in the house, but I'm sure you dear chaps don't want to cause any unpleasantness. You're broad-minded. Listen. Your name's Murphy, isn't it?"

"Donahue."

"I thought so. Well, you'll laugh at this. Only this morning I was saying to Mrs. Schnellenhamer that I must really slip down to head-quarters and give my old friend Donahue that ten dollars I owed him."

"What ten dollars?"

"I didn't say ten. I said a hundred. One hundred dollars, Donny, old man, and I'm not saying there mightn't be a little over for these two gentlemen here. How about it?"

The sergeant drew himself up. There was no sign of softening in his glance.

"Jacob Schnellenhamer," he said coldly, "you can't square me. When I tried for a job at the Colossal-Exquisite last spring I was turned down on account you said I had no sex-appeal."

The first patrolman, who had hitherto taken no part in the conversation, started.

"Is that so, Chief?"

"Yessir. No sex-appeal."

"Well, can you tie that!" said the first patrolman. "When I tried to crash the Colossal-Exquisite, they said my voice wasn't right."

"Me," said the second patrolman, eyeing Mr. Schnellenhamer sourly, "they had the nerve to beef at my left profile. Lookut, boys," he said, turning, "can you see anything wrong with that profile?"

His companions eyed him closely. The sergeant raised a hand and peered between his fingers with his head tilted back and his eyes half closed.

"Not a thing," he said.

"Why, Basil, it's a lovely profile," said the first patrolman.

"Well, that's how it goes," said the second patrolman moodily.

The sergeant had returned to his own grievance.

"No sex-appeal!" he said with rasping laugh. "And me that had specially taken sex-appeal in the College of Eastern Iowa course of Motion Picture Acting."

"Who says my voice ain't right?" demanded the first patrolman. "Listen. Mi-mi-mi-mi-mi."

"Swell," said the sergeant.

"Like a nightingale or something," said the second patrolman.

The sergeant flexed his muscles.

"Ready, boys?"

"Kayo, Chief."

"Wait!" cried Mr. Schnellenhamer. "Wait! Give me one more chance. I'm sure I can find parts for you all."

The sergeant shook his head.

"No. It's too late. You've got us mad now. You don't appreciate the sensitiveness of the artist. Does he, boys?"

"You're darned right he doesn't," said the first patrolman.

"I wouldn't work for the Colossal-Exquisite now," said the second patrolman with a petulant twitch of his shoulder, "not if they wanted me to play Romeo opposite Jean Harlow."

"Then let's go," said the sergeant. "Come along, lady, you show us where this cellar is."

For some moments after the officers of the Law, preceded by Vera Prebble, had left, nothing was to be heard in the silent sitting-room but the rhythmic beating of Mr. Fishbein's head against the wall and the rustling sound of Mr. Zizzbaum rolling round the floor. Mr. Schnellenhamer sat brooding with his chin in his hands, merely moving his legs slightly each time Mr. Zizzbaum came round. The failure of his diplomatic efforts had stunned him.

A vision rose before his eyes of Mrs. Schnellenhamer waiting in their sunlit patio for his return. As clearly as if he had been there now, he could see her swooning, slipping into the goldfish pond, and blowing bubbles with her head beneath the surface. And he was asking himself whether in such an event it would be better to raise her gently or just leave Nature to take its course. She would, he knew, be extremely full of that stormy emotion of which she had once been queen.

It was as he still debated this difficult point that a light step caught his ear. Vera Prebble was standing in the doorway.

"Mr. Schnellenhamer."

The magnate waved a weary hand.

"Leave me," he said. "I am thinking."

"I thought you would like to know," said Vera Prebble, "that I've just locked those cops in the coal-cellar."

As in the final reel of a super-super-film eyes brighten and faces light up at the entry of the United States Marines, so at these words did Mr. Schnellenhamer, Mr. Fishbein and Mr. Zizzbaum perk up as if after a draught of some magic elixir.

"In the coal-cellar?" gasped Mr. Schnellenhamer.

"In the coal-cellar."

"Then if we work quick..."

Vera Prebble coughed.

"One moment," she said. "Just one moment. Before you go, I have drawn up a little letter, covering our recent agreement. Perhaps you will all three just sign it."

Mr. Schnellenhamer clicked his tongue impatiently.

"No time for that now. Come to my office to-morrow. Where are you going?" he asked, as the girl started to withdraw.

"Just to the coal-cellar," said Vera Prebble. "I think those fellows may want to come out."

Mr. Schnellenhamer sighed. It had been worth trying, of course, but he had never really had much hope.

"Gimme," he said resignedly.

The girl watched as the three men attached their signatures. She took the document and folded it carefully.

"Would any of you like to hear me recite 'The Bells,' by Edgar Allan Poe?" she asked.

"No!" said Mr. Fishbein.

"No!" said Mr. Zizzbaum.

"No!" said Mr. Schnellenhamer. "We have no desire to hear you recite 'The Bells,' Miss Prebble."

The girl's eyes flashed haughtily.

"Miss Nordstrom," she corrected. "And just for that you'll get 'The Charge of the Light Brigade,' and like it."

Birth of a Salesman

The day was so fair, the breeze so gentle, the sky so blue and the sun so sunny, that Lord Emsworth, that vague and woollen-headed peer, who liked fine weather, should have been gay and carefree, especially as he was looking at flowers, a thing which always gave him great pleasure. But on his face, as he poked it over the hedge beyond which the flowers lay, a close observer would have noted a peevish frown. He was thinking of his younger son Freddie.

Coming to America to attend the wedding of one of his nieces to a local millionaire of the name Tipton Plimsoll, Lord Emsworth had found himself, in the matter of board and lodging, confronted with a difficult choice. The British Government, notoriously slow men with a dollar, having refused to allow him to take out of England a sum sufficient to enable him to live in a New York hotel, he could become the guest of the bridegroom's aunt, who was acting as M.C. of the nuptials, or he could dig in with Freddie in the Long Island suburb where the latter had made his home. Warned by his spies that Miss Plimsoll maintained in her establishment no fewer than six Pekinese dogs, a breed of animal which always made straight for his ankles, he had decided on Freddie and was conscious now of having done the wrong thing. Pekes chew the body, but Freddie seared the soul.

The flowers grew in the garden of a large white house at the end of the road, and Lord Emsworth had been goggling at them for some forty minutes, for he was a man who liked to take his time over these things, when his reverie was interrupted by the tooting of a horn and the sound of a discordant voice singing "Buttons and Bows." Freddie's car drew up, with Freddie at the wheel.

"Oh, there you are, guv'nor," said Freddie.

"Yes," said Lord Emsworth, who was. "I was looking at the flowers. A nice display. An attractive garden."

"Where every prospect pleases and only man is vile," said Freddie austerely. "Keep away from the owner of that joint, guv'nor. He lowers the tone of the neighbourhood."

"Indeed? Why is that?"

"Not one of the better element. His wife's away, and he throws parties. I've forgotten his name...Griggs or Follansbee or something...but we call him the Timber Wolf. He's something in the lumber business."

"And he throws parties?"

"Repeatedly. You might say incessantly. Entertains blondes in droves. All wrong. My wife's away, but do you find me festooned in blondes? No. I pine for her return. Well, I must be oozing along. I'm late."

"You are off somewhere?"

Freddie clicked his tongue.

"I told you yesterday, guv'nor, and I told you twice this morning, that I was giving a prospect lunch to-day at the golf club. I explained that I couldn't ask you to join us at the trough, because I shall be handing this bird a sales talk throughout the meal. You'll find your rations laid out on a tray. A cold collation to-day, because it's Thursday and on Thursdays the domestic staff downs tools."

He drove on, all briskness and efficiency, and Lord Emsworth tut-tutted an irritable tut-tut.

There, he was telling himself, you had in a nutshell what made Freddie such a nerve-rasping companion. He threw his weight about. He behaved as if he were the Spirit of Modern Commerce. He was like something out of one of those advertisements which show the employee who has taken the correspondence course in Confidence and Self-Reliance looking his boss in the eye and making him wilt.

Freddie worked for Donaldson's Inc., dealers in dog biscuits of Long Island City, and had been doing so now for three years. And in those three years some miracle had transformed him from a vapid young London lizard into a go-getter, a live wire and a man who thought on his feet and did it now. Every night since Lord Emsworth had come to enjoy his hospitality, if enjoy is the word, he had spoken lyrically and at length of his success in promoting the interests of Donaldson's Dog Joy ("Get Your Dog Thinking the Donaldson Way"), making no secret of his view that it had been a lucky day for the dear old firm when it had put him on the payroll. As a salesman he was good, a fellow who cooked with gas and did not spare himself, and he admitted it.

All of which might have been music to Lord Emsworth's ears, for a younger son earning his living in America is unquestionably a vast improvement on a younger son messing about and getting into debt in England, had it not been for one circumstance. He could not rid himself of a growing conviction that after years of regarding this child of his as a drone and a wastrel, the child was now regarding him as one. A world's worker himself, Freddie eyed with scorn one who, like Lord Emsworth, neither toiled nor spun. He patronized Lord Emsworth. He had never actually called Lord Emsworth a spiv, but he made it plain that it was in this category that he had mentally pencilled in the author of his being. And if there is one thing that pierces the armour of an English father of the upper classes, it is to be looked down on by his younger son. Little wonder that Lord Emsworth, as he toddled along the road, was gritting his teeth. A weaker man would have gnashed them.

His gloom was not lightened by the sight of the cold collation which leered at him on his return to the house. There was the tray of which Freddie had spoken, and on it a plate on which, like corpses after a battle, lay a slice of vermilion ham, a slice of sepia corned beef, a circle of mauve liverwurst and, of all revolting things, a large green pickle. It seemed to Lord Emsworth that Freddie's domestic staff was temperamentally incapable of distinguishing between the needs of an old gentleman who had to be careful what he ate and those of a flock of buzzards taking pot luck in the Florida Everglades.

For some moments he stood gaping at this unpleasant picture in still life; then there stole into his mind the thought that there might be eggs in the ice-box. He went thither and tested his theory and it was proved correct.

"Ha!" said Lord Emsworth. He remembered how he had frequently scrambled eggs at school.

But his school days lay half a century behind him, and time in its march robs us of our boyhood gifts. Since the era when he had worn Eton collars and ink spots on his face, he had lost the knack, and it all too speedily became apparent that Operation Eggs was not going to be the walkover he had anticipated. Came a moment when he would have been hard put to it to say whether he was scrambling eggs or the eggs were scrambling him. And he had paused to clarify his thoughts on this point, when there was a ring at the front door bell. Deeply incrusted in yolk, he shuffled off to answer the summons.

A girl was standing in the porch. He inspected her through his pince-nez with the vacant stare on which the female members of his family had so often commented adversely. She seemed to him, as he drank her slowly in, a nice sort of girl. A man with a great many nieces who were always bursting in on him and ballyragging him when he wanted to read his pig book, he had come to fear and distrust the younger members of the opposite sex, but this one's looks he liked immediately. About her there was none of that haughty beauty and stormy emotion in which his nieces specialized. She was small and friendly and companionable.

"Good morning," he said.

"Good morning. Would you like a richly bound encyclopaedia of Sport?"

"Not in the least," said Lord Emsworth cordially. "Can you scramble eggs?"

"Why, sure."

"Then come in," said Lord Emsworth. "Come in. And if you will excuse me leaving you, I will go and change my clothes."

Women are admittedly wonderful. It did not take Lord Emsworth long to remove his best suit, which he had been wearing in deference to the wishes of Freddie, who was a purist on dress, and don the older and shabbier one which made him look like a minor employee in some shady firm of private detectives, but, brief though the interval had been, the girl had succeeded in bringing order out of chaos. Not only had she quelled what had threatened to become an ugly revolt among the eggs, but she had found bacon and coffee and produced toast. What was virtually a banquet was set out in the living-room, and Lord Emsworth was about to square his elbows and have at it, when he detected an omission.

"Where is your plate?" he asked.

"Mine?" The girl seemed surprised. "Am I in on this?"

"Most certainly."

"That's mighty nice of you. I'm starving."

"These eggs," said Lord Emsworth some moments later, speaking thickly through a mouthful of them, "are delicious. Salt?"

"Thanks."

"Pepper? Mustard? Tell me," said Lord Emsworth, for it was a matter that had been perplexing him a good deal, "why do you go about the countryside offering people richly bound encyclopaedias of Sport? Deuced civil of you, of course," he added hastily, lest she might think he was criticizing, "but why do you?"

"I'm selling them."

"Selling them?"

"Yes."

A bright light shone upon Lord Emsworth. It had been well said of him that he had an I.Q. some thirty points lower than that of a not too agile-minded jellyfish, but he had grasped her point. She was selling them.

"Of course, yes. Quite. I see what you mean. You're *selling* them."

"That's right. They set you back five dollars and I get forty per cent. Only I don't."

"Why not?"

"Because people won't buy them."

"No?"

"No, sir."

"Don't people want richly bound encyclopaedias of Sport?"

"If they do, they keep it from me."

"Dear, dear." Lord Emsworth swallowed a piece of bacon emotionally. His heart was bleeding for this poor child. "That must be trying for you."

"It is."

"But why do you have to sell the bally things?"

"Well, it's like this. I'm going to have a baby."

"Good God!"

"Oh, not immediately. Next January. Well, that sort of thing costs money. Am I right or wrong?"

"Right, most decidedly," said Lord Emsworth, who had never been a young mother himself but knew the ropes. "I remember my poor wife complaining of the expense when my son Frederick was born. 'Oh dear, oh dear, oh dear,' I remember her saying. She was alive at the time," explained Lord Emsworth.

"Ed. works in a garage."

"Does he? I don't think I have met him. Who is Ed.?"

"My husband."

"Oh, your husband? You mean your husband. Works in a garage, does he?"

"That's right. And the take-home pay doesn't leave much over for extras."

"Like babies?"

"Like babies. So I got this job. I didn't tell Ed., of course. He'd have a fit."

"He is subject to fits?"

"He wants me to lie down and rest."

"I think he's right."

"Oh, he's right, all right, but how can I? I've got to hustle out and sell richly bound encyclopaedias."

"Of Sport?"

"Of Sport. And it's tough going. You do become discouraged. Besides getting blisters on the feet. I wish you could see my feet right now."

On the point of saying that he would be delighted, Lord Emsworth paused. He had had a bright idea and it had taken his breath away. This always happened when he had bright ideas. He had had one in the Spring of 1921 and another in the Summer of 1933, and those had taken his breath away, too.

"I will sell your richly bound encyclopaedias of Sport," he said.

"You?"

The bright idea which had taken Lord Emsworth's breath away was that if he went out and sold richly bound encyclopaedias of Sport, admitted by all the cognoscenti to be very difficult to dispose of, it would rid him once and for all of the inferiority complex which so oppressed him when in the society of his son Freddie. The brassiest of young men cannot pull that Spirit of Modern Commerce stuff on a father if the father is practically a Spirit of Modern Commerce himself.

"Precisely," he said.

"But you couldn't."

Lord Emsworth bridled. A wave of confidence and self-reliance was surging through him.

"Who says I couldn't? My son Frederick sells things, and I resent the suggestion that I am incapable of doing anything that Frederick can do." He wondered if it would be possible to explain to her what a turnip-headed young ass Frederick was, then gave up the attempt as hopeless. "Leave this to me," he said. "Lie down on that sofa and get a nice rest."

"But—"

"Don't argue," said Lord Emsworth dangerously, becoming the dominant male. "Lie down on that sofa."

Two minutes later, he was making his way down the road, still awash with that wave of confidence and self-reliance. His objective was the large white house where the flowers were. He was remembering what Freddie had said about its owner. The man, according to Freddie, threw par-

ties and entertained blondes in his wife's absence. And while
we may look askance from the moral standpoint at one who
does this, we have to admit that it suggests the possession
of sporting blood. That reckless, raffish type probably buys
its encyclopaedias of Sport by the gross.

But one of the things that make life so difficult is that
waves of confidence and self-reliance do not last. They
surge, but they recede, leaving us with dubious minds and
cooling feet. Lord Emsworth had started out in uplifted
mood, but as he reached the gate of the white house the
glow began to fade.

It was not that he had forgotten the technique of the thing.
Freddie had explained it too often for him to do that. You
rapped on the door. You said "I wonder if I could interest
you in a good dog biscuit?" And then by sheer personal mag-
netism you cast a spell on the householder so that he became wax in your hands. All perfectly simple and
straightforward. And yet, having opened the gate and advanced a few feet into the driveway, Lord Emsworth paused.
He removed his pince-nez, polished them, replaced them
on his nose, blinked, swallowed once or twice and ran a
finger over his chin. The first fine frenzy had abated. He
was feeling like a nervous man who in an impulsive moment has volunteered to go over Niagara Falls in a barrel.

He was still standing in the driveway, letting "I dare not"
wait upon "I would", as cats do in adages, when the air
became full of tooting horns and grinding brakes and
screaming voices.

"God bless my soul," said Lord Emsworth, coming out
of his coma.

The car which had so nearly caused a vacancy in the
House of Lords was bursting with blondes. There was a

blonde at the wheel, another at her side, further blondes in the rear seats and on the lap of the blonde beside the blonde at the wheel a blonde Pekinese dog. They were all shouting, and Pekinese dog was hurling abuse in Chinese.

"God bless my soul," said Lord Emsworth. "I beg your pardon. I really must apologize. I was plunged in thought."

"Oh, was that what you were plunged in?" said the blonde at the wheel, mollified by his suavity. Speak civilly to blondes, and they will speak civilly to you.

"I was thinking of dog biscuits. Of dog biscuits. Of...er...in short...dog biscuits. I wonder," said Lord Emsworth, striking while the iron was hot, "if I could interest you in a good dog biscuit?"

The blonde at the wheel weighed the question.

"Not me," she said. "I never touch 'em."

"Nor me," said a blonde at the back. "Doctor's orders."

"And if you're thinking of making a quick sale to Eisenhower here," said the blonde beside the driver, kissing the Pekinese on the tip of its nose, a feat of daring at which Lord Emsworth marvelled, "he only eats chicken."

Lord Emsworth corrected himself.

"When I said dog biscuit," he explained, "I meant a richly bound encyclopaedia of Sport."

The blondes exchanged glances.

"Look," said the one at the wheel. "If you don't know the difference between a dog biscuit and a richly bound encyclopaedia of Sport, seems to me you'd be doing better in some other line of business."

"Much better," said the blonde beside her.

"A whole lot better," agreed the blonde at the back.

"No future in it, the way you're going," said the blonde at the wheel, summing up. "That's the first thing you want to get straight on, the difference between dog biscuits and richly bound encyclopaedias of Sport. It's a thing that's cropping up all the time. There *is* a difference. I couldn't explain it to you offhand, but you go off into a corner somewheres and mull it over quietly and you'll find it'll suddenly come to you."

"Like a flash," said the blonde at the back.

"Like a stroke of lightning or sump'n," assented the blonde at the wheel. "You'll be amazed how you ever came to mix them up. Well, good-bye. Been nice seeing you."

The car moved on toward the house, and Lord Emsworth, closing his burning ears to the happy laughter proceeding from its interior, tottered out into the road. His spirit was broken. It was his intention to return home and stay there. And he had started on his way when there came stealing into his mind a disturbing thought.

That girl. That nice young Mrs. Ed. who was going to have a fit in January . . . or, rather, a baby. (It was her husband, he recalled, who had the fits). She was staking everything on his salesmanship. Could he fail her? Could he betray her simple trust?

The obvious answer was "Yes, certainly," but the inherited chivalry of a long line of ancestors, all of whom had been noted for doing the square thing by damsels in distress, caused Lord Emsworth to shrink from making it. In the old days when knighthood was in flower and somebody was needed to rescue a suffering female from a dragon or a two-headed giant, the cry was always "Let Emsworth do it!", and the Emsworth of the period had donned his suit of mail, stropped his sword, parked his chewing gum under the round table and snapped into it. A pretty state of things if the twentieth-century holder of the name were to allow himself to be intimidated by blondes.

Blushing hotly, Lord Emsworth turned and made for the gate again.

In the living-room of the white house, cool in the shade of the tree which stood outside its window, there had begun to burgeon one of those regrettable neo-Babylonian orgies which are so frequent when blondes and men who are something in the lumber business get together. Cocktails were circulating, and the blonde who had been at the wheel of the car was being the life and soul of the party with her imitation of the man outside who had been unable to get himself straightened out in the matter of dog biscuits and richly bound encyclopaedias. Her "Lord Emsworth" was a nice bit of impressionistic work, clever but not flattering.

She was giving a second encore when her performance was interrupted by a shrill yapping from without, and the blonde who had sat beside her knitted her brow in motherly concern.

"Somebody's teasing Eisenhower," she said.

"Probably found a cat," said the timber wolf. "Tell me more. What sort of a character was this character?"

"Tall," said a blonde.

"Old," said another blonde.

And a fourth blonde added that he had worn pince-nez.

A sudden gravity fell upon the timber wolf. He was remembering that on several occasions these last few days he had seen just such a man peering over his hedge in a furtive and menacing manner, like Sherlock Holmes on the trail. This very morning he had seen him. He had been standing there outside the hedge, motionless...watching...watching...

The fly in the ointment of men who throw parties for blondes when their wives are away, the thing that acts as a skeleton at the feast and induces goose pimples when the revelry is at its height, is the fact that they can never wholly dismiss the possibility that these wives, though they ought to be ashamed of themselves for entertaining unworthy suspicions, may have engaged firms of private detectives to detect them privately and report on their activities. It was this thought that now came whistling like an east wind through the mind of the timber wolf, whose name, just to keep the record straight, was not Griggs or Follansbee but Spenlow (George).

And as he quivered beneath its impact, one of his guests, who had hitherto taken no part in the conversation, spoke as follows:

"Oo, look! Eisenhower's got him up a tree!"

And George Spenlow, following her pointing finger, saw that she was correct. There the fellow was, roosting in the branches and adjusting his pince-nez as if the better to view the scene within. He quivered like a jelly and stared at Lord Emsworth. Lord Emsworth stared at him. Their eyes met.

Much has been written of the language of the eyes, but except between lovers it is never a very satisfactory medium of communication. George Spenlow, trying to read the message in Lord Emsworth's, completely missed the gist.

What Lord Emsworth was trying to convey with the language of the eye was an apology for behaviour which at first sight, he admitted, might seem a little odd. He had rapped on the door, he was endeavouring to explain, but, unable to attract attention to his presence, had worked his way round the house to where he heard voices, not a thought on his mind except a passionate desire to sell richly bound encyclopaedias of Sport, and suddenly something had exploded like a land mine on the ground beside him and, looking down, he had perceived a Pekinese dog advancing on him with bared teeth. This had left him no option but to climb the tree to avoid its slavering jaws. "Oh, for the wings of a dove!" he had said to himself, and had got moving. He concluded his remarks by smiling a conciliatory smile.

It pierced George Spenlow like a dagger. It seemed to him that this private investigator, elated at having caught him with the goods, was gloating evilly.

He gulped.

"You girls stay here," he said hoarsely. "I'll go talk to this fellow."

He climbed through the window, scooped up the Pekinese, restored it to its proprietress and addressed Lord Emsworth in a quavering voice.

"Now listen," he said.

These men high up in the lumber business are quick thinkers. George Spenlow had seen the way.

"Now listen," said George Spenlow.

He had taken Lord Emsworth affectionately by the arm and was walking him up and down the lawn. He was a stout, pink, globular man, so like Lord Emsworth's pig, Empress of Blandings, in appearance that the latter felt a wave of homesickness.

"Now listen," said George Spenlow. "I think you and I can get together."

Lord Emsworth, to show that his heart was in the right place, smiled another conciliatory smile.

"Yes, yes, I know," said George Spenlow, wincing. "But I think we can. I'll put my cards on the table. I know all about it. My wife. She gets ideas into her head. She imagines things."

Lord Emsworth, though fogged, was able to understand this.

"My wife was like that," he said.

"All women are like that," said George Spenlow. "It's something to do with the bone structure of their heads. They let their imagination run away with them. They entertain unworthy suspicions."

Here again Lord Emsworth was able to follow him. He said he had noticed the same thing in his sister Constance, and George Spenlow began to feel encouraged.

"Sure. Sisters, wives, late wives. . . they're all the same, and it doesn't do to let them get away with it. So here's what. What you tell her is that you found me enjoying a quiet home afternoon with a few old college friends. . . Wait, wait," said George Spenlow urgently. "Wait while I finish."

He had observed his guest shake his head. This was because a mosquito had just bitten Lord Emsworth on the ear, but he had no means of divining this. Shakes of the head are as hard to interpret as the language of the eyes.

"Wait while I finish," said George Spenlow. "Hear what I was going to say. You're a man of the world. You want to take the broad, sensible outlook. You want to study the situation from every angle and find out what there is in it for you. Now then how much?"

"You mean how many?"

"Eh?"

"How many would you like?"

"How many what?"

"Richly bound encyclopaedias of Sport."

"Oh yes, yes, yes," said George Spenlow, enlightened. "Oh, sure, sure, sure, sure, sure. I didn't get you for a moment. About how many would you suggest? Fifty?"

Lord Emsworth shook his head again—petulantly, it seemed to George Spenlow. The mosquito had returned.

"Well, naturally," proceeded George Spenlow, "when I

said fifty, I meant a hundred. I think that's a nice round number."

"Very nice," agreed Lord Emsworth. "Or would you care for a gross?"

"A gross might be better."

"You can give them to your friends."

"That's right. On their birthdays."

"Or at Christmas."

"Of course. So difficult to think of a suitable Christmas present."

"Extraordinarily difficult."

"Shall we say five hundred dollars on account?"

"That would be capital."

"And remember," said George Spenlow, with all the emphasis at his disposal. "Old college friends."

A passer-by, watching Lord Emsworth as he returned some twenty minutes later to Freddie's dream house down the road, would have said to himself that there went an old gentleman who had found the blue bird, and he would have been right. Lord Emsworth, as he fingered the crisp roll of bills in his trouser pocket, was not actually saying "Whooppee!", but it was a very near thing. He was feeling as if a great burden had been removed from his shoulders.

The girl was asleep when he reached the house. Gently, without disturbing her slumbers, Lord Emsworth reached for her bag and deposited the five hundred dollars in it. Then he tiptoed out and set a course for the golf club. He wanted to find his son Freddie.

"Ah, Frederick," he would say. "So you sell dog biscuits, do you? Pooh! Anyone can sell dog biscuits. Give me something tougher, like richly bound encyclopaedias of Sport. Now, I strolled out just now and sold a gross at the first house I visited. So don't talk to me about dog biscuits. In fact, don't talk to me at all, because I am sick of the sound of your voice. And STOP THAT SINGING!!"

Yes, when Freddie began singing "Buttons and Bows," that would be the moment to strike.

Two-Edged Talents

It's generally agreed that a man should be capable—but of what?

The Reverent Wooing of Archibald

The conversation in the bar-parlour of the Anglers' Rest, which always tends to get deepish towards closing time, had turned to the subject of the Modern Girl; and a Gin-and-Ginger-Ale sitting in the corner by the window remarked that it was strange how types die out.

"I can remember the days," said the Gin-and-Ginger-Ale, "when every other girl you met stood abut six feet two in her dancing-shoes, and had as many curves as a Scenic Railway. Now they are all five foot nothing and you can't see them sideways. Why is this?"

The Draught Stout shook his head.

"Nobody can say. It's the same with dogs. One moment the world is full of pugs as far as the eye can reach; the next, not a pug in sight, only Pekes and Alsatians. Odd!"

The Small Bass and the Double-Whisky-and-Splash admitted that these things were very mysterious, and supposed we should never know the reason for them. Probably we were not meant to know.

"I cannot agree with you, gentlemen," said Mr. Mulliner. He had been sipping his hot Scotch and lemon with a rather abstracted air: but now he sat up alertly, prepared to deliver judgment. "The reason for the disappearance of the dignified, queenly type of girl is surely obvious. It is Nature's method of ensuring the continuance of the species. A world full of the sort of young woman that Meredith used to put into his novels and du Maurier into his pictures in *Punch* would be a world full of permanent spinsters. The modern young man would never be able to summon up the nerve to propose to them."

"Something in that," assented the Draught Stout.

"I speak with authority on the point," said Mr. Mulliner, "because my nephew, Archibald, made me his confidant when he fell in love with Aurelia Cammarleigh. He worshipped that girl with a fervour which threatened to unseat his reason, such as it was: but the mere idea of asking her to be his wife gave him, he informed me, such a feeling of sick faintness that only by means of a very stiff brandy and soda, or some similar restorative, was he able to pull himself together on the occasions when he contemplated it. Had it not been for...But perhaps you would care to hear the story from the beginning?"

People who enjoyed a merely superficial acquaintance with my nephew Archibald (said Mr. Mulliner) were accustomed to set him down as just an ordinary pinheaded young man. It was only when they came to know him better that they discovered their mistake. Then they realised that his pinheadedness, so far from being ordinary, was exceptional. Even at the Drones Club, where the average of intellect is not high, it was often said of Archibald that, had his brain been constructed of silk, he would have been hard put to it to find sufficient material to make a canary a pair of cami-knickers. He sauntered through life with a cheerful insouciance, and up to the age of twenty-five had only once been moved by anything in the nature of a really strong emotion—on the occasion when, in the heart of Bond Street and at the height of the London season, he discovered that his man, Meadowes, had carelessly sent him out with odd spats on.

And then he met Aurelia Cammarleigh.

The first encounter between these two has always seemed

to me to bear an extraordinary resemblance to the famous meeting between the poet Dante and Beatrice Fortinari. Dante, if you remember, exchanged no remarks with Beatrice on that occasion. Nor did Archibald with Aurelia. Dante just goggled at the girl. So did Archibald. Like Archibald, Dante loved at first sight: and the poet's age at the time was, we are told, nine—which was almost exactly the mental age of Archibald Mulliner when he first set eye-glass on Aurelia Cammarleigh.

Only in the actual locale of the encounter do the two cases cease to be parallel. Dante, the story relates, was walking on the Ponte Vecchia, while Archibald Mulliner was having a thoughtful cocktail in the window of the Drones Club, looking out on Dover Street.

And he had just relaxed his lower jaw in order to examine Dover Street more comfortably when there swam into his line of vision something that looked like a Greek goddess. She came out of a shop opposite the club and stood on the pavement waiting for a taxi. And, as he saw her standing there, love at first sight seemed to go all over Archibald Mulliner like nettlerash.

It was strange that this should have been so, for she was not at all the sort of girl with whom Archibald had fallen in love at first sight in the past. I chanced, while in here the other day, to pick up a copy of one of the old yellow-back novels of fifty years ago—the property, I believe, of Miss Postlethwaite, our courteous and erudite barmaid. It was entitled *Sir Ralph's Secret*, and its heroine, the Lady Elaine, was described as a superbly handsome girl, divinely tall, with a noble figure, the arched Montresor nose, haughty eyes beneath delicately pencilled brows, and that indefinable air of aristocratic aloofness which marks the daughter of a hundred Earls. And Aurelia Cammarleigh might have been this formidable creature's double.

Yet Archibald, sighting her, reeled as if the cocktail he had just consumed had been his tenth instead of his first.

"Golly!" said Archibald.

To save himself from falling, he had clutched at a passing fellow-member: and how, examining his catch, he saw that it was young Algy Wymondham-Wymondham. Just the fellow-member he would have preferred to clutch at, for Algy was a man who went everywhere and knew everybody and could doubtless give him the information he desired.

"Algy, old prune," said Archibald in a low, throaty voice, "a moment of your valuable time, if you don't mind."

He paused, for he had perceived the need for caution. Algy was a notorious babbler, and it would be the height of rashness to give him an inkling of the passion which blazed within his breast. With a strong effort, he donned the mask. When he spoke again, it was with a deceiving nonchalance.

"I was just wondering if you happened to know who that girl is, across the street there. I suppose you don't know what her name is in rough numbers? Seems to me I've met her somewhere or something, or seen her, or something. Or something, if you know what I mean."

Algy followed his pointing finger and was in time to observe Aurelia as she disappeared into the cab.

"That girl?"

"Yes," said Archibald, yawning. "Who is she, if any?"

"Girl named Cammarleigh."

"Ah?" said Archibald, yawning again. "Then I haven't met her."

"Introduce you if you like. She's sure to be at Ascot. Look out for us there."

Archibald yawned for the third time.

"All right," he said, "I'll try to remember. Tell me about her. I mean, has she any fathers or mothers or any rot of that description?"

"Only an aunt. She lives with her in Park Street. She's potty."

Archibald stared, stung to the quick.

"Potty? That divine...I mean, that rather attractive-looking girl?"

"Not Aurelia. The aunt. She thinks Bacon wrote Shakespeare."

"Thinks who wrote what?" asked Archibald, puzzled, for the names were strange to him.

"You must have heard of Shakespeare. He's well known. Fellow who used to write plays. Only Aurelia's aunt says he didn't. She maintains that a bloke called Bacon wrote them for him."

"Dashed decent of him," said Archibald, approvingly. "Of course, he may have owed Shakespeare money."

"There's that, of course."

"What was the name again?"

"Bacon."

"Bacon," said Archibald, jotting it down on his cuff. "Right."

Algy moved on, and Archibald, his soul bubbling within him like a Welsh rabbit at the height of its fever, sank into a chair and stared sightlessly at the ceiling. Then, rising, he went off to the Burlington Arcade to buy socks.

The process of buying socks eased for awhile the turmoil that ran riot in Archibald's veins. But even socks with lavender clocks can only alleviate: they do not cure. Returning to his rooms, he found the anguish rather more overwhelming than ever. For at last he had leisure to think: and thinking always hurt his head.

Algy's careless words had confirmed his worst suspicions. A girl with an aunt who knew all about Shakespeare and Bacon must of necessity live in a mental atmosphere into which a lame-brained bird like himself could scarcely hope to soar. Even if he did meet her—even if she asked him to call—even if in due time their relations became positively cordial, what then? What had he to offer her?

Money?

Plenty of that, yes, but what was money?

Socks?

Of these he had the finest collection in London, but socks are not everything.

A loving heart?

A fat lot of use that was.

No, a girl like Aurelia Cammarleigh would, he felt, demand from the man who aspired to her hand something in the nature of gifts, of accomplishments. He would have to be a man who Did Things.

And what, Archibald asked himself, could he do? Absolutely nothing except give an imitation of a hen laying an egg.

That he could do. At imitating a hen laying an egg he was admittedly a master. His fame in that one respect had spread all over the West End of London. "Others abide our question. Thou art free," was the verdict of London's gilded youth on Archibald Mulliner when considered purely in the light of a man who could imitate a hen laying an egg. "Mulliner," they said to one another, "may be a pretty minus quantity in many ways, but he can imitate a hen laying an egg."

And, so far from helping him, this one accomplishment of his would, reason told him, be a positive handicap. A girl like Aurelia Cammarleigh would simply be sickened by such coarse buffoonery. He blushed at the very thought of her ever learning that he was capable of sinking to such depths.

And so, when some weeks later he was introduced to her in the paddock at Ascot and she, gazing at him with what seemed to his sensitive mind contemptuous loathing, said:

"They tell me you give an imitation of a hen laying an egg, Mr. Mulliner."

He replied with extraordinary vehemence:

"It is a lie—a foul and contemptible lie which I shall track to its source and nail to the counter."

Brave words! But had they clicked? Had she believed him? He trusted so. But her haughty eyes were very penetrating. They seemed to pierce through to the depths of his soul and lay it bare for what it was—the soul of a hen-imitator.

However, she did ask him to call. With a sort of queenly, bored disdain and only after he had asked twice if he might—but she did it. And Archibald resolved that, no matter what the mental strain, he would show her that her first impression of him had been erroneous; that, trivial and vapid though he might seem, there were in his nature deeps whose existence she had not suspected.

For a young man who had been super-annuated from Eton and believed everything he read in the Racing Expert's column in the morning paper, Archibald, I am bound to admit, exhibited in this crisis a sagacity for which few of his intimates would have given him credit. It may be that love stimulates the mind, or it may be that when the moment comes Blood will tell. Archibald, you must remember, was, after all, a Mulliner: and now the old canny strain of the Mulliners came out in him.

"Meadowes, my man," he said to Meadowes, his man.

"Sir," said Meadowes.

"It appears," said Archibald, "that there is—or was—a cove of the name of Shakespeare. Also a second cove of the name of Bacon. Bacon wrote plays, it seems, and Shakespeare went and put his own name on the programme and copped the credit."

"Indeed, sir?"

"If true, not right, Meadowes."

"Far from it, sir."

"Very well, then. I wish to go into this matter carefully. Kindly pop out and get me a book or two bearing on the business."

He had planned his campaign with infinite cunning. He knew that, before anything could be done in the direction of winning the heart of Aurelia Cammarleigh, he must first establish himself solidly with the aunt. He must court the aunt, ingratiate himself with her—always, of course, making it clear from the start that she was not the one. And, if reading about Shakespeare and Bacon could do it, he would, he told himself, have her eating out of his hand in a week.

Meadowes returned with a parcel of forbidding-looking volumes, and Archibald put in a fortnight's intensive study. Then, discarding the monocle which had up till then been his constant companion, and substituting for it a pair of horn-rimmed spectacles which gave him something of the look of an earnest sheep, he set out for Park Street to pay his first call. And within five minutes of his arrival he had declined a cigarette on the plea that he was a non-smoker, and had managed to say some rather caustic things about the practice, so prevalent among his contemporaries, of drinking cocktails.

Life, said Archibald, toying with his teacup, was surely given to us for some better purpose than the destruction of our brains and digestions with alcohol. Bacon, for instance, never took a cocktail in his life, and look at him.

At this, the aunt, who up till now had plainly been regarding him as just another of those unfortunate incidents, sprang to life.

"You admire Bacon, Mr. Mulliner?" she asked eagerly.

And, reaching out an arm like the tentacle of an octopus, she drew him into a corner and talked about Cryptograms for forty-seven minutes by the drawing-room clock. In short, to sum the thing up, my nephew Archibald, at his initial meeting with the only relative of the girl he loved, went like a sirocco. A Mulliner is always a Mulliner. Apply the acid test, and he will meet it.

It was not long after this that he informed me that he had sown the good seed to such an extent that Aurelia's aunt had invited him to pay a long visit to her country house, Brawstead Towers, in Sussex.

He was seated at the Savoy bar when he told me this, rather feverishly putting himself outside a Scotch and soda: and I was perplexed to note that his face was drawn and his eyes haggard.

"But you do not seem happy, my boy," I said.

"I'm not happy."

"But surely this should be an occasion for rejoicing. Thrown together as you will be in the pleasant surroundings of a country house, you ought easily to find an opportunity of asking this girl to marry you."

"And a lot of good that will be," said Archibald moodily. "Even if I do get a chance I shan't be able to make any use of it. I wouldn't have the nerve. You don't seem to realize what it means being in love with a girl like Aurelia. When

I look into those clear, soulful eyes, or see that perfect profile bobbing about on the horizon, a sense of my unworthiness seems to slosh me amidships like some blunt instrument. My tongue gets entangled with my front teeth, and all I can do is stand there feeling like a piece of Gorgonzola that has been condemned by the local sanitary inspector. I'm going to Brawstead Towers, yes, but I don't expect anything to come of it. I know exactly what's going to happen to me. I shall just buzz along through life, pining dumbly, and in the end slide into the tomb of a blasted, blighted bachelor. Another whisky, please, and jolly well make it a double."

Brawstead Towers, situated as it is in the pleasant Weald of Sussex, stands some fifty miles from London: and Archibald, taking the trip easily in his car, arrived there in time to dress comfortably for dinner. It was only when he reached the drawing-room at eight o'clock that he discovered that the younger members of the house-party had gone off in a body to dine and dance at a hospitable neighbour's, leaving him to waste the evening tie of a lifetime, to the composition of which he had devoted no less than twenty-two minutes, on Aurelia's aunt.

Dinner in these circumstances could hardly hope to be an unmixedly exhilarating function. Among the things which helped to differentiate it from a Babylonian orgy was the fact that, in deference to his known prejudices, no wine was served to Archibald. And, lacking artificial stimulus, he found the aunt even harder to endure philosophically than ever.

Archibald had long since come to a definite decision that what this woman needed was a fluid ounce of weed-killer, scientifically administered. With a good deal of adroitness

he contrived to head her off from her favourite topic during the meal: but after the coffee had been disposed of she
threw off all restraint. Scooping him up and bearing him
off into the recesses of the west wing, she wedged him into
a corner of a settee and began to tell him all about the
remarkable discovery which had been made by applying
the Plain Cipher to Milton's well-known Epitaph on
Shakespeare.

"The one beginning, 'What needs my Shakespeare for his
honoured bones?' said the aunt.

"Oh, that one?" said Archibald.

" 'What needs my Shakespeare for his honoured bones?
The labour of an Age in piled stones? Or that his hallowed
Reliques should be hid under a starry-pointing
Pyramid?' "said the aunt.

Archibald, who was not good at riddles, said he didn't
know.

"As in the Plays and Sonnets," said the aunt, "we substitute the name equivalents of the figure totals."

"We do what?"

"Substitute the name equivalents of the figure totals."

"The which?"

"The figure totals."

"All right," said Archibald. "Let it go. I daresay you know
best."

The aunt inflated her lungs.

"These figure totals," she said, "are always taken out in
the Plain Cipher, A equalling one to Z equals twenty-four.
The names are counted in the same way. A capital letter
with the figures indicates an occasional variation in the
Name Count. For instance, A equals twenty-seven, B
twenty-eight, until K equals ten is reached, when K, instead
of ten, becomes one, and T, instead of nineteen, is one, and

R or Reverse, and so on, until A equals twenty-four is reached. The short or single Digit is not used here. Reading the Epitaph in the light of this Cipher, it becomes: 'What need Verulam for Shakespeare? Francis Bacon England's King be hid under a W. Shakespeare? William Shakespeare. fame, what needst Francis Tudor, King of England? Francis. Francis W. Shakespeare. For Francis thy William Shakespeare hath England's King took W. Shakespeare. Then thou our W. Shakespeare Francis Tudor bereaving Francis Bacon Francis Tudor such a tomb William Shakespeare.' "

The speech to which he had been listening was unusually lucid and simple for a Baconian, yet Archibald, his eye catching a battle-axe that hung on the wall, could not but stifle a wistful sigh. How simple it would have been had he not been a Mulliner and a gentleman, to remove the weapon from its hook, spit on his hands, and haul off and dot this doddering old ruin one just above the imitation pearl necklace. Placing his twitching hands underneath him and sitting on them, he stayed where he was, until just as the clock on the mantlepiece chimed the hour of midnight, a merciful fit of hiccoughs on the part of his hostess enabled him to retire. As she reached the twenty-seventh "hic," his fingers found the door-handle and a moment later he was outside, streaking up the stairs.

The room they had given Archibald was at the end of a corridor, a pleasant, airy apartment with French windows opening upon a broad balcony. At any other time he would have found it agreeable to hop out onto this balcony and revel in the scents and sounds of the summer night, thinking the while long, lingering thoughts of Aurelia. But what with all that Francis Tudor Francis Bacon such a tomb William Shakespeare count seventeen drop one knit purl and set them up in the other alley stuff, not even thoughts of Aurelia could keep him from his bed.

Moodily tearing off his clothes and donning his pyjamas, Archibald Mulliner climbed in and instantaneously discovered that the bed was an apple-pie bed. When and how it had happened he did not know, but at a point during the day some loving hand had sewn up the sheets and put two hair-brushes and a branch of some prickly shrub between them.

Himself from the earliest boyhood an adept at the construction of booby-traps, Archibald, had his frame of mind been sunnier, would doubtless have greeted this really extremely sound effort with a cheery laugh. As it was, weighed down with Verulams and Francis Tudors, he swore for a while with considerable fervour: then, ripping off the sheets and tossing the prickly shrub wearily into a corner, crawled between the blankets and was soon asleep.

His last waking thought was that if the aunt hoped to catch him on the morrow, she would have to be considerably quicker on her pins than her physique indicated.

How long Archibald slept he could not have said. He woke some hours later with a vague feeling that a thunderstorm of unusual violence had broken out in his immediate neighbourhood. But this, he realized as the mists of slumber cleared away, was an error. The noise which had disturbed him was not thunder but the sound of someone snoring. Snoring like the dickens. The walls seemed to be vibrating like the deck of an ocean liner.

Archibald Mulliner might have had a tough evening with the aunt, but his spirit was not so completely broken as to make him lie supinely down beneath that snoring. The sound filled him as snoring fills every right-thinking man, with a seething resentment and a passionate yearning for justice, and he climbed out of bed with the intention of taking the proper steps through the recognised channels. It is the custom nowadays to disparage the educational methods of the English public-school and to maintain that they are not practical and of a kind to fit the growing boy for the problems of after-life. But you do learn one thing at a public-school, and that is how to act when somebody starts snoring.

You jolly well grab a cake of soap and pop in and stuff it down the blighter's throat. And this Archibald proposed—God willing—to do. It was the work of but a moment with him to dash to the washstand and arm himself. Then he moved softly out through the French windows onto the balcony.

The snoring, he had ascertained, proceeded from the next room. Presumably this room also would have French windows: and presumably, as the night was warm, these would be open. It would be a simple task to oil in, insert the soap, and buzz back undetected.

It was a lovely night, but Archibald paid no attention to it. Clasping his cake of soap, he crept on and was pleased to discover, on arriving outside the snorer's room, that his surmise had been correct. The windows were open. Beyond them, screening the interior of the room, were heavy curtains. And he had just placed his hand upon these when from inside a voice spoke. At the same moment the light was turned on.

"Who's that?" said the voice.

And it was as if Brawstead Towers with all its stabling, outhouses and messuages had fallen on Archibald's head. A mist rose before his eyes. He gasped and tottered.

The voice was that of Aurelia Cammarleigh.

For an instant, for a single long, sickening instant, I am compelled to admit that Archibald's love, deep as the sea though it was, definitely wobbled. It had received a grievous blow. It was not simply the discovery that the girl he adored was a snorer that unmanned him: it was the thought that she could snore like that. There was something about those snores that had seemed to sin against his whole conception of womanly purity.

Then he recovered. Even though this girl's slumber was not, as the poet Milton so beautifully puts it, "airy light," but rather reminiscent of a lumber-camp when the wood-sawing is proceeding at its briskest, he loved her still.

He had just reached this conclusion when a second voice spoke inside the room.

"I say, Aurelia."

It was the voice of another girl. He perceived now that the question "Who's that?" had been addressed not to him but to this newcomer fumbling at the door-handle.

"I say, Aurelia," said the girl complainingly, "you've simply got to do something about that bally bulldog of yours. I can't possibly get to sleep with him snoring like that. He's making the plaster come down from the ceiling in my room."

"I'm sorry," said Aurelia. "I've got so used to it that I don't notice."

"Well, I do. Put a green-baize cloth over him or something."

Out on the moonlit balcony Archibald Mulliner stood shaking like a blancmange. Although he had contrived to maintain his great love practically intact when he had supposed the snores to proceed from the girl he worshipped, it had been tough going, and for an instant, as I have said,

a very near thing. The relief that swept over him at the discovery that Aurelia could still justifiably remain on her pin-
nacle was so profound that it made him feel filleted. He
seemed for a moment in a daze. Then he was brought out
of the ether by hearing his name spoken.

"Did Archie Mulliner arrive to-night?" asked Aurelia's
friend.

"I suppose so," said Aurelia. "He wired that he was
motoring down."

"Just between us girls," said Aurelia's friend, "what do
you think of that bird?"

To listen to a private conversation—especially a private
conversation between two modern girls when you never
know what may come next—is rightly considered an action incompatible with the claim to be a gentleman. I regret
to say, therefore, that Archibald, ignoring the fact that he
belonged to a family whose code is as high as that of any
in the land, instead of creeping away to his room edged at
this point a step closer to the curtains and stood there with
his ears flapping. It might be an ignoble thing to eavesdrop,
but it was apparent that Aurelia Cammarleigh was about
to reveal her candid opinion of him: and the prospect of
getting the true facts—straight, as it were, from the horse's
mouth—held him so fascinated that he could not move.

"Archie Mulliner?" said Aurelia meditatively.

"Yes. The betting at the Junior Lipstick is seven to two
that you'll marry him."

"Why on earth?"

"Well, people have noticed he's always round at your
place, and they seem to think it significant. Anyway, that's
how the odds stood when I left London—seven to two."

"Get in on the short end," said Aurelia earnestly, "and
you'll make a packet."

"Is that official?"

"Absolutely," said Aurelia.

Out in the moonlight, Archibald Mulliner uttered a low, bleak moan rather like the last bit of wind going out of a dying duck. True, he had always told himself that he hadn't a chance, but, however much a man may say that, he never in his heart really believes it. And now from an authoritative source he had learned that his romance was definitely blue round the edges. It was a shattering blow. He wondered dully how the trains ran to the Rocky Mountains. A spot of grizzly-bear shooting seemed indicated.

Inside the room, the other girl appeared perplexed.

"But you told me at Ascot," she said, "just after he had been introduced to you, that you rather thought you had at last met your ideal. When did the good thing begin to come unstuck?"

A silvery sigh came through the curtains.

"I did think so then," said Aurelia wistfully. "There was something about him. I liked the way his ears wiggled. And I had always heard he was such a perfectly genial, cheery, merry old soul. Algy Wymondham-Wymondham told me that his imitation of a hen laying an egg was alone enough to keep any reasonable girl happy through a long married life."

"Can he imitate a hen?"

"No. It was nothing but an idle rumour. I asked him, and he stoutly denied that he had ever done such a thing in his life. He was quite stuffy about it. I felt a little uneasy then, and the moment he started calling and hanging about the house I knew that my fears had been well-founded. The man is beyond question a flat tire and a wet smack."

"As bad as that?"

"I'm not exaggerating a bit. Where people ever got the

idea that Archie Mulliner is a bonhomous old bean beats me. He is the world's worst monkey-wrench. He doesn't drink cocktails, he doesn't smoke cigarettes, and the thing he seems to enjoy most in the world is to sit for hours listening to the conversation of my aunt, who, as you know, is pure goof from the soles of the feet to the tortoiseshell comb and should long ago have been renting a padded cell in Earlswood. Believe me, Muriel, if you can really get seven to two, you are onto the best thing since Buttercup won the Lincolnshire."

"You don't say!"

"I do say. Apart from anything else, he's got a beastly habit of looking at me reverently. And if you knew how sick I am of being looked at reverently! They will do it, these lads. I suppose it's because I'm rather an out-size and modelled on the lines of Cleopatra."

"Tough!"

"You bet it's tough. A girl can't help her appearance. I may look as if my ideal man was the hero of a Viennese operetta, but I don't feel that way. What I want is some good sprightly sportsman who sets a neat booby-trap, and who'll rush up and grab me in his arms and say to me, 'Aurelia, old girl, you're the bee's roller-skates!'"

And Aurelia Cammarleigh emitted another sigh.

"Talking of booby-traps," said the other girl, "if Archie Mulliner has arrived he's in the next room, isn't he?"

"I suppose so. That's where he was to be. Why?"

"Because I made him an apple-pie bed."

"It was the right spirit," said Aurelia warmly. "I wish I'd thought of it myself."

"Too late now."

"Yes," said Aurelia. "But I'll tell you what I can and will do. You say you object to Lysander's snoring. Well, I'll go and pop him in at Archie Mulliner's window. That'll give him pause for thought."

"Splendid," agreed the girl Muriel. "Well, good night."

"Good night," said Aurelia.

There followed the sound of a door closing.

There was, as I have indicated, not much of my nephew Archibald's mind, but what there was of it was now in a whirl. He was stunned. Like every man who is abruptly called upon to revise his entire scheme of values, he felt as if he had been standing on top of the Eiffel Tower and some practical joker had suddenly drawn it away from under him. Tottering back to his room, he replaced the cake of soap in its dish and sat down on the bed to grapple with this amazing development.

Aurelia Cammarleigh had compared herself to Cleopatra. It is not too much to say that my nephew Archibald's emotions at this juncture were very similar to what Marc Antony's would have been had Egypt's queen risen from her throne at his entry and without a word of warning started to dance the Black Bottom.

He was roused from his thoughts by the sound of a light footstep on the balcony outside. At the same moment he heard a low woofly gruffle, the unmistakable note of a bulldog of regular habits who has been jerked out of his basket in the small hours and forced to take the night air.

She is coming, my own, my sweet!
Were it never so airy a tread,
My heart would hear her and beat,
Were it earth in an earthy bed,

whispered Archibald's soul, or words to that effect. He rose from his seat and paused for an instant, irresolute. Then inspiration descended on him. He knew what to do, and he did it.

Yes, gentlemen, in that supreme crisis of his life, with his whole fate hanging, as you might say, in the balance, Archibald Mulliner, showing for almost the first time in his career a well-nigh human intelligence, began to give his celebrated imitation of a hen laying an egg.

Archibald's imitation of a hen laying an egg was conceived on broad and sympathetic lines. Less violent than Salvini's *Othello*, it had in it something of the poignant wistfulness of Mrs. Siddons in the sleep-walking scene of *Macbeth*. The rendition started quietly, almost inaudibly, with a sort of soft, liquid crooning—the joyful yet half-incredulous murmur of a mother who can scarcely believe as yet that her union has really been blessed, and that it is indeed she who is responsible for that oval mixture of chalk and albumen which she sees lying beside her in the straw.

Then, gradually, conviction comes.

"It looks like an egg," one seems to hear her say. "It feels like an egg. It's shaped like an egg. Damme, it *is* an egg!"

And at that, all doubting resolved, the crooning changes; takes on a firmer note; soars into the upper register; and finally swells into a maternal paean of joy—a "Charawk-chawk-chawk-chawk" of such calibre that few had ever been able to listen to it dry-eyed. Following which, it was Archibald's custom to run round the room, flapping the sides of his coat, and then, leaping onto a sofa or some convenient chair, to stand there with his arms at right angles, crowing himself purple in the face.

All these things he had done many a time for the idle en-

tertainment of fellow-members in the smoking-room of the
Drones, but never with the gusto, the *brio*, with which he
performed them now. Essentially a modest man, like all the
Mulliners, he was compelled, nevertheless, to recognise that
to-night he was surpassing himself. Every artist knows when
the authentic divine fire is within him, and an inner voice
told Archibald Mulliner that he was at the top of his form
and giving the performance of a lifetime. Love thrilled
through every "Brt-t't-t't" that he uttered, animated each
flap of his arms. Indeed, so deeply did Love drive in its spur
that he tells me that, instead of the customary once, he actually made the circle of the room three times before coming to rest on top of the chest of drawers.

When at length he did so he glanced towards the window and saw that through the curtains the loveliest face
in the world was peering. And in Aurelia Cammarleigh's
glorious eyes there was a look he had never seen before,
the sort of look Kreisler or somebody like that beholds in
the eyes of the front row as he lowers his violin and brush-
es his forehead with the back of his hand. A look of worship.

There was a long silence. Then she spoke.

"Do it again!" she said.

And Archibald did it again. He did it four times and
could, he tells me, if he had pleased, have taken a fifth encore or at any rate a couple of bows. And then, leaping
lightly to the floor, he advanced towards her. He felt con-
quering, dominant. It was his hour. He reached out and
clasped her in his arms.

"Aurelia, old girl," said Archibald Mulliner in a clear,
firm voice, "you are the bee's roller-skates."

And at that she seemed to melt into his embrace. Her lovely face was raised to his.

"Archibald!" she whispered.

There was another throbbing silence, broken only by the beating of two hearts and the wheezing of the bulldog, who seemed to suffer a good deal in his bronchial tubes. Then Archibald released her.

"Well, that's that," he said. "Glad everything's all settled and hotsy-totsy. Gosh, I wish I had a cigarette. This is the sort of moment a bloke needs one."

She looked at him, surprised.

"But I thought you didn't smoke."

"Oh yes, I do."

"And do you drink as well?"

"Quite as well," said Archibald. "In fact, rather better. Oh, by the way."

"Yes?"

"There's just one other thing. Suppose that aunt of yours wants to come and visit us when we are settled down in our little nest, what, dearest, would be your reaction to the scheme of socking her on the base of the skull with a stuffed eel-skin?"

"I should like it," said Aurelia warmly, "above all things."

"Twin souls," cried Archibald. "That's what we are, when you come right down to it. I suspected it all along, and now I know. Two jolly old twin souls." He embraced her ardently. "And now," he said, "let us pop downstairs and put this bulldog in the butler's pantry, where he will come upon him unexpectedly in the morning and doubtless get a shock which will do him as much good as a week at the seaside. Are you on?"

"I am," whispered Aurelia. "Oh, I am!"

And hand in hand they wandered out together onto the broad staircase.

The Salvation of George Mackintosh

The young man came into the club-house. There was a frown on his usually cheerful face, and he ordered a ginger-ale in the sort of voice which an ancient Greek would have used when asking the executioner to bring on the hemlock.

Sunk in the recesses of his favourite settee the Oldest Member had watched him with silent sympathy.

"How did you get on?" he inquired.

"He beat me."

The Oldest Member nodded his venerable head.

"You have had a trying time, if I am not mistaken. I feared as much when I saw you go out with Pobsley. How many a young man have I seen go out with Herbert Pobsley exulting in his youth, and crawl back at eventide looking like a toad under the harrow! He talked?"

"All the time, confound it! Put me right off my stroke."

The Oldest Member sighed.

"The talking golfer is undeniably the most pronounced pest of our complex modern civilisation," he said, "and the most difficult to deal with. It is a melancholy thought that the noblest of games should have produced such a scourge. I have frequently marked Herbert Pobsley in action. As the crackling of thorns under a pot...He is almost as bad as poor George Mackintosh in his worst period. Did I ever tell you about George Mackintosh?"

"I don't think so."

"His," said the Sage, "is the only case of golfing garrulity I have ever known where a permanent cure was effected. If you would care to hear about it—?"

George Mackintosh (said the Oldest Member), when I first knew him, was one of the most admirable young fellows I have ever met. A handsome, well-set-up man, with no vices except a tendency to use the mashie for shots which should have been made with the light iron. And as for his positive virtues, they were too numerous to mention. He never swayed his body, moved his head, or pressed. He was always ready to utter a tactful grunt when his opponent foozled. And when he himself achieved a glaring fluke, his self-reproachful click of the tongue was music to his adversary's bruised soul. But of all his virtues the one that most endeared him to me and to all thinking men was the fact that, from the start of a round to the finish, he never spoke a word except when absolutely compelled to do so by the exigencies of the game. And it was this man who subsequently, for a black period which lives in the memory of all his contemporaries, was known as Gabby George and became a shade less popular than the germ of Spanish Influenza. Truly, *corruptio optimi pessima!*

One of the things that sadden a man as he grows older and reviews his life is the reflection that his most devastating deeds were generally the ones which he did with the best motives. The thought is disheartening. I can honestly say that, when George Mackintosh came to me and told me his troubles, my sole desire was to ameliorate his lot. That I might be starting on the downward path a man whom I liked and respected never once occurred to me.

One night after dinner when George Mackintosh came in, I could see at once that there was something on his mind, but what this could be I was at a loss to imagine, for I had been playing with him myself all the afternoon, and he had done an eighty-one and a seventy-nine. And, as I had not left the links till dusk was beginning to fall, it was practically impossible that he could have gone out again and done badly. The idea of financial trouble seemed equally out of the question. George had a good job with the old-established legal firm of Peabody, Peabody, Peabody, Peabody, Cootes, Toots, and Peabody. The third alternative, that he might be in love, I rejected at once. In all the time I had known him I had never seen a sign that George Mackintosh gave a thought to the opposite sex.

Yet this, bizarre as it seemed, was the true solution. Scarcely had he seated himself and lit a cigar when he blurted out his confession.

"What would you do in a case like this?" he asked.

"Like what?"

"Well—" He choked, and a rich blush permeated his surface. "Well, it seems a silly thing to say and all that, but I'm in love with Miss Tennant, you know!"

"You are in love with Celia Tennant?"

"Of course I am. I've got eyes, haven't I? Who else is there that any sane man could possibly be in love with? That," he went on, moodily, "is the whole trouble. There's a field of about twenty-nine, and I should think my place in the betting is about thirty-three to one."

"I cannot agree with you there," I said. "You have every advantage, it appears to me. You are young, amiable, good-looking, comfortably off, scratch—"

"But I can't talk, confound it!" he burst out. "And how is a man to get anywhere at this sort of game without talking?"

"You are talking perfectly fluently now."

"Yes, to you. But put me in front of Celia Tennant, and I simply make a sort of gurgling noise like a sheep with the botts. It kills my chances stone dead. You know these other men. I can give Claude Mainwaring a third and beat him.

I can give Eustace Brinkley a stroke a hole and simply trample on his corpse. But when it comes to talking to a girl, I'm not in her class."

"You must not be diffident."

"But I *am* diffident. What's the good of saying I mustn't be diffident when I'm the man who wrote the words and music, when Diffidence is my middle name and my telegraphic address? I can't help being diffident."

"Surely you could overcome it?"

"But how? It was in the hope that you might be able to suggest something that I came round to-night."

And this was where I did the fatal thing. It happened that, just before I took up "Braid on the Push-Shot," I had been dipping into the current number of a magazine, and one of the advertisements, I chanced to remember, might have been framed with a special eye to George's unfortunate case. It was that one, which I have no doubt you have seen, which treats of "How to Become a Convincing Talker." I picked up this magazine now and handed it to George.

He studied it for a few minutes in thoughtful silence. He looked at the picture of the man who had taken the course being fawned upon by lovely women, while the man who had let this opportunity slip stood outside the group gazing with a wistful envy.

"They never do that to me," said George.

"Do what, my boy?"

"Cluster round, clinging cooingly."

"I gather from the letterpress that they will if you write for the booklet."

"You think there is really something in it?"

"I see no reason why eloquence should not be taught by mail. One seems to be able to acquire every other desirable quality in that manner nowadays."

"I might try it. After all, it's not expensive. There's no doubt about it," he murmured, returning to his perusal, "that fellow does look popular. Of course, the evening dress may have something to do with it."

"Not at all. The other man, you will notice, is also wearing evening dress, and yet he is merely among those on the outskirts. It is simply a question of writing for the booklet."

"Sent post free."

"Sent, as you say, post free."

"I've got a good mind to try it."

"I see no reason why you should not."

"I will, by Duncan!" He tore the page out of the magazine and put it in his pocket. "I'll tell you what I'll do. I'll give this thing a trial for a week or two, and at the end of that time I'll go to the boss and see how he reacts when I ask for a rise of salary. If he crawls, it'll show there's something in this. If he flings me out, it will prove the thing's no good."

We left it at that, and I am bound to say—owing, no doubt, to my not having written for the booklet of the Memory Training Course advertised on the adjoining page of the magazine—the matter slipped from my mind. When, therefore, a few weeks later, I received a telegram from young Mackintosh which ran:

Worked like magic,

I confess I was intensely puzzled. It was only a quarter of an hour before George himself arrived that I solved the problem of its meaning.

"So the boss crawled?" I said, as he came in.

He gave a light, confident laugh. I had not seen him, as

I say, for some time, and I was struck by the alteration in his appearance. In what exactly this alteration consisted I could not at first have said; but gradually it began to impress itself on me that his eye was brighter, his jaw squarer, his carriage a trifle more upright than it had been. But it was his eye that struck me most forcibly. The George Mackintosh I had known had had a pleasing gaze, but, though frank and agreeable, it had never been more dynamic than a fried egg. This new George had an eye that was a combination of a gimlet and a searchlight. Coleridge's Ancient Mariner, I imagine, must have been somewhat similarly equipped. The Ancient Mariner stopped a wedding guest on his way to a wedding; George Mackintosh gave me the impression that he could have stopped the Twentieth Century Limited on its way to Chicago. Self-confidence—aye, and more than self-confidence—a sort of sinful, overbearing swank seemed to exude from his very pores.

"Crawled?" he said. "Well, he didn't actually lick my boots, because I saw him coming and side-stepped; but he did everything short of that. I hadn't been talking an hour when—"

"An hour!" I gasped. "Did you talk for an hour?"

"Certainly. You wouldn't have had me be abrupt, would you? I went into his private office and found him alone. I think at first he would have been just as well pleased if I had retired. In fact, he said as much. But I soon adjusted that outlook. I took a seat and a cigarette, and then I started to sketch out for him the history of my connection with the firm. He began to wilt before the end of the first ten minutes. At the quarter of an hour mark he was looking at me like a lost dog that's just found its owner. By the half-hour he was making little bleating noises and massaging my coat-sleeve. And when, after perhaps an hour and a half, I came to my peroration and suggested a rise, he choked back a sob, gave me double what I had asked, and invited me to dine at his club next Tuesday. I'm a little sorry now I cut the thing so short. A few minutes more, and I fancy he would have given me his sock-suspenders and made over his life insurance in my favour."

"Well," I said, as soon as I could speak, for I was finding my young friend a trifle overpowering, "this is most satisfactory."

"So-so," said George. "Not un-so-so. A man wants an addition to his income when he is going to get married."

"Ah!" I said. "That, of course, will be the real test."

"What do you mean?"

"Why, when you propose to Celia Tennant. You remember you were saying when we spoke of this before—"

"Oh, that!" said George, carelessly. "I've arranged all that."

"What!"

"Oh, yes. On my way up from the station. I looked in on Celia about an hour ago, and it's all settled."

"Amazing!"

"Well, I don't know. I just put the thing to her, and she seemed to see it."

"I congratulate you. So now, like Alexander, you have no more worlds to conquer."

"Well, I don't know so much about that," said George. "The way it looks to me is that I'm just starting. This eloquence is a thing that rather grows on one. You didn't hear about my after-dinner speech at the anniversary banquet of the firm, I suppose? My dear fellow, a riot! A positive stampede. Had 'em laughing and then crying and then laughing again and then crying once more till six of 'em had to be led out and the rest down with hiccoughs. Napkins waving...three tables broken...waiters in hysterics. I tell you, I played on them as on a stringed instrument..."

"Can you play on a stringed instrument?"

"As it happens, no. But as I would have played on a stringed instrument if I could play on a stringed instrument. Wonderful sense of power it gives you. I mean to go in pretty largely for that sort of thing in future."

"You must not let it interfere with your golf."

"Golf!" he said. "After all, what is golf? Just pushing a small ball into a hole. A child could do it. Indeed, children have done it with great success. I see an infant of fourteen has just won some sort of championship. Could that stripling convulse a roomful of banqueters? I think not! To sway your fellow-men with a word, to hold them with a gesture...that is the real salt of life. I don't suppose I shall play much more golf now. I'm making arrangements for a lecturing-tour, and I'm booked up for fifteen lunches already."

Those were his words. A man who had once done the lake-hole in one. A man whom the committee were grooming for the amateur championship. I am no weakling, but I confess they sent a chill shiver down my spine.

George Mackintosh did not, I am glad to say, carry out his mad project to the letter. He did not altogether sever himself from golf. He was still to be seen occasionally on the links. But now—and I know of nothing more tragic that can befall a man—he found himself gradually shunned, he who in the days of his sanity had been besieged with more offers of games than he could manage to accept. Men simply would not stand his incessant flow of talk. One by one they dropped off, until the only person he could find to go

round with him was old Major Moseby, whose hearing completely petered out as long ago as the year '98. And, of
course, Celia Tennant would play with him occasionally;
but it seemed to me that even she, greatly as no doubt she
loved him, was beginning to crack under the strain.

So surely had I read the pallor of her face and the wild
look of dumb agony in her eyes that I was not surprised
when, as I sat one morning in my garden reading Ray On
Taking Turf, my man announced her name. I had been half
expecting her to come to me for advice and consolation,
for I had known her ever since she was a child. It was I
who had given her her first driver and taught her infant lips
to lisp "Fore!" It is not easy to lisp the word "Fore!" but
I had taught her to do it, and this constituted a bond between us which had been strengthened rather than weakened
by the passage of time.

She sat down on the grass beside my chair, and looked
up at my face in silent pain. We had known each other so
long that I know that it was not my face that pained her,
but rather some unspoken *malaise* of the soul. I waited for
her to speak, and suddenly she burst out impetuously as
though she could hold back her sorrow no longer.

"Oh, I can't stand it! I can't stand it!"

"You mean...?" I said, though I knew only too well.

"This horrible obsession of poor George's," she cried passionately. "I don't think he has stopped talking once since
we have been engaged."

"He is chatty," I agreed. "Has he told you the story about
the Irishman?"

"Half a dozen times. And the one about the Swede oftener
than that. But I would not mind an occasional anecdote.
Women have to learn to bear anecdotes from the men they
love. It is the curse of Eve. It is his incessant easy flow of

chatter on all topics that is undermining even my devotion."

"But surely, when he proposed to you, he must have given you an inkling of the truth. He only hinted at it when he spoke to me, but I gather that he was eloquent."

"When he proposed," said Celia dreamily, "he was wonderful. He spoke for twenty minutes without stopping. He said I was the essence of his every hope, the tree on which the fruit of his life grew; his Present, his Future, his Past...oh, and all that sort of thing. If he would only confine his conversation now to remarks of a similar nature, I could listen to him all day long. But he doesn't. He talks politics and statistics and philosophy and...oh, and everything. He makes my head ache."

"And your heart also, I fear," I said gravely.

"I love him!" she replied simply. "In spite of everything, I love him dearly. But what to do? What to do? I have an awful fear that when we are getting married instead of answering 'I will,' he will go into the pulpit and deliver an address on Marriage Ceremonies of All Ages. The world to him is a vast lecture-platform. He looks on life as one long after-dinner, with himself as the principal speaker of the evening. It is breaking my heart. I see him shunned by his former friends. Shunned! They run a mile when they see him coming. The mere sound of his voice outside the club-house is enough to send brave men diving for safety beneath the sofas. Can you wonder that I am in despair? What have I to live for?"

"There is always golf."

"Yes, there is always golf," she whispered bravely.

"Come and have a round this afternoon."

"I had promised to go for a walk..." She shuddered, then pulled herself together. "...for a walk with George."

I hesitated for a moment.

"Bring him along," I said, and patted her hand. "It may be that together we shall find an opportunity of reasoning with him."

She shook her head.

"You can't reason with George. He never stops talking long enough to give you time."

"Nevertheless, there is no harm in trying. I have an idea that this malady of his is not permanent and incurable. The very violence with which the germ of loquacity has attacked him gives me hope. You must remember that before this seizure he was rather a noticeably silent man. Sometimes I think that it is just Nature's way of restoring the average, and that soon the fever may burn itself out. Or it may be that a sudden shock...At any rate, have courage."

"I will try to be brave."

"Capital! At half-past two on the first tee, then."

"You will have to give me a stroke on the third, ninth, twelfth, fifteen, sixteenth and eighteenth," she said, with a quaver in her voice. "My golf has fallen off rather lately."

I patted her hand again.

"I understand," I said gently. "I understand."

The steady drone of a baritone voice as I alighted from my car and approached the first tee told me that George had not forgotten the tryst. He was sitting on the stone seat under the chestnut-tree, speaking a few well-chosen words on the Labour Movement.

"To what conclusion, then, do we come?" he was saying. "We come to the foregone and inevitable conclusion that..."

"Good afternoon, George," I said.

He nodded briefly, but without verbal salutation. He seemed to regard my remark as he would have regarded the unmannerly heckling of some one at the back of the hall. He proceeded evenly with his speech, and was still talking when Celia addressed her ball and drove off. Her drive, coinciding with a sharp rhetorical question from George, wavered in mid-air, and the ball trickled off into the rough halfway down the hill. I can see the poor girl's tortured face even now. But she breathed no word of reproach. Such is the miracle of woman's love.

"Where you went wrong there," said George, breaking off his remarks on Labour, "was that you have not studied the dynamics of golf sufficiently. You did not pivot properly. You allowed your left heel to point down the course when you were at the top of your swing. This makes for instability and loss of distance. The fundamental laws of the dynamics of golf is that the left foot shall be solidly on the ground at the moment of impact. If you allow your heel to point down the course, it is almost impossible to bring it back in time to make the foot a solid fulcrum."

I drove and managed to clear the rough and reach the fairway. But it was not one of my best drives. George Mackintosh, I confess, had unnerved me. The feeling he gave me resembled the self-conscious panic which I used to experience in my childhood when informed that there was One Awful Eye that watched my every movement and saw my every act. It was only the fact that poor Celia appeared even more affected by his espionage that enabled me to win the first hole in seven.

On the way to the second tee George discoursed on the beauties of Nature, pointing out at considerable length how exquisitely the silver glitter of the lake harmonized with the vivid emerald turf near the hole and the duller green of the rough beyond it. As Celia teed up her ball, he directed her attention to the golden glory of the sand-pit to the left of the flag. It was not the spirit in which to approach the lake-hole, and I was not surprised when the unfortunate girl's ball fell with a sickening plop halfway across the water.

"Where you went wrong there," said George, "was that you made the stroke a sudden heave instead of a smooth, snappy flick of the wrists. Pressing is always bad, but with the mashie——"

"I think I will give you this hole," said Celia to me, for my shot had cleared the water and was lying on the edge of the green. "I wish I hadn't used a new ball."

"The price of golf-balls," said George, as we started to round the lake, "is a matter to which economists should give some attention. I am credibly informed that rubber at the present time is exceptionally cheap. Yet we see no decrease in the price of golf-balls, which, as I need scarcely inform you, are rubber-cored. Why should this be so? You will say that the wages of skilled labour have gone up. True. But——"

"One moment, George, while I drive," I said. For we had now arrived at the third tee.

"A curious thing, concentration," said George, "and why certain phenomena should prevent us from focussing our attention——This brings me to the vexed question of sleep. Why is it that we are able to sleep through some vast convulsion of Nature when a dripping tap is enough to keep us awake? I am told that there were people who slumbered peacefully through the San Francisco earthquake, merely stirring drowsily from time to time to tell an imaginary person to leave it on the mat. Yet these same people——"

Celia's drive bounded into the deep ravine which yawns some fifty yards from the tee. A low moan escaped her.

"Where you went wrong there..." said George.

"I know," said Celia. "I lifted my head."

I had never heard her speak so abruptly before. Her manner, in a girl less noticeably pretty, might almost have been called snappish. George, however, did not appear to have noticed anything amiss. He filled his pipe and followed her into the ravine.

"Remarkable," he said, "how fundamental a principle of golf is this keeping the head still. You will hear professionals tell their pupils to keep their eye on the ball. Keeping the eye on the ball is only a secondary matter. What they really mean is that the head should be kept rigid, as otherwise it is impossible to—"

His voice died away. I had sliced my drive into the woods on the right, and after playing another had gone off to try to find my ball, leaving Celia and George in the ravine behind me. My last glimpse of them showed me that her ball had fallen into a stone-studded cavity in the side of the hill, and she was drawing her niblick from her bag as I passed out of sight. George's voice, blurred by distance to a monotonous murmur, followed me until I was out of earshot.

I was just about to give up the hunt for my ball in despair, when I heard Celia's voice calling to me from the edge of the undergrowth. There was a sharp note in it which startled me.

I came out, trailing a portion of some unknown shrub which had twined itself about my ankle.

"Yes?" I said, picking twigs out of my hair.

"I want your advice," said Celia.

"Certainly. What is the trouble? By the way," I said, looking round, "where is your *fiance?*"

"I have no *fiance*," she said, in a dull, hard voice.

"You have broken off the engagement?"

"Not exactly. And yet—well, I suppose it amounts to that."

"I don't quite understand."

"Well, the fact is," said Celia, in a burst of girlish frankness, "I rather think I've killed George."

"Killed him, eh?"

It was a solution that had not occurred to me, but now that it was presented for my inspection I could see its merits. In these days of national effort when we are all working together to try to make our beloved land fit for heroes to live in, it was astonishing that nobody before had thought of a simple, obvious thing like killing George Mackintosh. George Mackintosh was undoubtedly better dead, but it had taken a woman's intuition to see it.

"I killed him with my niblick," said Celia.

I nodded. If the thing was to be done at all, it was unquestionably a niblick shot.

"I had just made my eleventh attempt to get out of that ravine," the girl went on, "with George talking all the time about the recent excavations in Egypt, when suddenly—you know what it is when something seems to snap—"

"I had the experience with my shoe-lace only this morning."

"Yes, it was like that. Sharp—sudden—happening all in a moment. I suppose I must have said something, for George stopped talking about Egypt and said that he was reminded by a remark of the last speaker's of a certain Irishman—"

I pressed her hand.

"Don't go on if it hurts you," I said, gently.

"Well, there is very little more to tell. He bent his head to light his pipe, and well—the temptation was too much for me. That's all."

"You were quite right."

"You really think so?"

"I certainly do. A rather similar action, under far less provocation, once made Jael the wife of Heber the most popular woman in Israel."

"I wish I could think so too," she murmured. "At the moment, you know, I was conscious of nothing but an awful elation. But—but—oh, he was such a darling before he got this dreadful affliction. I can't help thinking of G-George as he used to be."

She burst into a torrent of sobs.

"Would you care for me to view the remains?" I said.

"Perhaps it would be as well."

She led me silently into the ravine. George Mackintosh was lying on his back where he had fallen.

"There!" said Celia.

And, as she spoke, George Mackintosh gave a kind of snorting groan and sat up. Celia uttered a sharp shriek and sank on her knees before him. George blinked once or twice and looked about him dazedly.

"Save the women and children!" he cried. "I can swim."

"Oh, George!" said Celia.

"Feeling a little better?" I asked.

"A little. How many people were hurt?"

"Hurt?"

"When the express ran into us." He cast another glance around him. "Why, how did I get here?"

"You were here all the time," I said.

"Do you mean after the roof fell in or before?"

Celia was crying quietly down the back of his neck.

"Oh, George!" she said, again.

He groped out feebly for her hand and patted it.

"Brave little woman!" he said. "Brave little woman! She stuck by me all through. Tell me—I am strong enough to bear it—what caused the explosion?"

It seemed to me a case where much unpleasant explanation might be avoided by the exercise of a little tact.

"Well, some say one thing and some another," I said. "Whether it was a spark from a cigarette..."

Celia interrupted me. The woman in her made her revolt against this well-intentioned subterfuge.

"I hit you, George!"

"Hit me?" he repeated, curiously. "What with? The Eiffel Tower?"

"With my niblick."

"You hit me with your niblick? But why?"

She hesitated. Then she faced him bravely.

"Because you wouldn't stop talking."

He gaped.

"Me!" he said. "*I* wouldn't stop talking! But I hardly talk at all. I'm noted for it."

Celia's eyes met mine in agonised inquiry. But I saw what had happened. The blow, the sudden shock, had operated on George's brain-cells in such a way as to effect a complete cure. I have not the technical knowledge to be able to explain it, but the facts were plain.

"Lately, my dear fellow," I assured him, "you have dropped into the habit of talking rather a good deal. Ever since we started out this afternoon you have kept up an incessant flow of conversation!"

"Me! On the links! It isn't possible."

"It is only too true, I fear. And that is why this brave girl hit you with her niblick. You started to tell her a funny story just as she was making her eleventh shot to get her ball out of this ravine, and she took what she considered the necessary steps."

"Can you ever forgive me, George?" cried Celia.

George Mackintosh stared at me. Then a crimson blush mantled his face.

"So I did! It's all beginning to come back to me. Oh, heavens!"

Can you forgive me, George?" cried Celia again.

He took her hand in his.

"Forgive you?" he muttered. "Can *you* forgive *me?* Me—a tee-talker, a green-gabbler, a prattler on the links, the lowest form of life known to science! I am unclean, unclean!"

"It's only a little mud, dearest," said Celia, looking at the sleeve of his coat. "It will brush off when it's dry."

"How can you link your lot with a man who talks when people are making their shots?"

"You will never do it again."

"But I have done it. And you stuck to me all through! Oh, Celia!"

"I loved you, George!"

The man seemed to swell with a sudden emotion. His eyes lit up, and he thrust one hand into the breast of his coat while he raised the other in a sweeping gesture. For an instant he appeared on the verge of a flood of eloquence. And then, as if he had been made sharply aware of what it was that he intended to do, he suddenly sagged. The gleam died out of his eyes. He lowered his hand.

"Well, I must say that was rather decent of you," he said.

A lame speech, but one that brought an infinite joy to both his hearers. For it showed that George Mackintosh was cured beyond possibility of relapse.

"Yes, I must say you are rather a corker," he added.

"George!" cried Celia.

I said nothing, but I clasped his hand; and then, taking my clubs, I retired. When I looked round she was still in his arms. I left them there, alone together in the great silence.

And so (concluded the Oldest Member) you see that a cure is possible, though it needs a woman's gentle hand to bring it about. And how few women are capable of doing what Celia Tennant did. Apart from the difficulty of summoning up the necessary resolution, an act like hers requires a straight eye and a pair of strong and supple wrists. It seems to me that for the ordinary talking golfer there is no hope. And the race seems to be getting more numerous every day. Yet the finest golfers are always the least loquacious. It is related of the illustrious Sandy McHoots that when, on the occasion of his winning the British Open Championship, he was interviewed by reporters from the leading daily papers as to his views on Tariff Reform, Bimetallism, the Trial by Jury System, and the Modern Craze for Dancing, all they could extract from him was the single word "Mphm!" Having uttered which, he shouldered his bag and went home to tea. A great man. I wish there were more like him.

Run for the Hills!

When the call to loving arms brings out the draft-dodger in us.

Jeeves and the Yuletide Spirit

The letter arrived on the morning of the sixteenth. I was pushing a bit of breakfast into the Wooster face at the moment; and, feeling fairly well fortified with coffee and kippers, I decided to break the news to Jeeves without delay. As Shakespeare says, if you're going to do a thing you might just as well pop right at it and get it over. The man would be disappointed, of course, and possibly even chagrined; but, dash it all, a spot of disappointment here and there does a fellow good. Makes him realize that life is stern and life is earnest.

"Oh, Jeeves," I said.

"Sir?"

"We have here a communication from Lady Wickham. She has written inviting me to Skeldings for the festivities. So will you see about bunging the necessaries together? We repair thither on the twenty-third. We shall be there some little time, I expect."

There was a pause. I could feel he was directing a frosty gaze at me, but I dug into the marmalade and refused to meet it.

"I thought I understood you to say, sir, that you proposed to visit Monte Carlo immediately after Christmas."

"I know. But that's all off. Plans changed."

At this point the telephone bell rang, tiding over nicely what had threatened to be an awkward moment. Jeeves unhooked the receiver.

"Yes? . . . Yes, madam. . . . Very good, madam. Here is Mr. Wooster." He handed me the instrument. "Mrs. Spenser Gregson, sir."

You know, every now and then I can't help feeling that Jeeves is losing his grip. In his prime it would have been with him the work of a moment to have told my aunt Agatha that I was not at home. I gave him one of those reproachful glances, and took the machine.

"Hullo?" I said. "Yes? Yes? Yes? Bertie speaking. Hullo? Hullo? Hullo?"

"Don't keep on saying Hullo," yipped the old relative, in her customary curt manner. "You're not a parrot. Sometimes I wish you were, because then you might have a little sense."

Quite the wrong sort of tone to adopt toward a fellow in the early morning, of course, but what can one do?

"Bertie, Lady Wickham tells me she has invited you to Skeldings for Christmas. Are you going?"

"Rather!"

"Well, mind you behave yourself. Lady Wickham is an old friend of mine."

"I shall naturally endeavour, Aunt Agatha," I replied stiffly, "to conduct myself in a manner befitting an English gentleman paying a visit—"

"What did you say? Speak up. I can't hear."

"I said, 'Right ho.' "

"Oh? Well, mind you do. And there's another reason why I particularly wish you to be as little of an imbecile as you can manage while at Skeldings. Sir Roderick Glossop will be there."

"What!"

"Don't bellow like that."

"I did."

"You don't mean Tuppy Glossop?"

"I mean Sir Roderick Glossop. Which was my reason for saying Sir Roderick Glossop. Now, Bertie, I want you to listen to me attentively. Are you there?"

"Yes. Still here."

"Well, then, listen. I have at last succeeded, after incredible difficulty and in face of all the evidence, in almost persuading Sir Roderick that you are not actually insane. He is prepared to suspend judgment until he has seen you once more. On your behaviour at Skeldings, therefore—"

But I had hung up the receiver. Shaken. That's what I was. S. to the core.

This Glossop was a formidable old bird with a bald head and outsize eyebrows, by profession a loony-doctor. How it happened, I couldn't tell you to this day, but I once got engaged to his daughter Honoria, a ghastly dynamic exhibit who read Nietzsche and had a laugh like waves breaking on a stern and rock-bound coast. The fixture was scratched, owing to events occurring which convinced the old boy that I was off my napper; and since then he has always had my name at the top of his list of Loonies I Have Lunched With.

"Jeeves," I said, all of a twitter, "do you know what? Sir Roderick Glossop is going to be at Lady Wickham's."

"Very good, sir. If you have finished breakfast I will clear away."

Cold and haughty. No sympathy. None of the rallying-around spirit which one likes to see. As I had anticipated, Jeeves had been looking forward to a little flutter at the tables. We Woosters can wear the mask. I ignored his lack of decent feeling.

"Do so, Jeeves," I said proudly.

Going down to Skeldings in the car on the afternoon of the twenty-third, Jeeves was aloof and reserved. And before dinner on the first night of my visit he put the studs in my dress shirt in what I can only call a marked manner. The whole thing was extremely painful, and it seemed to me, as I lay in bed on the morning of the twenty-fourth, that the only step to take was to put the whole facts of the case before him and trust to his native good sense to effect an understanding.

My hostess, Lady Wickham, was a beaky female built far too closely on the lines of my aunt Agatha for comfort; but she had seemed matey enough on my arrival. Her daughter Roberta had welcomed me with a warmth which, I'm bound to say, had set the old heartstrings fluttering a bit. And Sir Roderick, in the brief moment we had had together, had said, "Ha, young man!"—not particularly chummily, but he said it; and my view was that it practically amounted to the lion lying down with the lamb.

So, all in all, life at this juncture seemed pretty well all to the mustard, and I decided to tell Jeeves exactly how matters stood.

"Jeeves," I said, as he appeared with the steaming.

"Sir?"

"I'm afraid scratching that Monte Carlo trip has been a bit of a jar for you, Jeeves."

"Not at all, sir."

"Oh, yes, it has. The heart was set on wintering in the world's good old plague spot, I know. I saw your eye light up when I said we were due for a visit there. You snorted a bit and your fingers twitched. I know, I know. And now that there has been a change of programme, the iron has entered into your soul."

"Not at all, sir."

"Oh, yes, it has. I've seen it. Very well, then. What I wish to impress upon you, Jeeves, is that it was through no light and airy caprice that I accepted this invitation to Lady Wickham's. I have been angling for it for weeks, prompted by many considerations. It was imperative that I should come to Skeldings for Christmas, Jeeves, because I knew that young Tuppy Glossop was going to be here."

"Sir Roderick Glossop, sir?"

"His nephew. You may have observed hanging about the place a fellow with light hair and Cheshire-cat grin. That is Tuppy, and I have been anxious for some time to get to grips with him. The Wooster honour is involved."

I took a sip of tea, for the mere memory of my wrongs had shaken me.

"In spite of the fact that young Tuppy is the nephew of Sir Roderick Glossop, at whose hands, Jeeves, as you are aware, I have suffered much, I fraternized with him freely. I said to myself that a man is not to be blamed for his relations, and that I should hate to have my pals hold my aunt Agatha, for instance, against me. Broad-minded, Jeeves, I think?"

"Extremely, sir."

"Well, then, as I say, I sought this Tuppy out, Jeeves, and hobnobbed; and what do you think he did?"

"I could not say, sir."

"I will tell you. One night, after dinner at the Drones' Club, he bet me I wouldn't swing myself across the swimming bath by the ropes and rings. I took him on, and was buzzing along in great style until I came to the last ring. And then I found that this fiend in human shape had looped it back against the rail, thus leaving me hanging in the void with no means of getting ashore to my home and loved ones.

"There was nothing for it but to drop into the water. And what I maintain, Jeeves, is that, if I can't get back at him somehow at Skeldings—with all the vast resources which a country house affords at my disposal—I am not the man I was."

"I see, sir."

"And now, Jeeves, we come to the most important reason why I had to spend Christmas at Skeldings. Jeeves,"
I said, diving into the old cup once more for a moment and
bringing myself out wreathed in blushes, "the fact of the
matter is, I'm in love."

"Indeed, sir."

"You've seen Miss Roberta Wickham?"

"Yes, sir."

"Very well, then."

There was a pause while I let it sink in.

"During your stay here, Jeeves," I said, "you will, no
doubt, be thrown a good deal together with Miss Wickham's
maid. On such occasions pitch it strong."

"Sir?"

"You know what I mean. Tell her I'm rather a good chap.
Mention my hidden depths. These things get round. A boost
is never wasted, Jeeves."

"Very good, sir. But—"

"But what?"

"Well, sir—"

"Carry on, Jeeves. We are always glad to hear from you,
always."

"What I was about to remark, if you will excuse me, sir,
was that I would scarcely have thought Miss Wickham a
suitable—"

"Jeeves," I said coldly, "what is your kick against Miss
Wickham?"

"Oh, really, sir!"

"Jeeves, I insist. This is a time for plain speaking. You
have beefed about Miss Wickham. I wish to know why."

"It merely crossed my mind, sir, that for a gentleman of
your description Miss Wickham is not a suitable mate."

"What do you mean by 'a gentleman of my description'?"

"I beg your pardon, sir. The expression escaped me inadvertently. I was about to observe, sir, that though Miss Wickham is a charming young lady—"

"There, Jeeves, you spoke an imperial quart. What eyes!"

"Yes, sir."

"What hair!"

"Very true, sir."

"And what *espieglerie*—if that's the word I want."

"The exact word, sir."

"All right, then. Carry on."

"I grant Miss Wickham the possession of all these desirable qualities, sir. Nevertheless, considered as a matrimonial prospect for a gentleman of your description, I cannot look upon her as suitable. In my opinion, Miss Wickham lacks seriousness, sir. She is too volatile and frivolous. To qualify as Miss Wickham's husband, a gentleman would need to possess a commanding personality and considerable strength of character."

"Exactly!"

"I would always hesitate to recommend as a life's companion a young lady with such a vivid shade of red hair. Red hair, sir, is dangerous."

I eyed the blighter squarely.

"Jeeves," I said, "you're talking rot."

"Very good, sir."

"Absolute drivel."

"Very good, sir."

"Pure mashed potatoes."

"Very good, sir."

"Very good, sir—I mean very good, Jeeves; that will be all," I said.

And I drank a modicum of tea with a good deal of hauteur.

It isn't often that I find myself able to prove Jeeves in the wrong; but by dinner time that night I was in a position to do so, and I did it without delay.

"Touching on that matter we were touching on, Jeeves," I said, coming in from the bath and tackling him as he studded the shirt, "I should be glad if you would give me your careful attention for a moment. I warn you that what I am about to say is going to make you look pretty silly."

"Indeed, sir?"

"Yes, Jeeves. Pretty dashed silly it's going to make you look. This morning, if I remember rightly, you stated that Miss Wickham was volatile, frivolous, and lacking in seriousness. Am I correct?"

"Quite correct, sir."

"Then what I have to tell you may cause you to alter that opinion. I went for a walk with Miss Wickham this afternoon; and, as we walked I told her about what young Tuppy Glossop did to me in he swimming bath at the Drones'. She hung upon my words, Jeeves, and was full of sympathy."

"Indeed, sir?"

"Dripping with it. And that's not all. Almost before I had finished she was suggesting the ripest, fruitiest, brainiest scheme for bringing young Tuppy's gray hairs in sorrow to the grave that anyone could possibly imagine."

"That is very gratifying, sir."

" 'Gratifying' is the word. It appears that at the school where Miss Wickham was educated, Jeeves, it used to become necessary from time to time for the right-thinking element to slip it across certain of the baser sort. Do you know what they did, Jeeves?"

"No, sir."

"They took a long stick, Jeeves, and—follow me closely

here—they tied a darning needle to the end of it. Then, at dead of night, it appears, they sneaked into the party of the second part's cubicle and shoved the needle through the bedclothes and punctured her hot-water bottle.

"Girls are much subtler in these matters than boys, Jeeves. At my old school one would occasionally heave a jug of water over another bloke during the night watches, but we never though of effecting the same result in this particularly neat and scientific manner.

"Well, Jeeves, that was the scheme which Miss Wickham suggested I should work on young Tuppy, and that is the girl you call frivolous and lacking in seriousness. Any girl who can think up a wheeze like that is my idea of a helpmate.

"I shall be glad, Jeeves, if by the time I come to bed tonight you have waiting for me in this room a stout stick with a good sharp darning needle attached."

"Well, sir—"

I raised my hand.

"Jeeves," I said, "not another word. Stick, one, and needle, darning, good, sharp, one, without fail, in this room at eleven-thirty to-night."

"Very good, sir."

"Have you any idea where young Tuppy sleeps?"

"I could ascertain, sir."

"Do so, Jeeves."

In a few minutes he was back with the necessary informash.

"Mr. Glossop is established in the Moat Room, sir."

"Where's that?"

"The second door on the floor below, sir."

"Right ho, Jeeves. Are the studs in my shirt?"

"Yes, sir."

"And the links also?"
"Yes, sir."
"Then push me into it."

The task to which I had set myself was one that involved hardship and discomfort, for it meant sitting up till well into the small hours, and then padding down a cold corridor. But I did not shrink from it. After all, there is a lot to be said for family tradition. We Woosters did our bit in the Crusades.

It being Christmas Eve, there was, as I had foreseen, a good deal of revelry and what not; so that it wasn't till past one that I got to my room. Allowing for everything, it didn't seem that it was going to be safe to start my little expedition till half-past two at the earliest; and I'm bound to say that it was only the utmost resolution that kept me from snuggling into the sheets and calling it a day. I'm not much of a lad now for late hours.

However, by half-past two everything appeared to be quiet. I shook off the mists of sleep, grabbed the good old stick and needle, and was off along the corridor. And presently, pausing outside the Moat Room, I turned the handle, found the door wasn't locked, and went in.

At first, when I had beetled in, the room had seemed as black as a coal cellar; but after a bit things began to lighten. The curtains weren't quite drawn over the window, and I could see a trifle of the scenery here and there.

The bed was opposite the window, with the head against the wall and the end where the feet were jutting out toward where I stood, thus rendering it possible after one had sown the seed, so to speak, to make a quick get-away.

There only remained now the rather tricky problem of locating the old hot-water bottle. I mean to say, the one thing you can't do if you want to carry a job like this through with secrecy and dispatch is to stand at the end of a fellow's bed, jabbing at random.

I was a good deal cheered, at this juncture, to hear a fruity snore from the direction of the pillows. Reason told me that a bloke who could snore like that wasn't going to be awakened by a trifle. I edged forward and ran a hand in a gingerly sort of way over the coverlet. A moment later I had found the bulge. I steered the good old darning needle on to it, gripped the sick, and shoved. Then, pulling out the weapon, I sidled toward the door, and in an another moment would have been outside, buzzing for home and the good night's rest, when suddenly there was a crash that sent my spine shooting up through the top of my head, and the contents of the bed sat up like a jack-in-the-box and said:

"Who's that?"

It just shows how your most careful strategic moves can be the very ones that dish your campaign. In order to facilitate the orderly retreat according to plan, I had left the door open, and the beastly thing had slammed like a bomb.

But I wasn't giving much thought to the causes of the explosion. What was disturbing me was the discovery that, whoever else the bloke in the bed might be, he was not young Tuppy. Tuppy has one of those high squeaky voices that sound like the tenor of the village choir failing to hit a high note. This one was something in between the last trump and a tiger calling for breakfast after being on a diet for a day or two. It was the sort of nasty, rasping voice you hear shouting "Fore!" when you're one of a slow foursome on the links and are holding up a couple of retired colonels.

I did not linger. Getting swiftly off the mark, I dived for the door handle, and was off and away, banging the door behind me. I may be a chump in many ways, as my aunt Agatha will freely attest, but I know when and when not to be among those present.

And I was just about to do the stretch of corridor leading to the stairs in a split second under the record time for the course, when something brought me up with a sudden jerk. An irresistible force was holding me straining at leash, as it were.

You know, sometimes it seems to me as if Fate were going out of its way to such an extent to snooter you that you wonder if it's worth while to struggle. The night being a trifle chillier than the dickens, I had donned for this expedition a dressing gown. It was the tail of this infernal garment that had caught in the door and pipped me at the eleventh hour.

The next moment the door had opened, light was streaming through it, and the bloke with the voice had grabbed me by the arm.

It was Sir Roderick Glossop.

For about three and a quarter seconds, or possibly more, we just stood there, drinking each other in, so to speak, the old boy still attached with a limpetlike grip to my elbow. If I hadn't been in a dressing gown and he in pink pajamas with a blue stripe, and if he hadn't been glaring quite so much as if he were shortly going to commit a murder, the tableau would have looked rather like one of those advertisements you see in the magazines, where the experienced elder is patting the young man's arm and saying to him: "My boy, if you subscribe to the Mutt-Jeff Correspondence School of Oswego, Kansas, as I did, you may some day, like me, become Third Assistant Vice President of the Schenectady Consolidated Nail File and Eyebrow Tweezer Corporation."

"You!" said Sir Roderick finally. And in this connection I want to state that it's all rot to say you can't hiss a word that hasn't an *s* in it. The way he pushed out that "You!" sounded like an angry cobra.

By rights, I suppose, at this point I ought to have said something. The best I could manage, however was a faint, soft, bleating sound.

"Come in here," he said, lugging me into the room. "We don't want to wake the whole house. Now," he said, depositing me on the carpet and closing the door, and doing a bit of eyebrow work, "kindly inform me what is this latest manifestation of insanity?"

It seemed to me that a light and cheery laugh might help. So I had a pop at one.

"Don't gibber!" said my genial host. And I'm bound to admit that the light and cheery hadn't come out quite as I'd intended.

I pulled myself together with a strong effort.

"Awfully sorry about all this," I said in a hearty sort of voice. "The fact is, I thought you were Tuppy."

"Kindly refrain from inflicting your idiotic slang on me. What do you mean by the adjective 'tuppy'?"

"It isn't so much an adjective, don't you know. More of a noun, I should think, if you examine it squarely. What I mean to say is, I thought you were your nephew."

"You thought I was my nephew? Why should I be my nephew?"

"What I'm driving at is, I thought this was his room."

"My nephew and I changed rooms. I have a great dislike for sleeping on an upper floor. I am nervous about fire."

For the first time since this interview had started I braced up a trifle. I lost that sense of being a toad under the harrow which had been cramping my style up till now. I even went so far as to eye this pink-pajamaed poltroon with a good deal of contempt and loathing. Just because he had this craven fear of fire and this selfish preference for letting Tuppy be cooked instead of himself, should the emergency occur, my nicely reasoned plans had gone up the spout. I gave him a look, and I think I may even have snorted a bit.

"I should have thought that your manservant would have informed you," said Sir Roderick, "that we contemplated making this change. I met him shortly before luncheon and told him to tell you."

This extraordinary statement staggered me. That Jeeves had been aware all along that this old crumb would occupy the bed which I was proposing to prod with darning needles and had let me rush upon my doom without a word of warning was almost beyond belief. You might say I was aghast. Yes, practically aghast.

"You told Jeeves that you were going to sleep in this room?" I gasped.

"I did. I was aware that you and my nephew were on terms of intimacy, and I wished to spare myself the possibility of a visit from you. I confess that it never occurred to me that such a visit was to be anticipated at three o'clock in the morning. What the devil do you mean," he barked, suddenly hotting up, "by prowling about the house at this hour? And what is that thing in your hand?"

I looked down, and found that I was still grasping the stick. I give you my honest word that, what with the maelstrom of emotions into which his revelation about Jeeves had cast me, the discovery came as an absolute surprise.

"This?" I said. "Oh, yes."

"What do you mean, 'Oh, yes'? What is it?"

"Well, it's a long story."

"We have the night before us."

"It's this way: I will ask you to picture me some weeks ago, perfectly peaceful and inoffensive, after dinner at the Drones', smoking a thoughtful cigarette and—"

I broke off. The man wasn't listening. He was goggling in a rapt sort of way at the end of the bed, from which there had now begun to drip on to the carpet a series of drops.

"Good heavens!"

"—thoughtful cigarette and chatting pleasantly of this and that—"

I broke off again. He had lifted the sheets and was gazing at the corpse of the hot-water bottle.

"Did you do this?" he said in a low, strangled sort of voice.

"Er—yes. As a matter of fact, yes. I was going to tell you—"

"And your aunt tried to persuade me that you were not insane!"

"I'm not. Absolutely not. If you'll just let me explain—"

"I will do nothing of the kind."

"It all began—"

"Silence!"

"Right ho."

He did some deep-breathing exercises.

"My bed is drenched!"

"The way it all began—"

"Be quiet!" He heaved somewhat for a while. "You wretched, miserable idiot," he said, "kindly inform me which bedroom you are supposed to be occupying."

"It's on the floor above. The Clock Room."

"Thank you. I will find it."

"Eh?"

He gave me the eyebrow.

"I propose," he said, "to pass the remainder of the night

in your room, where, I presume, there is a bed in a condition to be slept in. You may bestow yourself as comfortably as you can here. I will wish you good-night."

He buzzed off, leaving me flat.

Well, we Woosters are old campaigners. We can take the rough with the smooth. But to say that I liked the prospect now before me would be paltering with the truth. One glance at the bed told me that any idea of sleeping there was out. A goldfish could have done it, but not Bertram. After a bit of a look round I decided that the best chance of getting any night's rest was to doze as well as I could in the armchair. I pinched a couple of pillows off the bed, shoved the hearthrug over my knees, and sat down and started counting sheep.

But it wasn't any good. The old lemon was sizzling much too much to admit of anything in the nature of slumber. This hideous revelation of the blackness of Jeeves's treachery kept coming back to me every time I nearly succeeded in dropping off. I was just wondering if I would ever get to sleep again in this world when a voice at my elbow said, "Good-morning, sir," and I sat up with a jerk.

I could have sworn I hadn't so much as dozed off for even a minute; but apparently I had. For the curtains were drawn back and daylight was coming in through the window, and there was Jeeves with a cup of tea on a tray.

"Merry Christmas, sir!"

I reached out a feeble hand for the restoring brew. I swallowed a mouthful or two, and felt a little better. I was aching in every limb, and the dome felt like lead; but I was now able to think with a certain amount of clearness, and I fixed the man with a stony eye and prepared to let him have it.

"You think so, do you?" I said. "Much, let me tell you,

depends on what you mean by the adjective 'merry.' If, moreover, you suppose that it is going to be merry for you, correct that impression. Jeeves," I said, taking another half oz. of tea and speaking in a cold, measured voice, "I wish to ask you one question. Did you or did you not know that Sir Roderick Glossop was sleeping in this room last night?"

"Yes, sir."

"You admit it!"

"Yes, sir."

"And you didn't tell me!"

"No, sir. I thought it would be more judicious not to do so."

"Jeeves—"

"If you will allow me to explain, sir."

"Explain!"

"I was aware that my silence might lead to something in the nature of an embarrassing contretemps, sir—"

"You thought that, did you?"

"Yes, sir."

"You were a good guesser," I said, sucking down further bohea.

"But it seemed to me, sir, that whatever might occur was all for the best."

I would have put in a crisp word or two here, but he carried on without giving me the opp.

"I thought that possibly, on reflection, sir, your views being what they are, you would prefer your relations with Sir Roderick Glossop and his family to be distant rather than cordial."

"My views? What do you mean,'my views'?"

"As regards a matrimonial alliance with Miss Honoria Glossop, sir."

Something like an electric shock seemed to zip through

me. The man had opened up a new line of thought. I suddenly saw what he was driving at, and realized all in a flash
that I had been wronging this faithful fellow. All the while
I supposed he had been landing me in the soup he had really been steering me away from it.

It was like those stories one used to read as a kid, about
the traveller going along on a dark night, and his dog grabs
him by the leg of his trousers, and he says, "Down, sir! What
are you doing, Rover?" And the dog hangs on, and he gets
rather hot under the collar and curses a bit, but the dog
won't let him go, and then suddenly the moon shines
through the clouds and he finds he's been standing on the
edge of a precipice and one more step would have—well,
anyway, you get the idea. And what I'm driving at is that
much the same thing seemed to be happening now.

I give you my honest word, it had never struck me till
this moment that my aunt Agatha had been scheming to
get me in right with Sir Roderick so that I should eventually be received back into the fold, if you see what I mean,
and subsequently pushed off on Honoria.

"My God, Jeeves!" I said, paling.

"Precisely, sir."

"You think there was a risk!"

"I do, sir. A very grave risk."

A disturbing thought struck me.

"But, Jeeves, on calm reflection, won't Sir Roderick have
gathered by now that my objective was young Tuppy, and
that puncturing his hot-water bottle was just one of those
things that occur when the Yuletide spirit is abroad—one
of those things that have to be overlooked and taken with
the indulgent smile and fatherly shake of the head? What
I mean is, he'll realize that I wasn't trying to snooter him,
and then all the good work will have been wasted."

"No, sir. I fancy not. That might possibly have been Sir Roderick's mental reaction, had it not been for the second incident."

"During the night, sir, while Sir Roderick was occupying your bed, somebody entered the room, pierced his hot-water bottle with some sharp instrument, and vanished in the darkness."

I could make nothing of this.

"What! Do you think I walked in my sleep?"

"No, sir. It was young Mr. Glossop who did it. I encountered him this morning, sir, shortly before I came here. He was in cheerful spirits, and inquired of me how you were feeling about the incident—not being aware that his victim had been Sir Roderick."

"But, Jeeves, what an amazing coincidence!"

"Sir?"

"Why, young Tuppy getting exactly the same idea as I did. Or, rather, as Miss Wickham did. You can't say that's not a miracle."

"Not altogether, sir. It appears that he received the suggestion from her."

"From Miss Wickham?"

"Yes, sir."

"You mean to say that, after she had put me up to the scheme of puncturing Tuppy's hot-water bottle, she went off and tipped Tuppy off to puncturing mine?"

"Precisely, sir. She is a young lady with a keen sense of humour, sir."

I say there—you might say, stunned. When I thought how near I had come to offering the Wooster heart and hand to a girl capable of double-crossing a strong man's honest love like that, I shivered.

"Are you cold, sir?"

"No, Jeeves. Just shuddering."

"The occurrence, if I may take the liberty of saying so, sir, will perhaps lend colour to the view which I put forward yesterday that Miss Wickham, though in many respects a charming young lady—"

I raised the hand.

"Say no more, Jeeves," I replied. "Love is dead."

I brooded for a while.

"You've seen Sir Roderick this morning?"

"Yes, sir."

"How did he seem?"

"A trifle feverish, sir."

"Feverish?"

"A little emotional, sir. He expressed a strong desire to meet you, sir."

"What would you advise?"

"If you were to slip out by the back entrance, sir, it would be possible for you to make your way across the field without being observed and reach the village, where you could hire an automobile to take you to London. I could bring on your effects later in your own car."

"But London. Jeeves? Is any man safe? My aunt Agatha is in London."

"Yes, sir."

"Well, then?"

He regarded me for a moment with a fathomless eye.

"I think the best plan, sir, would be for you to leave England, which is not pleasant at this time of the year, for some little while. I would not take the liberty of dictating your movements, sir, but, as you already have accommodation engaged on the Blue Train for Monte Carlo for the day after to-morrow—"

"But you cancelled the booking?"

"No, sir."

"I told you to."

"Yes, sir. It was remiss of me, but the matter slipped my mind."

"Oh?"

"Yes, sir."

"All right, Jeeves. Monte Carlo, ho, then."

"Very good, sir."

"It's lucky, as things have turned out, that you forgot to cancel that booking."

"Very fortunate indeed, sir. If you will wait here, sir, I will return to your room and procure a suit of clothes."

Honeysuckle Cottage

"Do you believe in ghosts?" asked Mr. Mulliner, abruptly.

I weighed the question thoughtfully. I was a little surprised, for nothing in our previous conversation had suggested the topic.

"Well," I replied, "I don't like them, if that's what you mean. I was once butted by one as a child."

"Ghosts. Not goats."

"Oh, ghosts? Do I believe in ghosts?"

"Exactly."

"Well, yes—and no."

"Let me put it another way," said Mr. Mulliner, patiently. "Do you believe in haunted houses? Do you believe that it is possible for a malign influence to envelop a place and work a spell on all who come within its radius?"

I hesitated.

"Well, no—and yes."

Mr. Mulliner sighed a little. He seemed to be wondering if I was always as bright as this.

"Of course," I went on, "one has read stories. Henry James's *Turn of the Screw*—"

"I am not talking about fiction."

"Well, in real life—Well, look here, I once, as a matter of fact, did meet a man who knew a fellow—"

"My distant cousin James Rodman spent some weeks in a haunted house," said Mr. Mulliner, who, if he has a fault, is not a very good listener. "It cost him five thousand pounds. That is to say, he sacrificed five thousand pounds by not remaining there. Did you ever," he asked, wandering, it seemed to me, from the subject, "hear of Leila J. Pinckney?"

Naturally I had heard of Leila J. Pinckney. Her death
some years ago has diminished her vogue, but at one time
it was impossible to pass a book-shop or a railway book-
stall without seeing a long row of her novels. I had never
myself actually read any of them, but I knew that in her
particular line of literature, the Squashily Sentimental, she
had always been regarded by those entitled to judge as preeminent. The critics usually headed their reviews of her stories with the words:—

ANOTHER PINCKNEY

or sometimes, more offensively:—

ANOTHER PINCKNEY!!!

And once, dealing with, I think, *The Love Which Prevails*,
the literary expert of the *Scrutinizer* had compressed his entire critique into the single phrase, "Oh, God!"

"Of course," I said. "But what about her?"

"She was James Rodman's aunt."

"Yes?"

"And when she died James found that she had left him
five thousand pounds and the house in the country where
she had lived for the last twenty years of her life."

"A very nice little legacy."

"Twenty years," repeated Mr. Mulliner. "Grasp that, for
it has a vital bearing on what follows. Twenty years, mind
you, and Miss Pinckney turned out two novels and twelve
short stories regularly every year, besides a monthly page
of Advice to Young Girls in one of the magazines. That is
to say, forty of her novels and no fewer than two hundred
and forty of her short stories were written under the roof

of Honeysuckle Cottage."

"A pretty name."

"A nasty, sloppy name," said Mr. Mulliner, severely, "which should have warned my distant cousin James from the start. Have you a pencil and a piece of paper?" He scribbled for a while, poring frowningly over columns of figures. "Yes," he said, looking up, "if my calculations are correct, Leila J. Pinckney wrote in all a matter of nine million and one hundred and forty thousand words of glutinous sentimentality at Honeysuckle Cottage, and it was a condition of her will that James should reside there for six months in every year. Failing to do this, he was to forfeit the five thousand pounds."

"It must be great fun making a freak will," I mused. "I often wish I was rich enough to do it."

"This was not a freak will. The conditions are perfectly understandable. James Rodman was a writer of sensational mystery stories, and his Aunt Leila had always disapproved of his work. She was a great believer in the influence of environment, and the reason why she inserted that clause in her will was that she wished to compel James to move from London to the country. She considered that living in London hardened him and made his outlook on life sordid. She often asked him if he thought it quite nice to harp so much on sudden death and blackmailers with squints. Surely, she said, there were enough squinting blackmailers in the world without writing about them.

"The fact that Literature meant such different things to these two had, I believe, caused something of a coolness between them, and James had never dreamed that he would be remembered in his aunt's will. For he had never concealed his opinion that Leila J. Pinckney's style of writing revolted him, however dear it might be to her enormous public.

He held rigid views on the art of the novel, and always maintained that an artist with a true reverence for his craft should
not descend to goo-ey love stories, but should stick austerely
to revolvers, cries in the night, missing papers, mysterious
Chinamen and dead bodies—with or without gash in throat.
And not even the thought that his aunt had dandled him
on her knee as a baby could induce him to stifle his literary
conscience to the extent of pretending to enjoy her work.
First, last, and all the time, James Rodman had held the
opinion—and voiced it fearlessly—that Leila J. Pinckney
wrote bilge.

"It was a surprise to him, therefore, to find that he had
been left this legacy. A pleasant surprise, of course. James
was making a decent income out of the three novels and
eighteen short stories which he produced annually, but an
author can always find a use for five thousand pounds. And,
as for the cottage, he had actually been looking about for
a little place in the country at the very moment when he
received the lawyer's letter. In less than a week he was in-
stalled at his new residence."

James's first impressions of Honeysuckle Cottage were,
he tells me, wholly favourable. He was delighted with the
place. It was a low, rambling, picturesque old house with
funny little chimneys and a red roof, placed in the middle
of the most charming country. With its oak beams, its trim
garden, its trilling birds and its rose-hung porch, it was the
ideal spot for a writer. It was just the sort of place, he reflected whimsically, which his aunt had loved to write about
in her books. Even the apple-cheeked old housekeeper who
attended to his needs might have stepped straight out of
one of them.

It seemed to James that his lot had been cast in pleasant

places. He had brought down his books, his pipes, and his golf clubs, and was hard at work finishing the best thing he had ever done. *The Secret Nine* was the title of it; and on the beautiful summer afternoon on which this story opens he was in the study, hammering away at his type-writer, at peace with the world. The machine was running sweetly, the new tobacco he had bought the day before was proving admirable, and he was moving on all six cylinders to the end of a chapter.

He shoved in a fresh sheet of paper, chewed his pipe thoughtfully for a moment, then wrote rapidly:

> For an instant Lester Gage thought that he must have been mistaken. Then the noise came again, faint but unmistakable—a soft scratching on the outer panel.
>
> His mouth set in a grim line. Silently, like a panther, he made one quick step to the desk, noiselessly opened a draw-er, drew out his automatic. After that affair of the poisoned needle, he was taking no chances. Still in dead silence, he tiptoed to the door; then, flinging it suddenly open, he stood there, his weapon poised.
>
> On the mat stood the most beautiful girl he had ever be-held. A veritable child of Faerie. She eyed him for a mo-ment with a saucy smile; then with a pretty, roguish look of reproof shook a dainty forefinger at him.
>
> "I believe you've forgotten me, Mr. Gage!" she fluted with a mock severity which her eyes belied.

James stared at the paper dumbly. He was utterly per-plexed. He had not had the slightest intention of writing anything like this. To begin with, it was a rule with him, and one which he never broke, to allow no girls to appear in his stories. Sinister landladies, yes, and naturally any amount of adventuresses with foreign accents, but never under any pretext what may be broadly described as girls.

A detective story, he maintained, should have no heroine. Heroines only held up the action and tried to flirt with the hero when he should have been busy looking for clues, and then went and let the villain kidnap them by some childishly simple trick. In his writing, James was positively monastic.

And yet here was this creature with her saucy smile and her dainty forefinger horning in at the most important point in the story. It was uncanny.

He looked once more at his scenario. No, the scenario was all right.

In perfectly plain words it stated that what happened when the door opened was that a dying man fell in and after gasping, "The beetle! Tell Scotland Yard that the blue beetle is—" expired on the hearthrug, leaving Lester Gage not unnaturally somewhat mystified. Nothing whatever about any beautiful girls.

In a curious mood of irritation, James scratched out the offending passage, wrote in the necessary corrections, and put the cover on the machine. It was at this point that he heard William whining.

The only blot on this paradise which James had so far been able to discover was the infernal dog, William. Belonging nominally to the gardener, on the very first morning he had adopted James by acclamation, and he maddened and infuriated James. He had a habit of coming and whining under the window when James was at work. The latter would ignore this as long as he could; then, when the thing became insupportable, would bound out of his chair, to see the animal standing on the gravel, gazing expectantly up at him with a stone in his mouth. William had a weak-minded passion for chasing stones; and on the first day James, in a rash spirit of camaraderie, had flung one for him. Since then James had thrown no more stones; but he had thrown any number of other solids, and the garden was littered with objects ranging from match boxes to a plaster statuette of the young Joseph prophesying before Pharaoh. And still William came and whined, an optimist to the last.

The whining, coming now at a moment when he felt irritable and unsettled, acted on James much as the scratching on the door had acted on Lester Gage. Silently, like a panther, he made one quick step to the mantelpiece, removed from it a china mug bearing the legend A Present From Clacton-on-Sea, and crept to the window.

And as he did so a voice outside said, "Go away, sir, go away!" and there followed a short, high-pitched bark which was certainly not William's. William was a mixture of Airedale, setter, bull terrier, and mastiff; and when in a vocal mood, favoured the mastiff side of his family.

James peered out. There on the porch stood a girl in blue. She held in her arms a small fluffy dog, and she was endeavouring to foil the upward movement toward this of the blackguard William. William's metality had been arrested some years before at the point where he imagined that everything in the world had been created for him to eat. A bone, a boot, a steak, the back wheel of a bicycle—it was all one to William. If it was there he tried to eat it. He had even made a plucky attempt to devour the remains of the young Joseph prophesying before Pharaoh. And it was perfectly plain now that he regarded the curious wriggling object in the girl's arms purely in the light of a snack to keep body and soul together till dinner-time.

"William!" bellowed James.

William looked courteously over his shoulder with eyes that beamed with the pure light of a life's devotion, wagged the whiplike tail which he had inherited from his bull-terrier ancestor and resumed his intent scrutiny of the fluffy dog.

"Oh, please!" cried the girl. "This great rough dog is frightening poor Toto."

The man of letters and the man of action do not always go hand in hand, but practice had made James perfect in handling with a swift efficiency any situation that involved William. A moment later that canine moron, having received the present from Clacton in the short ribs, was scuttling round the corner of the house, and James had jumped through the window and was facing the girl.

She was an extraordinarily pretty girl. Very sweet and fragile she looked as she stood there under the honeysuckle with the breeze ruffling a tendril of golden hair that strayed from beneath her coquettish little hat. Her eyes were very big and very blue, her rose-tinted face becomingly flushed. All wasted on James, though. He disliked all girls, and particularly the sweet, droopy type.

"Did you want to see somebody?" he asked, stiffly.

"Just the house," said the girl, "if it wouldn't be giving any trouble. I do so want to see the room where Miss Pinckney wrote her books. This is where Leila J. Pinckney used to live, isn't it?"

"Yes; I am her nephew. My name is James Rodman."

"Mine is Rose Maynard."

James led the way into the house, and she stopped with a cry of delight on the threshold of the morning room.

"Oh, how too perfect!" she cried. "So this was her study?"

"Yes."

"What a wonderful place it would be for you to think in if you were a writer, too."

James held no high opinion of women's literary taste, but nevertheless he was conscious of an unpleasant shock.

"I am a writer," he said, coldly. "I write detective stories."

"I—I'm afraid"—she blushed—"I'm afraid I don't often

read detective stories."

"You no doubt prefer," said James, still more coldly, "the sort of thing my aunt used to write."

"Oh, I love her stories!" cried the girl, clasping her hands ecstatically. "Don't you?"

"I cannot say that I do."

"What?"

"They are pure apple sauce," said James, sternly; "just nasty blobs of sentimentality, thoroughly untrue to life."

The girl stared.

"Why, that's just what's so wonderful about them, their trueness to life! You feel they might all have happened. I don't understand what you mean."

They were walking down the garden now. James held the gate open for her and she passed through into the road.

"Well, for one thing," he said, "I decline to believe that a marriage between two young people is invariably preceded by some violent and sensational experience in which they both share."

"Are you thinking of *Scent o' the Blossom*, where Edgar saves Maud from drowning?"

"I am thinking of every single one of my aunt's books." He looked at her curiously. He had just got the solution of a mystery which had been puzzling him for some time. Almost from the moment he had set eyes on her she had seemed somehow strangely familiar. It now suddenly came to him why it was that he disliked her so much. "Do you know," he said, "you might be one of my aunt's heroines yourself? You're just the sort of girl she used to love to write about."

Her face lit up.

"Oh, do you really think so?" She hesitated. "Do you know what I have been feeling ever since I came here? I've been feeling that you are exactly like one of Miss Pinckney's heroes."

"No, I say, really!" said James, revolted.

"Oh, but you are! When you jumped through that window it gave me quite a start. You were so exactly like Claude Masterson in *Heather o' the Hills.*"

"I have not read *Heather o' the Hills,*" said James, with a shudder.

"He was very strong and quiet, with deep, dark, sad eyes."

James did not explain that his eyes were sad because her society gave him a pain in the neck. He merely laughed scornfully.

"So now, I suppose," he said, "a car will come and knock you down and I shall carry you gently into the house and lay you—Look out!" he cried.

It was too late. She was lying in a little huddled heap at his feet. Round the corner a large automobile had come bowling, keeping with an almost affected precision to the wrong side of the road. It was now receding into the distance, the occupant of the tonneau, a stout red-faced gentleman in a fur coat, leaning out over the back. He had bared his head—not, one fears, as a pretty gesture of respect and regret, but because he was using his hat to hide the number plate.

The dog Toto was unfortunately uninjured.

James carried the girl gently into the house and laid her on the sofa in the morning-room. He rang the bell and the apple-cheeked housekeeper appeared.

"Send for the doctor," said James. "There has been an accident."

The housekeeper bent over the girl.

"Eh, dearie, dearie!" she said. "Bless her sweet pretty

face!"

The gardener, he who technically owned William, was routed out from among the young lettuces and told to fetch Doctor Brady. He separated his bicycle from William, who was making a light meal off the left pedal, and departed on his mission. Doctor Brady arrived and in due course he made his report.

"No bones broken, but a number of nasty bruises. And, of course, the shock. She will have to stay here for some time, Rodman. Can't be moved."

"Stay here! But she can't! It isn't proper."

"Your housekeeper will act as a chaperone."

The doctor sighed. He was a stolid-looking man of middle age with side whiskers.

"A beautiful girl, that, Rodman," he said.

"I suppose so," said James.

"A sweet, beautiful girl. An elfin child."

"A what?" cried James, starting.

The imagery was very foreign to Doctor Brady as he knew him. On the only previous occasion on which they had had any extended conversation, the doctor had talked exclusively about the effect of too much protein on the gastric juices.

"An elfin child; a tender, fairy creature. When I was looking at her just now, Rodman, I nearly broke down. Her little hand lay on the coverlet like some white lily floating on the surface of a still pool, and her dear, trusting eyes gazed up at me."

He pottered off down the garden, still babbling, and James stood staring after him blankly. And slowly, like some cloud athwart a summer sky, there crept over James's heart the chill shadow of a nameless fear.

It was about a week later that Mr. Andrew McKinnon,

the senior partner in the well-known firm of literary agents, McKinnon & Gooch, sat in his office in Chancery Lane, frowning thoughtfully over a telegram. He rang the bell.

"Ask Mr. Gooch to step in here." He resumed his study of the telegram. "Oh, Gooch," he said when his partner appeared, "I've just had a curious wire from young Rodman. He seems to want to see me very urgently."

Mr. Gooch read the telegram.

"Written under the influence of some strong mental excitement," he agreed. "I wonder why he doesn't come to the office if he wants to see you so badly."

"He's working very hard, finishing that novel for Prodder & Wiggs. Can't leave it, I suppose. Well, it's a nice day. If you will look after things here I think I'll motor down and let him give me lunch."

As Mr. McKinnon's car reached the crossroads a mile from Honeysuckle Cottage, he was aware of a gesticulating figure by the hedge. He stopped the car.

"Morning, Rodman."

"Thank God, you've come!" said James. It seemed to Mr. McKinnon that the young man looked paler and thinner. "Would you mind walking the rest of the way? There's something I want to speak to you about."

Mr. McKinnon alighted; and James, as he glanced at him, felt cheered and encouraged by the very sight of the man. The literary agent was a grim, hard-bitten person, to whom, when he called at their offices to arrange terms, editors kept their faces turned so that they might at least retain their back collar studs. There was no sentiment in Andrew McKinnon. Editresses of society papers practised their blandishments on him in vain, and many a publisher had waked screaming in the night, dreaming that he was signing a

McKinnon contract.

"Well, Rodman," he said, "Prodder & Wiggs have agreed to our terms. I was writing to tell you so when your wire arrived. I had a lot of trouble with them, but it's fixed at 20 per cent., rising to 25, and two hundred pounds advance royalties on day of publication."

"Good!" said James, absently. "Good! McKinnon, do you remember my aunt, Leila J. Pinckney?"

"Remember her? Why, I was her agent all her life."

"Of course. Then you know the sort of tripe she wrote."

"No author," said Mr. McKinnon, reprovingly "who pulls down a steady twenty thousand pounds a year writes tripe."

"Well, anyway, you know her stuff."

"Who better?"

"When she died she left me five thousand pounds and her house, Honeysuckle Cottage. I'm living there now. McKinnon, do you believe in haunted houses?"

"No."

"Yet I tell you solemnly that Honeysuckle Cottage is haunted!"

"By your aunt?" said Mr. McKinnon, surprised.

"By her influence. There's a malignant spell over the place; a sort of miasma of sentimentalism. Everybody who enters it succumbs."

"Tut-tut! You mustn't have these fancies."

"They aren't fancies."

"You aren't seriously meaning to tell me—"

"Well, how do you account for this? That book you were speaking about, which Prodder & Wiggs are to publish— *The Secret Nine*. Every time I sit down to write it a girl keeps trying to sneak in."

"Into the room?"

"Into the story."

"You don't want a love interest in your sort of book,"
said Mr. McKinnon, shaking his head. "It delays the action."

"I know it does. And every day I have to keep shooing
this infernal female out. An awful girl, McKinnon. A sop-
py, soupy, treacly, drooping girl with a roguish smile. This
morning she tried to butt in on the scene where Lester Gage
is trapped in the den of the mysterious leper."

"No!"

"She did, I assure you. I had to rewrite three pages before I could get her out of it. And that's not the worst. Do
you know, McKinnon, that at this moment I am actually
living the plot of a typical Leila Jo Pinckney novel in just
the setting she always used! And I can see the happy ending coming nearer every day! A week ago a girl was knocked
down by a car at my door and I've had to put her up, and
every day I realise more clearly that sooner or later I shall
ask her to marry me."

"Don't do it," said Mr. McKinnon, a stout bachelor.
"You're too young to marry."

"So was Methuselah," said James, a stouter. "But all the
same I know I'm going to do it. It's the influence of this
awful house weighing upon me. I feel like an eggshell in
a maelstrom. I am being sucked on by a force too strong
for me to resist. This morning I found myself kissing her
dog!"

"No!"

"I did! And I loathe the little beast. Yesterday I got up
at dawn and plucked a nosegay of flowers for her, wet with
the dew."

"Rodman!"

"It's a fact. I laid them at her door and went downstairs
kicking myself all the way. And there in the hall was the
apple-cheeked housekeeper regarding me archly. If she

didn't murmur 'Bless their sweet young hearts!' my ears deceived me."

"Why don't you pack up and leave?"

"If I do I lose the five thousand pounds."

"Ah!" said Mr. McKinnon.

"I can understand what has happened. It's the same with all haunted houses. My aunt's subliminal ether vibrations have woven themselves into the texture of the place, creating an atmosphere which forces the ego of all who come in contact with it to attune themselves to it. It's either that or something to do with the fourth dimension."

Mr. McKinnon laughed scornfully.

"Tut-tut!" he said again. "This is pure imagination. What has happened is that you've been working too hard. You'll see this precious atmosphere of yours will have no effect on me."

"That's exactly why I asked you to come down. I hoped you might break the spell."

"I will that," said Mr. McKinnon, jovially.

The fact that the literary agent spoke little at lunch caused James no apprehension. Mr. McKinnon was ever a silent trencherman. From time to time James caught him stealing a glance at the girl, who was well enough to come down to meals now, limping pathetically; but he could read nothing in his face. And yet the mere look of his face was a consolation. It was so solid, so matter of fact, so exactly like an unemotional coconut.

"You've done me good," said James with a sigh of relief, as he escorted the agent down the garden to his car after lunch. "I felt all along that I could rely on your rugged common sense. The whole atmosphere of the place seems different now."

Mr. McKinnon did not speak for a moment. He seemed

to be plunged in thought.

"Rodman," he said, as he got into his car, "I've been thinking over that suggestion of yours of putting a love interest
into *The Secret Nine*. I think you're wise. The story needs
it. After all, what is there greater in the world than love?
Love—love—aye, it's the sweetest word in the language.
Put in a heroine and let her marry Lester Gage."

"If," said James, grimly, "she does succeed in worming
her way in she'll jolly well marry the mysterious leper. But
look here, I don't understand—"

"It was seeing the girl that changed me," proceeded Mr.
McKinnon. And as James stared at him aghast, tears suddenly filled his hard-boiled eyes. He openly snuffled. "Aye,
seeing her sitting there under the roses, with all that smell
of honeysuckle and all. And the birdies singing so sweet
in the garden and the sun lighting up her bonny face. The
puir wee lass!" he muttered, dabbing at his eyes. "The puir
bonny wee lass! Rodman," he said, his voice quivering, "I've
decided that we're being hard on Prodder & Wiggs. Wiggs
has had sickness in his home lately. We mustn't be hard
on a man who's had sickness in his home, hey, laddie? No,
no! I'm going to take back that contract and alter it to a
flat 12 per cent. and no advance royalties."

"What!"

"But you shan't lose by it, Rodman. No, no, you shan't
lose by it, my manny. I am going to waive my commis-
sion. The puir bonny wee lass!"

The car rolled off down the road. Mr. McKinnon, seated in the back, was blowing his nose violently.

"This is the end!" said James.

It is necessary at this point to pause and examine James
Rodman's position with an unbiassed eye. The average man,
unless he puts himself in James's place, will be unable to

appreciate it. James, he will feel, was making a lot of fuss about nothing. Here he was, drawing daily closer and closer to a charming girl with big blue eyes, and surely rather to be envied than pitied.

But we must remember that James was one of Nature's bachelors. And no ordinary man, looking forward dreamily to a little home of his own with a loving wife putting out his slippers and changing the gramophone records, can realise the intensity of the instinct for self-preservation which animates Nature's bachelors in times of peril.

James Rodman had a congenital horror of matrimony. Though a young man, he had allowed himself to develop a great many habits which were as the breath of life to him; and these habits, he knew instinctively, a wife would shoot to pieces within a week of the end of the honeymoon.

James liked to breakfast in bed; and, having breakfasted, to smoke in bed and knock the ashes out on the carpet. What wife would tolerate this practice?

James liked to pass his days in a tennis shirt, grey flannel trousers and slippers. What wife ever rests until she has inclosed her husband in a stiff collar, tight boots, and a morning suit and taken him with her to *thes musicales?*

These and a thousand other thoughts of the same kind flashed through the unfortunate young man's mind as the days went by, and every day that passed seemed to draw him nearer to the brink of the chasm. Fate appeared to be taking a malicious pleasure in making things as difficult for him as possible. Now that the girl was well enough to leave her bed, she spent her time sitting in a chair on the sun-sprinkled porch, and James had to read to her—and poetry, at that; and not the jolly, wholesome sort of poetry the boys are turning out nowadays, either—good, honest stuff about sin and gas works and decaying corpses—but the old-

fashioned kind with rhymes in it, dealing almost exclusively with love. The weather, moreover, continued superb. The
honeysuckle cast its sweet scent on the gentle breeze; the
roses over the porch stirred and nodded; the flowers in the
garden were lovelier than ever; the birds sang their little
throats sore. And every evening there was a magnificent
sunset. It was almost as if Nature were doing it on purpose.

At last James intercepted Doctor Brady as he was leaving after one of his visits and put the thing to him squarely:

"When is that girl going?"

The doctor patted him on the arm.

"Not yet, Rodman," he said in a low, understanding
voice. "No need to worry yourself about that. Mustn't be
moved for days and days and days—I might almost say
weeks and weeks and weeks."

"Weeks and weeks!" cried James.

"And weeks," said Doctor Brady. He prodded James
roguishly in the abdomen. "Good luck to you, my boy,
good luck to you," he said.

It was some small consolation to James that the mushy
physician immediately afterward tripped over William on
his way down the path and broke his stethoscope. When
a man is up against it like James every little bit helps.

He was walking dismally back to the house after this conversation when he was met by the apple-cheeked housekeeper.

"The little lady would like to speak to you, sir," said the
apple-cheeked exhibit, rubbing her hands.

"Would she?" said James, hollowly.

"So sweet and pretty she looks, sir—oh, sir, you wouldn't
believe! Like a blessed angel sitting there with her dear eyes
all a-shining."

"Don't do it!" cried James with extraordinary vehemence. "Don't do it!"

He found the girl propped up on the cushions and thought once again how singularly he disliked her. And yet, even as he thought this, some force against which he had to fight madly was whispering to him, "Go to her and take that little hand! Breathe into that little ear the burning words that will make that little face turn away crimsoned with blushes!" He wiped a bead of perspiration from his forehead and sat down.

"Mrs. Stick-in-the-Mud—what's her name?—says you want to see me."

The girl nodded.

"I've had a letter from Uncle Henry. I wrote to him as soon as I was better and told him what had happened, and he is coming here to-morrow morning."

"Uncle Henry?"

"That's what I call him, but he's really no relation. He is my guardian. He and daddy were officers in the same regiment, and when daddy was killed, fighting on the Afghan frontier, he died in Uncle Henry's arms and with his last breath begged him to take care of me."

James started. A sudden wild hope had waked in his heart. Years ago, he remembered, he had read a book of his aunt's entitled *Rupert's Legacy*, and in that book—

"I'm engaged to marry him," said the girl, quietly.

"Wow!" shouted James.

"What?" asked the girl, startled.

"Touch of cramp," said James. He was thrilling all over. That wild hope had been realised.

"It was daddy's dying wish that we should marry," said the girl.

"And dashed sensible of him, too; dashed sensible," said

James, warmly.

"And yet," she went on, a little wistfully, "I sometimes wonder—"

"Don't!" said James. "Don't! You must respect daddy's dying wish. There's nothing like daddy's dying wish; you can't beat it. So he's coming here to-morrow, is he? Capital, capital! To lunch, I suppose? Excellent! I'll run down and tell Mrs. Who-Is-It to lay in another chop."

It was with a gay and uplifted heart that James strolled the garden and smoked his pipe the next morning. A great cloud seemed to have rolled itself away from him. Everything was for the best in the best of all possible worlds. He had finished *The Secret Nine* and shipped it off to Mr. McKinnon, and now as he strolled there was shaping itself in his mind a corking plot about a man with only half a face who lived in a secret den and terrorised London with a series of shocking murders. And what made them so shocking was the fact that each of the victims, when discovered, was found to have only half a face, too. The rest had been chipped off, presumably by some blunt instrument.

The thing was coming out magnificently, when suddenly his attention was diverted by a piercing scream. Out of the bushes fringing the river that ran beside the garden burst the apple-cheeked housekeeper.

"Oh, sir! Oh, sir! Oh, sir!"

"What is it?" demanded James, irritably.

"Oh, sir! Oh, sir! Oh, sir!

"Yes, and then what?"

"The little dog, sir! He's in the river!"

"Well, whistle him to come out."

"Oh, sir, do come quick! He'll be drowned!"

James followed her through the bushes, taking off his coat

as he went. He was saying to himself, "I will not rescue this dog. I do not like the dog. It is high time he had a bath, and in any case it would be much simpler to stand on the bank and fish for him with a rake. Only an ass out of a Leila J. Pinckney book would dive into a beastly river to save—"

At this point he dived. Toto, alarmed by the splash, swam rapidly for the bank, but James was too quick for him. Grasping him firmly by the neck, he scrambled ashore and ran for the house, followed by the housekeeper.

The girl was seated on the porch. Over her there bent the tall soldierly figure of a man with keen eyes and graying hair. The housekeeper raced up.

"Oh, miss! Toto! In the river! He saved him! He plunged in and saved him!"

The girl drew a quick breath.

"Gallant, damme! By Jove! By gad! Yes, gallant, by George!" exclaimed the soldierly man.

The girl seemed to wake from a reverie.

"Uncle Henry, this is Mr. Rodman. Mr. Rodman, my guardian, Colonel Carteret."

"Proud to meet you, sir," said the colonel, his honest blue eyes glowing as he fingered his short crisp moustache. "As fine a thing as I ever heard of, damme!"

"Yes, you are brave—brave," the girl whispered.

"I am wet—wet," said James, and went upstairs to change his clothes.

When he came down for lunch, he found to his relief that the girl had decided not to join them, and Colonel Carteret was silent and preoccupied. James, exerting himself in his capacity of host, tried him with the weather, golf, India, the Government, the high cost of living, first-class cricket, the modern dancing craze, and murderers he had met, but the other still preserved that strange, absent-minded silence. It was only when the meal was concluded and James had produced cigarettes that he came abruptly out of his trance.

"Rodman," he said, "I should like to speak with you."

"Yes?" said James, thinking it was about time.

"Rodman," said Colonel Carteret, "or rather, George—I may call you George?" he added, with a sort of wistful diffidence that had a singular charm.

"Certainly," replied James, "if you wish it. Though my name is James."

"James, eh? Well, well, it amounts to the same thing, eh, what, damme, by gad?" said the colonel with a momentary return of his bluff soldierly manner. "Well, then, James, I have something that I wish to say to you. Did Miss Maynard—did Rose happen to tell you anything about myself in—er—in connection with herself?"

"She mentioned that you and she were engaged to be married."

The colonel's tightly drawn lips quiverd.

"No longer," he said.

"What?"

"No, John, my boy."

"James."

"No, James, my boy, no longer. While you were upstairs changing your clothes she told me—breaking down, poor child, as she spoke—that she wished our engagement to be at an end."

James half rose from the table, his cheeks blanched.

"You don't mean that!" he gasped.

Colonel Carteret nodded. He was staring out of the window, his fine eyes set in a look of pain.

"But this is nonsense!" cried James. "This is absurd! She—

she mustn't be allowed to chop and change like this. I mean to say, it—it isn't fair—"

"Don't think of me, my boy."

"I'm not—I mean, did she give any reason?"

"Her eyes did."

"Her eyes did?"

"Her eyes, when she looked at you on the porch, as you stood there—young, heroic—having just saved the life of the dog she loves. It is you who have won that tender heart, my boy."

"Now listen," protested James, "you aren't going to sit there and tell me that a girl falls in love with a man just because he saves her dog from drowning?"

"Why, surely," said Colonel Carteret, surprised. "What better reason could she have?" He sighed. "It is the old, old story, my boy. Youth to youth. I am an old man. I should have known—I should have foreseen—yes, youth to youth."

"You aren't a bit old."

"Yes, yes."

"No, no."

"Yes, yes."

"Don't keep on saying 'yes, yes'!" cried James, clutching at his hair. "Besides, she wants a steady old buffer—a steady, sensible man of medium age—to look after her."

Colonel Carteret shook his head with a gentle smile.

"This is mere quixotry, my boy. It is splendid of you to take this attitude; but no, no."

"Yes, yes."

"No, no." He gripped James's hand for an instant, then rose and walked to the door. "That is all I wished to say, Tom."

"James."

"James. I just thought that you ought to know how matters stood. Go to her, my boy, go to her, and don't let any thought of an old man's broken dream keep you from pouring out what is in your heart. I am an old soldier, lad, an old soldier. I have learned to take the rough with the smooth. But I think—I think I will leave you now. I—I should—should like to be alone for a while. If you need me you will find me in the raspberry bushes."

He had scarcely gone when James also left the room. He took his hat and stick and walked blindly out of the garden, he knew not whither. His brain was numbed. Then, as his powers of reasoning returned, he told himself that he should have foreseen this ghastly thing. If there was one type of character over which Leila J. Pinckney had been wont to spread herself, it was the pathetic guardian who loves his ward but relinquishes her to the younger man. No wonder the girl had broken off the engagement. Any elderly guardian who allowed himself to come within a mile of Honeysuckle Cottage was simply asking for it. And then, as he turned to walk back, a sort of dull defiance gripped James. Why, he asked, should he be put upon in this manner? If the girl liked to throw over this man, why should he be the goat?

He saw his way clearly now. He just wouldn't do it, that was all. And if they didn't like it they could lump it.

Full of a new fortitude, he strode in at the gate. A tall, soldierly figure emerged from the raspberry bushes and came to meet him.

"Well?" said Colonel Carteret.

"Well?" said James, defiantly.

"Am I to congratulate you?"

James caught his keen blue eye and hesitated. It was not going to be so simple as he had supposed.

"Well—er—" he said.

Into the keen blue eyes there came a look that James had not seen there before. It was the stern, hard look which—probably—had caused men to bestow upon this old soldier the name of Cold-Steel Carteret.

"You have not asked Rose to marry you?"

"Er—no; not yet."

The keen blue eyes grew keener and bluer.

"Rodman," said Colonel Carteret in a strange, quiet voice, "I have known that little girl since she was a tiny child. For years she has been all in all to me. Her father died in my arms and with his last breath bade me see that no harm came to his darling. I have nursed her through mumps, measles—aye, and chicken pox—and I live but for her happiness." He paused, with a significance that made James's toes curl. "Rodman, he said, "do you know what I would do to any man who trifled with that little girl's affections?" He reached in his hip pocket and an ugly-looking revolver glittered in the sunlight. "I would shoot him like a dog."

"Like a dog?" faltered James.

"Like a dog," said Colonel Carteret. He took James's arm and turned toward the house. "She is on the porch. Go to her. And if—" He broke off. "But tut!" he said in a kindlier tone. "I am doing you an injustice, my boy. I know it."

"Oh, you are," said James, fervently.

"Your heart is in the right place."

"Oh, absolutely," said James.

"Then go to her, my boy. Later on you may have something to tell me. You will find me in the strawberry beds."

It was very cool and fragrant on the porch. Overhead, little breezes played and laughed among the roses. Somewhere in the distance sheep bells tinkled, and in the shrubbery a thrush was singing its even-song.

Seated in her chair behind a wicker table laden with tea things, Rose Maynard watched James as he shambled up the path.

"Tea's ready," she called, gaily. "Where is Uncle Henry?" A look of pity and distress flitted for a moment over her flower-like face. "Oh, I—I forgot," she whispered.

"He is in the strawberry beds," said James in a low voice.

She nodded unhappily.

"Of course, of course. Oh, why is life like this?" James heard her whisper.

He sat down. He looked at the girl. She was leaning back with closed eyes, and he thought he had never seen such a little squirt in his life. The idea of passing his remaining days in her society revolted him. He was stoutly opposed to the idea of marrying anyone; but if, as happens to the best of us, he ever were compelled to perform the wedding glide, he had always hoped it would be with some lady golf champion who would help him with his putting, and thus, by bringing his handicap down a notch or two, enable him to save something from the wreck, so to speak. But to link his lot with a girl who read his aunt's books and liked them; a girl who could tolerate the presence of the dog Toto; a girl who clasped her hands in pretty, childish joy when she saw a nasturtium in bloom—it was too much. Nevertheless, he took her hand and began to speak.

"Miss Maynard—Rose—"

She opened her eyes and cast them down. A flush had come into her cheeks. The dog Toto at her side sat up and begged for cake, disregarded.

"Let me tell you a story. Once upon a time there was a lonely man who lived in a cottage all by himself—"

He stopped. Was it James Rodman who was talking this bilge?

"Yes?" whispered the girl.

"—but one day there came to him out of nowhere a little fairy princess. She—"

He stopped again, but this time not because of the sheer shame of listening to his own voice. What caused him to interrupt his tale was the fact that at this moment the tea table suddenly began to rise slowly in the air, tilting as it did so a considerable quantity of hot tea on to the knees of his trousers.

"Ouch!" cried James, leaping.

The table continued to rise, and then fell sideways, revealing the homely contenance of William, who, concealed by the cloth, had been taking a nap beneath it. He moved slowly forward, his eyes on Toto. For many a long day William had been desirous of putting to the test, once and for all, the problem of whether Toto was edible or not. Sometimes he thought yes, at other times no. Now seemed an admirable opportunity for a definite decision. He advanced on the object of his experiment, making a low whistling noise through his nostrils, not unlike a boiling kettle. And Toto, after one long look of incredulous horror, tucked his shapely tail between his legs and, turning, raced for safety. He had laid a course in a bee line for the open garden gate, and William, shaking a dish of marmalade off his head a little petulantly, galloped ponderously after him. Rose Maynard staggered to her feet.

"Oh, save him!" she cried.

Without a word James added himself to the procession. His interest in Toto was but tepid. What he wanted was to get near enough to William to discuss with him that matter of the tea on his trousers. He reached the road and found that the order of the runners had not changed. For so small a dog, Toto was moving magnificently. A cloud of dust rose as he skidded round the corner. William followed. James followed William.

And so they passed Farmer Birkett's barn, Farmer Giles's cow shed, the place where Farmer Willetts's pigsty used to be before the big fire, and the Bunch of Grapes public house, Jno. Biggs propr., licensed to sell tobacco, wines, and spirits. And it was as they were turning down the lane that leads past Farmer Robinson's chicken run that Toto, thinking swiftly, bolted abruptly into a small drain pipe.

"William!" roared James, coming up at a canter. He stopped to pluck a branch from the hedge and swooped darkly on.

William had been crouching before the pipe, making a noise like a bassoon into its interior; but now he rose and came beamingly to James. His eyes were aglow with chumminess and affection; and placing his forefeet on James's chest, he licked him three times on the face in rapid succession. And as he did so, something seemed to snap in James. The scales seemed to fall from James's eyes. For the first time he saw William as he really was, the authentic type of dog that saves his master from a frightful peril. A wave of emotion swept over him.

"William!" he mutterd. "William!"

William was making an early supper off a half brick he had found in the road. James stopped and patted him fondly.

"William," he whispered, "you knew when the time had come to change the conversation, didn't you, old boy!" He straightened himself. "Come, William," he said. "Another four miles and we reach Meadowsweet Junction. Make it snappy and we shall just catch the up express, first stop London."

William looked up into his face and it seemed to James

that he gave a brief nod of comprehension and approval. James turned. Through the trees to the east he could see the red roof of Honeysuckle Cottage, lurking like some evil dragon in ambush.

Then, together, man and dog passed silently into the sunset.

That (concluded Mr. Mulliner) is the story of my distant cousin James Rodman. As to whether it is true, that, of course, is an open question. I, personally, am of opinion that it is. There is no doubt that James did go to live at Honeysuckle Cottage and, while there, underwent some experience which has left an ineradicable mark upon him. His eyes to-day have that unmistakable look which is to be seen only in the eyes of confirmed bachelors whose feet have been dragged to the very brink of the pit and who have gazed at close range into the naked face of matrimony.

And, if further proof be needed, there is William. He is now James's inseparable companion. Would any man be habitually seen in public with a dog like William unless he had some solid cause to be grateful to him,—unless they were linked together by some deep and imperishable memory? I think not. Myself, when I observe William coming along the street, I cross the road and look into a shop window till he has passed. I am not a snob, but I dare not risk my position in Society by being seen talking to that curious compound.

Nor is the precaution an unnecessary one. There is about William a shameless absence of appreciation of class distinctions which recalls the worst excesses of the French Revolution. I have seen him with these eyes chivvy a pomeranian belonging to a Baroness in her own right from near the Achilles Statue to within a few yards of the Marble Arch.

And yet James walks daily with him in Piccadilly. It is surely significant.

The Heel of Achilles

On the young man's face, as he sat sipping his ginger-ale in the club-house smoking-room, there was a look of disillusionment.

"Never again!" he said.

The Oldest Member glanced up from his paper.

"You are proposing to give up golf once more?" he queried.

"Not golf. Betting on golf." The Young Man frowned. "I've just been let down badly. Wouldn't you have thought I had a good thing, laying seven to one on McTavish against Robinson?"

"Undoubtedly," said the Sage. "The odds, indeed, generous as they are, scarcely indicate the former's superiority. Do you mean to tell me that the thing came unstitched?"

"Robinson won in a walk, after being three down at the turn."

"Strange! What happened?"

"Why, they looked in at the bar to have a refresher before starting for the tenth," said the young man, his voice quivering, "and McTavish suddenly discovered that there was a hole in his trouser-pocket and a dime had dropped out. He worried so frightfully about it that on the second nine he couldn't do a thing right. Went completely off his game and didn't win a hole."

The Sage shook his head gravely.

"If this is really going to be a lesson to you, my boy, never to bet on the result of a golf-match, it will be a blessing in disguise. There is no such thing as a certainty in golf. I wonder if I ever told you a rather curious episode in the career of Vincent Jopp?"

"*The* Vincent Jopp? The Chicago multimillionaire?"

"The same. You never knew he once came within an ace of winning the American Amateur Championship, did you?"

"I never heard of his playing golf."

"He played for one season. After that he gave it up and has not touched a club since. Ring the bell and get me a small lime-juice, and I will tell you all."

It was long before your time (said the Oldest Member) that the events which I am about to relate took place. I had just come down from Harvard, and was feeling particularly pleased with myself because I had secured the job of private and confidential secretary to Vincent Jopp, then a man in the early thirties, busy in laying the foundations of his present remarkable fortune. He engaged me, and took me with him to Chicago.

Jopp was, I think, the most extraordinary personality I have encountered in a long and many sided life. He was admirably equipped for success in finance, having the steely eye and square jaw without which it is hopeless for a man to enter that line of business. He possessed also an overwhelming confidence in himself, and the ability to switch a cigar from one corner of his mouth to the other without wiggling his ears, which, as you know, is the stamp of the true Monarch of the Money Market. He was the nearest approach to the financier on the films, the fellow who makes his jaw-muscles jump when he is telephoning, that I have ever seen.

Like all successful men, he was a man of method. He kept a pad on his desk on which he would scribble down his appointments, and it was my duty on entering the office each morning to take this pad and type its contents neatly in a loose-leaved ledger. Usually, of course, these entries referred to business appointments and deals which he was contemplating, but one day I was interested to note, against the date May 3rd, the entry:—

"Propose to Amelia."

I was interested, as I say, but not surprised. Though a man of steel and iron, there was nothing of the celibate about Vincent Jopp. He was one of those men who marry early and often. On three separate occasions before I joined his service he had jumped off the dock, to scramble back to shore again later by means of the Divorce Court lifebelt. Scattered here and there about the country there were three ex-Mrs. Jopps, drawing their monthly envelope, and now, it seemed, he contemplated the addition of a fourth to the platoon.

I was not surprised, I say, at this resolve of his. What did seem a little remarkable to me was the thorough way in which he had thought the thing out. This iron-willed man recked nothing of possible obstacles. Under the date of June 1st was the entry:—

"Marry Amelia";

while in March of the following year he had arranged to have his first-born christened Thomas Reginald. Later on, the short-coating of Thomas Reginald was arranged for, and there was a note about sending him to school. Many hard things have been said of Vincent Jopp, but nobody has ever accused him of not being a man who looked ahead.

On the morning of May 4th Jopp came into the office,

looking, I fancied, a little thoughtful. He sat for some moments staring before him with his brow a trifle furrowed; then he seemed to come to himself. He rapped his desk.

"Hi! You!" he said. It was thus that he habitually addressed me.

"Mr. Jopp?" I replied.

"What's golf?"

I had at this time just succeeded in getting my handicap down into single figures, and I welcomed the opportunity of dilating on the noblest of pastimes. But I had barely begun my eulogy when he stopped me.

"It's a game, is it?"

"I suppose you could call it that," I said, "but it is an offhand way of describing the holiest—"

"How do you play it?"

"Pretty well," I said. "At the beginning of the season I didn't seem able to keep 'em straight at all, but lately I've been doing fine. Getting better every day. Whether it was that I was moving my head or gripping too tightly with the right hand—"

"Keep the reminiscences for your grandchildren during the long winter evenings," he interrupted, abruptly, as was his habit. "What I want to know is what a fellow does when he plays golf. Tell me in as few words as you can just what it's all about."

"You hit a ball with a stick till it falls into a hole."

"Easy!" he snapped. "Take dictation."

I produced my pad.

"May the fifth, take up golf. What's an Amateur Championship?"

"It is the annual competition to decide which is the best player among the amateurs. There is also a Professional Championship, and an Open event."

"Oh, there are golf professionals, are there? What do they do?"

"They teach golf."

"Which is the best of them?"

"Sandy McHoots won both British and American Open events last year."

"Wire him to come here at once."

"But McHoots is in Inverlochty, in Scotland."

"Never mind. Get him; tell him to name his own terms. When is the Amateur Championship?"

"I think it is on September the twelfth this year."

"All right, take dictation. September twelfth, win Amateur Championship."

I stared at him in amazement, but he was not looking at me.

"Got that?" he said. "September thir—Oh, I was forgetting! Add September twelfth, corner wheat. September thirteenth, marry Amelia."

"Marry Amelia," I echoed, moistening my pencil.

"Where do you play this—what's-its-name—golf?"

"There are clubs all over the country. I belong to the Wissahicky Glen."

"That a good place?"

"Very good."

"Arrange to-day for my becoming a member."

Sandy McHoots arrived in due course, and was shown into the private office.

"Mr. McHoots?" said Vincent Jopp.

"Mphm!" said the Open Champion.

"I have sent for you, Mr. McHoots, because I hear that you are the greatest living exponent of this game of golf."

"Aye," said the champion, cordially. "I am that."

"I wish you to teach me the game. I am already somewhat behind schedule owing to the delay incident upon your
long journey, so let us start at once. Name a few of the most
important points in connection with the game. My secretary will make notes of them, and I will memorise them.
In this way we shall save time. Now, what is the most important thing to remember when playing golf?"

"Keep your head still."

"A simple task."

"Na sae simple as it soonds."

"Nonsense!" said Vincent Jopp, curtly. "If I decide to keep
my head still, I shall keep it still. What next?"

"Keep yer ee on the ba'."

"It shall be attended to. And the next?"

"Dinna press."

"I won't. And to resume."

Mr. McHoots ran through a dozen of the basic rules, and
I took them down in shorthand. Vincent Jopp studied the
list.

"Very good. Easier than I had supposed. On the first tee
at Wissahicky Glen at eleven sharp to-morrow, Mr.
McHoots. Hi! You!"

"Sir?" I said.

"Go out and buy me a set of clubs, a red jacket, a cloth
cap, a pair of spiked shoes, and a ball."

"One ball?"

"Certainly. What need is there of more?"

"It sometimes happens," I explained, "that a player who
is learning the game fails to hit his ball straight, and then
he often loses it in the rough at the side of the fairway."

"Absurd!" said Vincent Jopp. "If I set out to drive my
ball straight, I shall drive it straight. Good morning, Mr.
McHoots. You will excuse me now. I am busy cornering

Woven Textiles."

Golf is in its essence a simple game. You laugh in a sharp, bitter, barking manner when I say this, but nevertheless it is true. Where the average man goes wrong is in making the game difficult for himself. Observe the non-player, the man who walks round with you for the sake of the fresh air. He will hole out with a single care-free flick of his umbrella the twenty-foot putt over which you would ponder and hesitate for a full minute before sending it right off the line. Put a driver in his hands, and he pastes the ball into the next county without a thought. It is only when he takes to the game in earnest that he becomes self-conscious and anxious, and tops his shots even as you and I. A man who could retain through his golfing career the almost scornful confidence of the non-player would be unbeatable. Fortunately such an attitude of mind is beyond the scope of human nature.

It was not, however, beyond the scope of Vincent Jopp, the superman. Vincent Jopp was, I am inclined to think, the only golfer who ever approached the game in a spirit of Pure Reason. I have read of men who, never having swum in their lives, studied a text-book on their way down to the swimming bath, mastered its contents, and dived in and won the big race. In just such a spirit did Vincent Jopp start to play golf. He committed McHoots's hints to memory, and then went out on the links and put them into practice. He came to the tee with a clear picture in his mind of what he had to do, and he did it. He was not intimidated, like the average novice, by the thought that if he pulled in his hands he would slice, or if he gripped too tightly with the right he would pull. Pulling in the hands was an error, so he did not pull in his hands. Gripping too tightly was a defect, so he did not grip too tightly. With that weird concentration which had served him so well in business he did precisely what he had set out to do—no less and no more. Golf with Vincent Jopp was an exact science.

The annals of the game are studded with the names of those who have made rapid progress in their first season. Colonel Quill, we read in our Vardon, took up golf at the age of fifty-six, and by devising an ingenious machine consisting of a fishing-line and a sawn-down bedpost was enabled to keep his head so still that he became a scratch player before the end of the year. But no one, I imagine, except Vincent Jopp, has ever achieved scratch on his first morning on the links.

The main difference, we are told, between the amateur and the professional golfer is the fact that the latter is always aiming at the pin, while the former has in his mind a vague picture of getting somewhere reasonably near it. Vincent Jopp invariably went for the pin. He tried to hole out from anywhere inside two hundred and twenty yards. The only occasion on which I ever heard him express any chagrin or disappointment was during the afternoon round on his first day out, when from the tee on the two hundred and eighty yard seventh he laid his ball within six inches of the hole.

"A marvellous shot!" I cried, genuinely stirred.

"Too much to the right," said Vincent Jopp, frowning.

He went on from triumph to triumph. He won the monthly medal in May, June, July, August, and September. Towards the end of May he was heard to complain that Wissahicky Glen was not a sporting course. The Greens Committee sat up night after night trying to adjust his handicap so as to give other members an outside chance against him. The golf experts of the daily papers wrote columns about his play. And it was pretty generally considered throughout the country that it would be a pure formality for anyone else to enter against him in the Amateur Championship—an opinion which was borne out when he got through into the final without losing a hole. A safe man to have betted on, you would have said. But mark the sequel.

The Amateur Championship was held that year in Detroit. I had accompanied my employer there; for, though engaged on this nerve-wearing contest, he refused to allow his business to be interfered with. As he had indicated in his schedule, he was busy at the time cornering wheat; and it was my task to combine the duties of caddy and secretary. Each day I accompanied him round the links with my notebook and his bag of clubs, and the progress of his various matches was somewhat complicated by the arrival of a stream of telegraph-boys bearing important messages. He would read these between the strokes and dictate replies to me, never, however, taking more than the five minutes allowed by the rules for an interval between strokes. I am inclined to think that it was this that put the finishing touch on his opponents' discomfiture. It is not soothing for a nervous man to have the game hung up on the green while his adversary dictates to his caddy, a letter beginning "Yours of the 11th inst. received and contents noted. In reply would state—" This sort of thing puts a man off his game.

I was resting in the lobby of our hotel after a strenuous day's work, when I found that I was being paged. I answered the summons, and was informed that a lady wished to see me. Her card bore the name "Miss Amelia Merridew." Amelia! The name seemed familiar. Then I remembered. Amelia was the name of the girl Vincent Jopp intended to marry, the fourth of the long line of Mrs. Jopps. I hurried to present myself, and found a tall, slim girl, who was plainly labouring under a considerable agitation.

"Miss Merridew?" I said.

"Yes," she murmured. "My name will be strange to you."

"Am I right," I queried, "in supposing that you are the lady to whom Mr. Jopp—"

"I am! I am!" she replied, "And, oh, what shall I do?"

"Kindly give me particulars," I said, taking out my pad from force of habit.

She hesitated a moment, as if afraid to speak.

"You're caddying for Mr. Jopp in the Final to-morrow?" she said at last.

"I am."

"Then could you—would you mind—would it be giving you too much trouble if I asked you to shout 'Boo!' at him when he is making his stroke, if he looks like winning?"

I was perplexed.

"I don't understand."

"I see that I must tell you all. I am sure you will treat what I say as absolutely confidential."

"Certainly."

"I am provisionally engaged to Mr. Jopp."

"Provisionally?"

She gulped.

"Let me tell you my story. Mr. Jopp asked me to marry him, and I would rather do anything on earth than marry him. But how could I say 'No!' with those awful eyes of his boring me through? I knew that if I said 'No,' he would argue me out of it in two minutes. I had an idea. I gathered that he had never played golf, so I told him that I would marry him if he won the Amateur Championship this year. And now I find that he has been a golfer all along, and, what is more, a plus man! It isn't fair!"

"He was not a golfer when you made that condition," I said. "He took up the game on the following day."

"Impossible! How could he have become as good as he is in this short time?"

"Because he is Vincent Jopp! In his lexicon there is no such word as impossible."

She shuddered.

"What a man! But I can't marry him," she cried. "I want to marry somebody else. Oh, won't you help me? Do shout 'Boo!' at him when he is starting his down-swing!"

I shook my head.

"It would take more than a single 'boo' to put Vincent Jopp off his stroke."

"But won't you try it?"

"I cannot. My duty is to my employer."

"Oh, do!"

"No, no. Duty is duty, and paramount with me. Besides, I have a hundred dollars down on him to win."

The stricken girl uttered a faint moan, and tottered away.

I was in our suite shortly after dinner that night, going over some of the notes I had made that day, when the telephone rang. Jopp was out at the time, taking a short stroll with his after-dinner cigar. I unhooked the receiver, and a female voice spoke.

"Is that Mr. Jopp?"

"Mr. Jopp's secretary speaking. Mr. Jopp is out."

"Oh, it's nothing important. Will you say that Mrs. Luella Mainprice Jopp called up to wish him luck? I shall be on the course to-morrow to see him win the final."

I returned to my notes. Soon afterwards the telephone rang again.

"Vincent, dear?"

"Mr. Jopp's secretary speaking."

"Oh, will you say that Mrs. Jane Jukes Jopp called up to wish him luck? I shall be there to-morrow to see him play."

I resumed my work. I had hardly started when the telephone rang for the third time.

"Mr. Jopp?"

"Mr. Jopp's secretary speaking."

"This is Mrs. Agnes Parsons Jopp. I just called to wish him luck. I shall be looking on to-morrow."

I shifted my work nearer to the telephone-table so as to be ready for the next call. I had heard that Vincent Jopp had only been married three times, but you never knew.

Presently Jopp came in.

"Anybody called up?" he asked.

"Nobody on business. An assortment of your wives were on the wire wishing you luck. They asked me to say that they will be on the course to-morrow."

For a moment it seemed to me that the man's iron repose was shaken.

"Luella?" he asked.

"She was the first."

"Jane?"

"And Jane."

"And Agnes?"

"Agnes," I said, "is right."

"H'im!" said Vincent Jopp. And for the first time since I had known him I thought that he was ill at ease.

The day of the final dawned bright and clear. At least, I was not awake at the time to see, but I suppose it did; for at nine o'clock, when I came down to breakfast, the sun was shining brightly. The first eighteen holes were to be played before lunch, starting at eleven. Until twenty minutes before the hour Vincent Jopp kept me busy taking dictation, partly on matters connected with his wheat deal and partly on a signed article dealing with the Final, entitled "How I Won." At eleven sharp we were out on the first tee.

Jopp's opponent was a nice-looking young man, but obviously nervous. He giggled in a distraught sort of way as he shook hands with my employer.

"Well, may the best man win," he said.

"I have arranged to do so," replied Jopp, curtly, and started to address his ball.

There was a large crowd at the tee, and, as Jopp started his down-swing, from somewhere on the outskirts of this crowd there came suddenly a musical "Boo!" It rang out in the clear morning air like a bugle.

I had been right in my estimate of Vincent Jopp. His forceful stroke never wavered. The head of his club struck the ball, despatching it a good two hundred yards down the middle of the fairway. As we left the tee I saw Amelia Merridew being led away with bowed head by two members of the Greens Committee. Poor girl! My heart bled for her. And yet, after all, Fate had been kind in removing her from the scene, even in custody, for she could hardly have borne to watch the proceedings. Vincent Jopp made rings around his antagonist. Hole after hole he won in his remorseless, machine-like way, until when lunch-time came at the end of the eighteenth he was ten up. All the other holes had been halved.

It was after lunch, as we made our way to the first tee, that the advance-guard of the Mrs. Jopps appeared in the person of Luella Mainprice Jopp, a kittenish little woman with blonde hair and a Pekingese dog. I remembered reading in the papers that she had divorced my employer for persistent and aggravated mental cruelty, calling witnesses to bear out her statement that he had said he did not like her in pink, and that on two separate occasions had insisted on her dog eating the leg of a chicken instead of the breast; but Time, the great healer, seemed to have removed all bitterness, and she greeted him affectionately.

"Wassums going to win great big championship against nasty rough strong man?" she said.

"Such," said Vincent Jopp, "is my intention. It was kind of you, Luella, to trouble to come and watch me. I wonder if you know Mrs. Agnes Parsons Jopp?" he said, courteously, indicating a kind-looking, motherly woman who had just come up. "How are you, Agnes?"

"If you had asked me that question this morning, Vincent," replied Mrs. Agnes Parsons Jopp, "I should have been obliged to say that I felt far from well. I had an odd throbbing feeling in the left elbow, and I am sure my temperature was above the normal. But this afternoon I am a little better. How are you, Vincent?"

Although she had, as I recalled from the reports of the case, been compelled some years earlier to request the Court to sever her marital relations with Vincent Jopp on the ground of calculated and inhuman brutality, in that he had callously refused, in spite of her pleadings, to take old Dr. Bennett's Tonic Swamp-Juice three times a day, her voice, as she spoke, was kind and even anxious. Badly as this man had treated her—and I remember hearing that several of the jury had been unable to restrain their tears when she was in the witness-box giving her evidence—there still seemed to linger some remnants of the old affection.

"I am quite well, thank you, Agnes," said Vincent Jopp.

"Are you wearing your liver-pad?"

A frown flitted across my employer's strong face.

"I am not wearing my liver-pad," he replied, brusquely.

"Oh, Vincent, how rash of you!"

He was about to speak, when a sudden exclamation from his rear checked him. A genial-looking woman in a sports coat was standing there, eyeing him with a sort of humorous horror.

"Well, Jane," he said.

I gathered that this was Mrs. Jane Jukes Jopp, the wife who had divorced him for systematic and ingrowing fiendishness on the ground that he had repeatedly outraged her feelings by wearing a white waistcoat with a dinner-jacket. She continued to look at him dumbly, and then uttered a sort of strangled, hysterical laugh.

"Those legs!" she cried. "Those legs!"

Vincent Jopp flushed darkly. Even the strongest and most silent of us have our weaknesses, and my employer's was the rooted idea that he looked well in knickerbockers. It was not my place to try to dissuade him, but there was no doubt that they did not suit him. Nature, in bestowing upon him a massive head and a jutting chin, had forgotten to finish him off at the other end. Vincent Jopp's legs were skinny.

"You poor dear man!" went on Mrs. Jane Jukes Jopp. "What practical joker ever lured you into appearing in public in knickerbockers?"

"I don't object to the knickerbockers," said Mrs. Agnes Parsons Jopp, "but when he foolishly comes out in quite a strong east wind without his liver-pad—"

"Little Tinky-Ting don't need no liver-pad, he don't," said Mrs. Luella Mainprice Jopp, addressing the animal in her arms, "because he was his muzzer's pet, he was."

I was standing quite near to Vincent Jopp, and at this moment I saw a bead of perspiration spring out on his forehead, and into his steely eyes there came a positively hunted look. I could understand and sympathise. Napoleon himself would have wilted if he had found himself in the midst of a trio of females, one talking baby-talk, another fussing about his health, and the third making derogatory observations of his lower limbs. Vincent Jopp was becoming unstrung.

"May as well be starting, shall we?"

It was Jopp's opponent who spoke. There was a strange, set look on his face—the look of a man whose back is against the wall. Ten down on the morning's round, he had drawn on his reserves of courage and was determined to meet the inevitable bravely.

Vincent Jopp nodded absently, then turned to me.

"Keep those women away from me," he whispered tensely. "They'll put me off my stroke!"

"Put *you* off your stroke!" I exclaimed, incredulously.

"Yes, me! How the deuce can I concentrate, with people babbling about liver-pads, and—and knickerbockers all round me? Keep them away!"

He started to address his ball, and there was a weak uncertainty in the way he did it that prepared me for what was to come. His club rose, wavered, fell; and the ball, badly topped, trickled two feet and sank into a cuppy lie.

"Is that good or bad?" inquired Mrs. Luella Mainprice Jopp.

A sort of desperate hope gleamed in the eye of the other competitor in the final. He swung with renewed vigour. His ball sang through the air, and lay within chip-shot distance of the green.

"At the very least," said Mrs. Agnes Parsons Jopp, "I hope, Vincent, that you are wearing flannel next your skin."

I heard Jopp give a stifled groan as he took his spoon from

the bag. He made a gallant effort to retrieve the lost ground, but the ball struck a stone and bounded away into the long grass to the side of the green. His opponent won the hole.

We moved to the second tee.

"Now, *that* young man," said Mrs. Jane Jukes Jopp, indicating her late husband's blushing antagonist, "is quite right to wear knickerbockers. He can carry them off. But a glance in the mirror must have shown you that you—"

"I'm sure you're feverish, Vincent," said Mrs. Agnes Parsons Jopp, solicitously. "You are quite flushed. There is a wild gleam in your eyes."

"Muzzer's pet's got little buttons of eyes, that don't never have no wild gleam in zem because he's muzzer's own darling, he was!" said Mrs. Luella Mainprice Jopp.

A hollow groan escaped Vincent Jopp's ashen lips.

I need not recount the play hole by hole, I think. There are some subjects that are too painful. It was pitiful to watch Vincent Jopp in his downfall. By the end of the first nine his lead had been reduced to one, and his antagonist, rendered a new man by success, was playing magnificent golf. On the next hole he drew level. Then with a superhuman effort Jopp contrived to halve the eleventh, twelfth, and thirteenth. It seemed as though his iron will might still assert itself, but on the fourteenth, the end came.

He had driven a superb ball, outdistancing his opponent by a full fifty yards. The latter played a good second to within a few feet of the green. And then, as Vincent Jopp was shaping for his stroke, Luella Mainprice gave tongue.

"Vincent!"

"Well?"

"Vincent, that other man—bad man—not playing fair. When your back was turned just now, he gave his ball a great bang. *I* was watching him."

"At any rate," said Mrs. Agnes Parsons Jopp, "I do hope, when the game is over, Vincent, that you will remember to cool slowly."

"Flesho!" cried Mrs. Jane Jukes Jopp triumphantly. "I've been trying to remember the name all the afternoon. I saw about it in one of the papers. The advertisements speak most highly of it. You take it before breakfast and again before retiring, and they guarantee it to produce firm, healthy flesh on the most sparsely-covered limbs in next to no time. Now, *will* you remember to get a bottle to-night? It comes in two sizes, the dollar (or large) size and the smaller at fifty cents. Irvin Cobb writes that he used it regularly for years."

Vincent Jopp uttered a quavering moan, and his hand, as he took the mashie from his bag, was trembling like an aspen.

Ten minutes later, he was on his way back to the clubhouse, a beaten man.

And so (concluded the Oldest Member) you see that in golf there is no such thing as a soft snap. You can never be certain of the finest player. Anything may happen to the greatest expert at any stage of the game. In a recent competition George Duncan took eleven shots over a hole which eighteen-handicap men generally do in five. No! Back horses or go down to Throckmorton Street and try to take it away from the Rothschilds, and I will applaud you as a shrewd and cautious financier. But to bet at golf is pure gambling.

Little Girls Grow Bigger Every Day

Their youth and innocence is no protection—for hapless adult world.

Lord Emsworth and the Girl Friend

The day was so warm, so fair, so magically a thing of sunshine and blue skies and birdsong that anyone acquainted with Clarence, ninth Earl of Emsworth, and aware of his liking for fine weather, would have pictured him going about the place on this summer morning with a beaming smile and an uplifted heart. Instead of which, humped over the breakfast table, he was directing at a blameless kippered herring a look of such intense bitterness that the fish seemed to sizzle beneath it. For it was August Bank Holiday, and Blandings Castle on August Bank Holiday became, in his lordship's opinion, a miniature Inferno.

This was the day when his park and grounds broke out into a noisome rash of swings, roundabouts, marquees, toy balloons and paper bags; when a tidal wave of the peasantry and its squealing young engulfed those haunts of immemorial peace. On August Bank Holiday he was not allowed to potter pleasantly about his gardens in an old coat: forces beyond his control shoved him into a stiff collar and a top-hat and told him to go out and be genial. And in the cool of the quiet evenfall they put him on a platform and made him make a speech. To a man with a day like that in front of him fine weather was a mockery.

His sister, Lady Constance Keeble, looked brightly at him over the coffee-pot.

"What a lovely morning!" she said.

Lord Emsworth's gloom deepened. He chafed at being called upon—by this woman of all others—to behave as if everything was for the jolliest in the jolliest of all possible worlds. But for his sister Constance and her hawk-like vigilance, he might, he thought, have been able at least to dodge the top-hat.

"Have you got your speech ready?"

"Yes."

"Well, mind you learn it by heart this time and don't stammer and dodder as you did last year."

Lord Emsworth pushed plate and kipper away. He had lost his desire for food.

"And don't forget you have to go to the village this morning to judge the cottage gardens."

"All right, all right, all right," said his lordship testily. "I've not forgotten."

"I think I will come to the village with you. There are a number of those Fresh Air London children staying there now, and I must warn them to behave properly when they come to the Fete this afternoon. You know what London children are. McAllister says he found one of them in the gardens the other day, picking his flowers."

At any other time the news of this outrage would, no doubt, have affected Lord Emsworth profoundly. But now, so intense was his self-pity, he did not even shudder. He drank coffee with the air of a man who regretted that it was not hemlock.

"By the way, McAllister was speaking to me again last night about that gravel path through the yew alley. He seems very keen on it."

"Glug!" said Lord Emsworth—which, as any philologist will tell you, is the sound which peers of the realm make when stricken to the soul while drinking coffee.

Concerning Glasgow, that great commercial and manufacturing city in the county of Lanarkshire in Scotland, much has been written. So lyrically does the *Encyclopaedia Brittanica* deal with the place that it covers twenty-seven pages before it can tear itself away and go on to Glass, Glastonbury, Glatz and Glauber. The only aspect of it, however, which immediately concerns the present historian is the fact that the citizens it breeds are apt to be grim, dour, persevering, tenacious men; men with red whiskers who know what they want and mean to get it. Such a one was Angus McAllister, head-gardener at Blandings Castle.

For years Angus McAllister had set before himself as his earthly goal the construction of a gravel path through the Castle's famous yew alley. For years he had been bringing the project to the notice of his employer, though in any one less whiskered the latter's unconcealed loathing would have caused embarrassment. And now, it seemed, he was at it again.

"Gravel path!" Lord Emsworth stiffened through the whole length of his stringy body. Nature, he had always maintained, intended a yew alley to be carpeted with a mossy growth. And, whatever Nature felt about it, he personally was dashed if he was going to have men with Clydeside accents and faces like dissipated potatoes coming along and mutilating that lovely expanse of green velvet. "Gravel path, indeed! Why not asphalt? Why not a few hoardings with advertisements of liver pills and a filling-station? That's what the man would really like."

Lord Emsworth felt bitter, and when he felt bitter he could be terribly sarcastic.

"Well, I think it is a very good idea," said his sister. "One could walk there in wet weather then. Damp moss is ruinous to shoes."

Lord Emsworth rose. He could bear no more of this. He left the table, the room and the house and, reaching the yew alley some minutes later, was revolted to find it infested by Angus McAllister in person. The head-gardener was standing gazing at the moss like a high priest of some ancient religion about to stick the gaff into the human sacrifice.

"Morning, McAllister," said Lord Emsworth coldly.

"Good morrrrning, your lorrudsheep."

There was a pause. Angus McAllister, extending a foot that looked like a violin-case, pressed it on the moss. The meaning of the gesture was plain. It expressed contempt, dislike, a generally anti-moss spirit: and Lord Emsworth, wincing, surveyed the man unpleasantly through his pincenez. Though not often given to theological speculation, he was wondering why Providence, if obliged to make headgardeners, had found it necessary to make them so Scotch. In the case of Angus McAllister, why, going a step farther, have made him a human being at all? All the ingredients of a first-class mule simply thrown away. He felt that he might have liked Angus McAllister if he had been a mule.

"I was speaking to her leddyship yesterday."

"Oh?"

"About the gravel path I was speaking to her leddyship."

"Oh?"

"Her leddyship likes the notion fine."

"Indeed! Well..."

Lord Emsworth's face had turned a lively pink, and he was about to release the blistering words which were forming themselves in his mind when suddenly he caught the head-gardener's eye and paused. Angus McAllister was looking at him in a peculiar manner, and he knew what that look meant. Just one crack, his eye was saying—in Scotch, of course—Just one crack out of you and I tender my resignation. And with a sickening shock it came home to Lord Emsworth how completely he was in this man's clutches.

He shuffled miserably. Yes, he was helpless. Except for

that kink about gravel paths, Angus McAllister was a head-gardener in a thousand, and he needed him. He could not do without him. That, unfortunately, had been proved by experiment. Once before, at the time when they were grooming for the Agricultural Show that pumpkin which had subsequently romped home so gallant a winner, he had dared to flout Angus McAllister. And Angus had resigned, and he had been forced to plead—yes, plead—with him to come back. An employer cannot hope to do this sort of thing and still rule with an iron hand. Filled with the coward rage that dares to burn but does not dare to blaze, Lord Emsworth coughed a cough that was undisguisedly a bronchial white flag.

"I'll—er—I'll think it over, McAllister."

"Mphm."

"I have to go to the village now. I will see you later."

"Mphm."

"Meanwhile, I will—er—think it over."

"Mphm."

The task of judging the floral displays in the cottage gardens of the little village of Blandings Parva was one to which Lord Emsworth had looked forward with pleasurable anticipation. It was the sort of job he liked. But now, even though he had managed to give his sister Constance the slip and was free from her threatened society, he approached the task with a downcast spirit. It is always unpleasant for a proud man to realize that he is no longer captain of his soul ; that he is to all intents and purposes ground beneath the number twelve heel of a Glaswegian head-gardener; and, brooding on this, he judged the cottage gardens with a distrait eye. It was only when he came to the last on his list that anything like animation crept into his demeanour.

This, he perceived, peering over its rickety fence, was not at all a bad little garden. It demanded closer inspection. He unlatched the gate and pottered in. And a dog, dozing behind a water-butt, opened one eye and looked at him. It was one of those hairy, nondescript dogs, and its gaze was cold, wary and suspicious, like that of a stockbroker who thinks someone is going to play the confidence trick on him.

Lord Emsworth did not observe the animal. He had pottered to a bed of wallflowers and now, stooping, he took a sniff at them.

As sniffs go, it was an innocent sniff, but the dog for some reason appeared to read into it criminality of a high order. All the indignant householder in him woke in a flash. The next moment the world had become full of hideous noises, and Lord Emsworth's preoccupation was swept away in a passionate desire to save his ankles from harm.

As these chronicles of Blandings Castle have already shown, he was not at his best with strange dogs. Beyond saying "Go away, sir!" and leaping to and fro with an agility surprising in one of his years, he had accomplished little in the direction of a reasoned plan of defence when the cottage door opened and a girl came out.

"Hoy!" cried the girl.

And on the instant, at the mere sound of her voice, the mongrel, suspending hostilities, bounded at the newcomer and writhed on his back at her feet with all four legs in the air. The spectacle reminded Lord Emsworth irresistibly of his own behaviour when in the presence of Angus McAllister.

He blinked at his preserver. She was a small girl, of uncertain age—possibly twelve or thirteen, though a combination of London fogs and early cares had given her face a sort of wizened motherliness which in some odd way caused his lordship from the first to look on her as belonging to his own generation. She was the type of girl you see in back streets carrying a baby nearly as large as herself and still retaining sufficient energy to lead one little brother by the hand and shout recrimination at another in the distance. Her cheeks shone from recent soaping, and she was dressed in a velveteen frock which was obviously the pick of her wardrobe. Her hair, in defiance of the prevailing mode, she wore drawn tightly back into a short pigtail.

"Er—thank you," said Lord Emsworth.

"Thank you, sir," said the girl.

For what she was thanking him, his lordship was not able to gather. Later, as their acquaintance ripened, he was to discover that this strange gratitude was a habit with his new friend. She thanked everybody for everything. At the moment, the mannerism surprised him. He continued to blink at her through his pince-nez.

Lack of practice had rendered Lord Emsworth a little rusty in the art of making conversation to members of the other sex. He sought in his mind for topics.

"Fine day."

"Yes, sir. Thank you, sir."

"Are you"—Lord Emsworth furtively consulted his list—"are you the daughter of—ah—Ebenezer Sprockett?" he asked, thinking, as he had often thought before, what ghastly names some of his tenantry possessed.

"No, sir. I'm from London, sir."

"Ah? London, eh? Pretty warm it must be there." He paused. Then, remembering a formula of his youth: "Er—been out much this Season?"

"No, sir."

"Everybody out of town now, I suppose? What part of London?"

"Drury Line, sir."

"What's your name? Eh, what?"

"Gladys, sir. Thank you, sir. This is Ern."

A small boy had wandered out of the cottage, a rather hard-boiled specimen with freckles, bearing surprisingly in his hand a large and beautiful bunch of flowers. Lord Emsworth bowed courteously and with the addition of this third party to the *tete-a-tete* felt more at his ease.

"How do you do," he said. "What pretty flowers."

With her brother's advent, Gladys, also, had lost diffidence, and gained conversational aplomb.

"A treat, ain't they?" she agreed eagerly. "I got 'em for 'im up at the big 'ahse. Coo! The old josser the plice belongs to didn't arf chase me. 'E found me picking 'em and 'e sharted somefin at me and come runnin' after me, but I copped 'im on the shin wiv a stone and 'e stopped to rub it and I come away."

Lord Emsworth might have corrected her impression that Blandings Castle and its gardens belonged to Angus McAllister, but his mind was so filled with admiration and gratitude that he refrained from doing so. He looked at the girl almost reverently. Not content with controlling savage dogs with a mere word, this super-woman actually threw stones at Angus McAllister—a thing which he had never been able to nerve himself to do in an association which had lasted nine years—and, what was more, copped him on the shin with them. What nonsense, Lord Emsworth felt, the papers talked about the Modern Girl. If this was a specimen, the Modern Girl was the highest point the sex had yet reached.

"Ern," said Gladys, changing the subject, "is wearin' 'air-oil todiy."

Lord Emsworth had already observed this and had, indeed, been moving to windward as she spoke.

"For the Feet," explained Gladys.

"For the feet?" It seemed unusual.

"For the Feet in the pork this afternoon."

"Oh, you are going to the Fete?"

"Yes, sir, thank you, sir."

For the first time, Lord Emsworth found himself regarding that grisly social event with something approaching favour.

"We must look out for one another there," he said cordially. "You will remember me again? I shall be wearing"— he gulped—"a top-hat."

"Ern's going to wear a stror penamaw that's been give 'im."

Lord Emsworth regarded the lucky young devil with frank envy. He rather fancied he knew that panama. It had been his constant companion for some six years and then had been torn from him by his sister Constance and handed over to the vicar's wife for her rummage-sale.

He sighed.

"Well, good-bye."

"Good-bye, sir. Thank you, sir."

Lord Emsworth walked pensively out of the garden and, turning into the little street, encountered Lady Constance.

"Oh, there you are, Clarence."

"Yes," said Lord Emsworth, for such was the case.

"Have you finished judging the gardens?"

"Yes."

"I am just going into this end cottage here. The vicar tells me there is a little girl from London staying there. I want to warn her to behave this afternoon. I have spoken to the others."

Lord Emsworth drew himself up. His pince-nez were slightly askew, but despite this his gaze was commanding and impressive.

"Well, mind what you say," he said authoritatively. "None of your district visiting stuff, Constance."

"What do you mean?"

"You know what I mean. I have the greatest respect for the young lady to whom you refer. She behaved on a certain recent occasion—on two recent occasions—with notable gallantry and resource, and I won't have her ballyragged. Understand that!"

The technical title of the orgy which broke out annually on the first Monday in August in the park of Blandings Castle was the Blandings Parva School Treat, and it seemed to Lord Emsworth, wanly watching the proceedings from under the shadow of his top-hat, that if this was the sort of thing schools looked on as pleasure he and they were mentally poles apart. A function like the Blandings Parva School Treat blurred his conception of Man as Nature's Final Word.

The decent sheep and cattle to whom this park normally belonged had been hustled away into regions unknown, leaving the smooth expanse of turf to children whose vivacity scared Lord Emsworth and adults who appeared to him to have cast aside all dignity and every other noble quality which goes to make a one hundred per cent British citizen. Look at Mrs. Rossiter over there, for instance, the wife of Jno. Rossiter, Provisions, Groceries and Home-Made Jams. On any other day of the year, when you met her, Mrs. Rossiter was a nice, quiet, docile woman who gave at the knees respectfully as you passed. To-day, flushed in the face and with her bonnet on one side, she seemed to have gone completely native. She was wandering to and fro drinking lemonade out of a bottle and employing her mouth, when not so occupied, to make a devastating noise with what he believed was termed a squeaker.

The injustice of the thing stung Lord Emsworth. This park was his own private park. What right had people to come and blow squeakers in it? How would Mrs. Rossiter like it if one afternoon he suddenly invaded her neat little garden in the High Street and rushed about over her lawn, blowing a squeaker?

And it was always on these occasions so infernally hot. July might have ended in a flurry of snow, but directly the first Monday in August arrived and he had to put on a stiff collar out came the sun, blazing with tropic fury.

Of course, admitted Lord Emsworth, for he was a fair-minded man, this cut both ways. The hotter the day, the more quickly his collar lost its starch and ceased to spike him like a javelin. This afternoon, for instance, it had resolved itself almost immediately into something which felt like a wet compress. Severe as were his sufferings, he was compelled to recognize that he was that much ahead of the game.

A masterful figure loomed at his side.

"Clarence!"

Lord Emsworth's mental and spiritual state was now such that not even the advent of his sister Constance could add noticeably to his discomfort.

"Clarence, you look a perfect sight."

"I know I do. Who wouldn't in a rig-out like this? Why in the name of goodness you always insist..."

"Please don't be childish, Clarence. I cannot understand the fuss you make about dressing for once in your life like a reasonable English gentleman and not like a tramp."

"It's this top-hat. It's exciting the children."

"What on earth do you mean, exciting the children?"

"Well, all I can tell you is that just now, as I was passing the place where they're playing football—Football! In weather like this!—a small boy called out something derogatory and threw a portion of a coconut at it."

"If you will identify the child," said Lady Constance warmly, "I will have him severely punished."

"How the dickens," replied his lordship with equal warmth, "can I identify the child? They all look alike to me. And if I did identify him, I would shake him by the hand. A boy who throws coconuts at top-hats is fundamentally sound in his views. And stiff collars..."

"Stiff! That's what I came to speak to you about. Are you aware that your collar looks like a rag? Go in and change it at once."

"But, my dear Constance..."

"At once, Clarence. I simply cannot understand a man having so little pride in his appearance. But all your life you have been like that. I remember when we were children..."

Lord Emsworth's past was not of such a purity that he was prepared to stand and listen to it being lectured on by a sister with a good memory.

"Oh, all right, all right, all right," he said. "I'll change it, I'll change it."

"Well, hurry. They are just starting tea."

Lord Emsworth quivered.

"Have I got to go into that tea-tent?"

"Of course you have. Don't be so ridiculous. I do wish you would realize your position. As master of Blandings Castle..."

A bitter, mirthless laugh from the poor peon thus ludicrously described drowned the rest of the sentence.

It always seemed to Lord Emsworth, in analyzing these entertainments, that the August Bank Holiday Saturnalia at Blandings Castle reached a peak of repulsiveness when tea was served in the big marquee. Tea over, the agony abated, to become acute once more at the moment when he stepped to the edge of the platform and cleared his throat and tried to recollect what the deuce he had planned to say to the goggling audience beneath him. After that, it subsided again and passed until the following August.

Conditions during the tea hour, the marquee having stood all day under a blazing sun, were generally such that Shadrach, Meshach and Abednego, had they been there, could have learned something new about burning fiery furnaces. Lord Emsworth, delayed by the revision of his toilet, made his entry when the meal was half over and was pleased to find that his second collar almost instantaneously began to relax its iron grip. That, however, was the only gleam of happiness which was to be vouchsafed him. Once in the tent, it took his experienced eye but a moment to discern that the present feast was eclipsing in frightfulness all its predecessors.

Young Blandings Parva, in its normal form, tended rather to the stolidly bovine than the riotous. In all villages, of course, there must of necessity be an occasional tough egg—in the case of Blandings Parva the names of Willie Drake and Thomas (Rat-Face) Blenkiron spring to the mind—but it was seldom that the local infants offered anything beyond the power of a curate to control. What was giving the present gathering its striking resemblance to a reunion of *sans-culottes* at the height of the French Revolution was the admixture of the Fresh Air London visitors.

About the London child, reared among the tin cans and

cabbage stalks of Drury Lane and Clare Market, there is a breezy insouciance which his country cousin lacks. Years of back-chat with annoyed parents and relatives have cured him of any tendency he may have had towards shyness, with the result that when he requires anything he grabs for it, and when he is amused by any slight peculiarity in the personal appearance of members of the governing classes he finds no difficulty in translating his thoughts into speech. Already, up and down the long tables, the curate's unfortunate squint was coming in for hearty comment, and the front teeth of one of the school-teachers ran it a close second for popularity. Lord Emsworth was not, as a rule, a man of swift inspirations, but it occurred to him at this juncture that it would be a prudent move to take off his top-hat before his little guests observed it and appreciated its humorous possibilities.

The action was not, however, necessary. Even as he raised his hand a rock cake, singing through the air like a shell, took it off for him.

Lord Emsworth had had sufficient. Even Constance, unreasonable woman though she was, could hardly expect him to stay and beam genially under conditions like this. All civilized laws had obviously gone by the board and Anarchy reigned in the marquee. The curate was doing his best to form a provisional government consisting of himself and the two school-teachers, but there was only one man who could have coped adequately with the situation and that was King Herod, who—regrettably—was not among those present. Feeling like some aristocrat of the old regime sneaking away from the tumbril, Lord Emsworth edged to the exit and withdrew.

Outside the marquee the world was quieter but only comparatively so. What Lord Emsworth craved was solitude, and in all the broad park there seemed to be but one spot where it was to be had. This was a red-tiled shed, standing beside a small pond, used at happier times as a lounge or retiring-room for cattle. Hurrying thither, his lordship had just begun to revel in the cool, cow-scented dimness of its interior when from one of the dark corners, causing him to start and bite his tongue, there came the sound of a sub-dued sniff.

He turned. This was persecution. With the whole park to mess about in, why should an infernal child invade this one sanctuary of his? He spoke with angry sharpness. He came of a line of warrior ancestors and his fighting blood was up.

"Who's that?"

"Me, sir. Thank you, sir."

Only one person of Lord Emsworth's acquaintance was capable of expressing gratitude for having been barked at in such a tone. His wrath died away and remorse took its place. He felt like a man who in error has kicked a favourite dog.

"God bless my soul!" he exclaimed. "What in the world are you doing in a cow-shed?"

"Please, sir, I was put."

"Put? How do you mean, put? Why?"

"For pinching things, sir."

"Eh? What? Pinching things? Most extraordinary. What did you—er—pinch?"

"Two buns, two jem-sengwiches, two apples and a slicer cake."

The girl had come out of her corner and was standing correctly at attention. Force of habit had caused her to in-tone the list of the purloined articles in the sing-song voice in which she was wont to recite the multiplication-table at school, but Lord Emsworth could see that she was deeply moved. Tear-stains glistened on her face, and no Emsworth had ever been able to watch unstirred a woman's tears. The ninth Earl was visibly affected.

"Blow your nose," he said, hospitably extending his handkerchief.

"Yes, sir. Thank you, sir."

"What did you say you had pinched? Two buns..."

"...Two jem-sengwiches, two apples and a slicer cake."

"Did you eat them?"

"No, sir. They wasn't for me. They was for Ern."

"Ern? Oh, ah, yes. Yes, to be sure. For Ern, eh?"

"Yes, sir."

"But why the dooce couldn't Ern have—er—pinched them for himself? Strong, able-bodied young feller, I mean."

Lord Emsworth, a member of the old school, did not like this disposition on the part of the modern young man to shirk the dirty work and let the woman pay.

"Ern wasn't allowed to come to the treat, sir."

"What! Not allowed? Whos said he mustn't?"

"The lidy, sir."

"What lidy?"

"The one that come in just after you'd gorn this morning."

A fierce snort escaped Lord Emsworth. Constance! What the devil did Constance mean by taking it upon herself to revise his list of guests without so much as a...Constance, eh? He snorted again. One of these days Constance would go too far.

"Monstrous!" he cried.

"Yes, sir."

"High-handed tyranny, by Gad. Did she give any reason?"

"The lidy didn't like Ern biting 'er in the leg, sir."

"Ern bit her in the leg?"

"Yes, sir. Pliying 'e was a dorg. And the lidy was cross and Ern wasn't allowed to come to the treat, and I told 'im I'd bring 'im back somefing nice."

Lord Emsworth breathed heavily. He had not supposed that in these degenerate days a family like this existed. The sister copped Angus McAllister on the shin with stones, the brother bit Constance in the leg. . . It was like listening to some grand old saga of the exploits of heroes and demigods.

"I thought if I didn't 'ave nothing myself it would make it all right."

"Nothing?" Lord Emsworth started. "Do you mean to tell me you have not had tea?"

"No, sir. Thank you, sir. I thought if I didn't 'ave none, then it would be all right Ern 'aving what I would 'ave 'ad if I 'ad 'ave 'ad."

His lordship's head, never strong, swam a little. Then it resumed its equilibrium. He caught her drift.

"God bless my soul!" said Lord Emsworth. "I never heard anything so monstrous and appalling in my life. Come with me immediately."

"The lidy said I was to stop 'ere, sir."

Lord Emsworth gave vent to his loudest snort of the afternoon.

"Confound the lidy!"

"Yes, sir. Thank you, sir."

Five minutes later Beach, the butler, enjoying a siesta in the housekeeper's room, was roused from his slumbers by the unexpected ringing of a bell. Answering its summons, he found his employer in the library, and with him a surprising young person in a velveteen frock, at the sight of whom his eyebrows quivered and, but for his iron self-restraint, would have risen.

"Beach!"

"Your lordship?"

"This young lady would like some tea."

"Very good, your lordship."

"Buns, you know. And apples, and jem—I mean jam-sandwiches, and cake, and that sort of thing."

"Very good, your lordship."

"And she has a brother, Beach."

"Indeed, your lordship?"

"She will want to take some stuff away for him." Lord Emsworth turned to his guest. "Ernest would like a little chicken, perhaps?"

"Coo!"

"I beg your pardon?"

"Yes, sir. Thank you, sir."

"And a slice or two of ham?"

"Yes, sir. Thank you, sir."

"And—he has no gouty tendency?"

"No, sir. Thank you, sir."

"Capital! Then a bottle of that new lot of port, Beach. It's some stuff they've sent me down to try," explained his lordship. "Nothing special, you understand," he added apologetically, "but quite drinkable. I should like your brother's opinion of it. See that all that is put together in a parcel, Beach, and leave it on the table in the hall. We will pick it up as we go out."

A welcome coolness had crept into the evening air by the time Lord Emsworth and his guest came out of the great door of the castle. Gladys, holding her host's hand and clutching the parcel, sighed contentedly. She had done herself well at the tea-table. Life seemed to have nothing more to offer.

Lord Emsworth did not share this view. His spacious mood had not yet exhausted itself.

"Now, is there anything else you can think of that Ernest would like?" he asked. "If so, do not hesitate to mention it. Beach, can you think of anything?"

The butler, hovering respectfully, was unable to do so.

"No, your lordship. I ventured to add—on my own responsibility, your lordship—some hard-boiled eggs and a pot of jam to the parcel."

"Excellent! You are sure there is nothing else?"

A wistful look came into Gladys's eyes.

"Could he 'ave some flarze?"

"Certainly," said Lord Emsworth. "Certainly, certainly, certainly. By all means. Just what I was about to suggest my—er—what *is* flarze?"

Beach, the linguist, interpreted.

"I think the young lady means flowers, your lordship."

"Yes, sir. Thank you, sir. Flarze."

"Oh?" said Lord Emsworth. "Oh? Flarze?" he said slowly. "Oh, ah, yes. Yes, I see. H'm!"

He removed his pince-nez, wiped them thoughtfully, replaced them, and gazed with wrinkling forehead at the gardens that stretched gaily out before him. Flarze! It would be idle to deny that those gardens contained flarze in full measure. They were bright with Achillea, Bignonia Radicans, Campanula, Digitalis, Euphorbia, Funkia, Gypsophila, Helianthus, Iris, Liatris, Monarda, Phlox Drummondi, Salvia, Thalictrum, Vinca and Yucca. But the devil of it was that Angus McAllister would have a fit if they were picked. Across the threshold of this Eden the ginger whiskers of Angus McAllister lay like a flaming sword.

As a general rule, the procedure for getting flowers out of Angus McAllister was as follows. You waited till he was

in one of his rare moods of complaisance, then you led the
conversation gently round to the subject of interior deco-
ration, and then, choosing your moment, you asked if he
could possibly spare a few to be put in vases. The last thing
you thought of doing was to charge in and start helping
yourself.

"I—er—..." said Lord Emsworth.

He stopped. In a sudden blinding flash of clear vision he
had seen himself for what he was—the spineless, unspeak-
ably unworthy descendant of ancestors who, though they
may have had their faults, had certainly known how to handle employees. It was "How now, varlet!" and "Marry come
up, thou malapert knave!" in the days of previous Earls of
Emsworth. Of course, they had possessed certain advantages which he lacked. It undoubtedly helped a man in his
dealings with the domestic staff to have, as they had had,
the rights of the high, the middle and the low justice—which
meant, broadly, that if you got annoyed with your head-
gardener you could immediately divide him into four head-
gardeners with a battle axe and no questions asked: but even
so, he realized that they were better men than he was and
that, if he allowed craven fear of Angus McAllister to stand
in the way of this delightful girl and her charming brother
getting all the flowers they required, he was not worthy to
be the last of their line.

Lord Emsworth wrestled with his tremors.

"Certainly, certainly, certainly," he said, though not
without a qualm. "Take as many as you want."

And so it came about that Angus McAllister, crouched
in his potting-shed like some dangerous beast in its den, be-
held a sight which first froze his blood and then sent it boiling through his veins. Flitting to and fro through his sacred
gardens, picking his sacred flowers, was a small girl in a

velveteen frock. And—which brought apoplexy a step closer—it was the same small girl who two days before had copped him on the shin with a stone. The stillness of the summer evening was shattered by a roar that sounded like boilers exploding, and Angus McAllister came out of the potting-shed at forty-five miles per hour.

Gladys did not linger. She was a London child, trained from infancy to bear herself gallantly in the presence of alarms and excursions, but this excursion had been so sudden that it momentarily broke her nerve. With a horrified yelp she scuttled to where Lord Emsworth stood and, hiding behind him, clutched the tails of his morning-coat.

"Oo-er!" said Gladys.

Lord Emsworth was not feeling so frightfully good himself. We have pictured him a few moments back drawing inspiration from the nobility of his ancestors and saying, in effect, "That for McAllister!" but truth now compels us to admit that this hardy attitude was largely due to the fact that he believed the head-gardener to be a safe quarter of a mile away among the swings and roundabouts of the Fete. The spectacle of the man charging vengefully down on him with gleaming eyes and bristling whiskers made him feel like a nervous English infantryman at the Battle of Bannockburn. His knees shook and the soul within him quivered.

And then something happened, and the whole aspect of the situation changed.

It was, in itself, quite a trivial thing, but it had an astoundingly stimulating effect on Lord Emsworth's morale. What happened was that Gladys, seeking further protection, slipped at this moment a small, hot hand into his.

It was a mute vote of confidence, and Lord Emsworth intended to be worthy of it.

"He's coming," whispered his lordship's Inferiority Complex agitatedly.

"What of it?" replied Lord Emsworth stoutly.

"Tick him off," breathed his lordship's ancestors in his other ear.

"Leave it to me," replied Lord Emsworth.

He drew himself up and adjusted his pince-nez. He felt filled with a cool masterfulness. If the man tendered his resignation, let him tender his damned resignation.

"Well, McAllister?" said Lord Emsworth coldly.

He removed his top-hat and brushed it aginst his sleeve.

"What is the matter, McAllister?"

He replaced his top-hat.

"You appear agitated, McAllister."

He jerked his head militantly. The hat fell off. He let it lie. Freed from its loathsome weight he felt more masterful than ever. It had just needed that to bring him to the top of his form.

"This young lady," said Lord Emsworth, "has my full permission to pick all the flowers she wants, McAllister. If you do not see eye to eye with me in this matter, McAllister, say so and we will discuss what you are going to do about it, McAllister. These gardens, McAllister, belong to me, and if you do not—er—appreciate that fact you will, no doubt, be able to find another employer—ah—more in tune with your views. I value your services highly, McAllister, but I will not be dictated to in my own garden, McAllister. Er— dash it," added his lordship, spoiling the whole effect.

A long moment followed in which Nature stood still, breathless. The Achillea stood still. So did Bignonia Radicans. So did the Campanula, the Digitalis, the Euphorbia, the Funkia, the Gypsophila, the Helianthus, the Iris, the Liatris, the Monarda, the Phlox Drummondi, the Salvia, the Thalictrum, the Vinca and the Yucca. From far off in the direction of the park there sounded the happy howls of children who were probably breaking things, but even these seemed hushed. The evening breeze had died away.

Angus McAllister stood glowering. His attitude was that of one sorely perplexed. So might the early bird have looked if the worm ear-marked for its breakfast had suddenly turned and snapped at it. It had never occurred to him that his employer would voluntarily suggest that he sought another position, and now that he had suggested it Angus McAllister disliked the idea very much. Blandings Castle was in his bones. Elsewhere, he would feel an exile. He fingered his whiskers, but they gave him no comfort.

He made his decision. Better to cease to be a Napoleon than be a Napoleon in exile.

"Mphm," said Angus McAllister.

"Oh, and by the way, McAllister," said Lord Emsworth, "that matter of the gravel path through the yew alley. I've been thinking it over, and I won't have it. Not on any account. Mutilate my beautiful moss with a beastly gravel path? Make an eyesore of the loveliest spot in one of the finest and oldest gardens in the United Kingdom? Certainly not. Most decidedly not. Try to remember, McAllister, as you work in the gardens of Blandings Castle, that you are not back in Glasgow, laying out recreation grounds. That is all, McAllister. Er—dash it—that is all."

"Mphm," said Angus McAllister.

He turned. He walked away. The potting-shed swallowed him up. Nature resumed its breathing. The breeze began to blow again. And all over the gardens birds who had stopped on their high note carried on according to plan.

Lord Emsworth took out his handkerchief and dabbed with it at his forehead. He was shaken, but a novel sense of being a man among men thrilled him. It might seem bravado, but he almost wished—yes, dash it, he almost wished—that his sister Constance would come along and start something while he felt like this.

He had his wish.

"Clarence!"

Yes, there she was, hurrying towards him up the garden path. She, like McAllister, seemed agitated. Something was on her mind.

"Clarence!"

"Don't keep saying 'Clarence!' as if you were a dashed parrot," said Lord Emsworth haughtily. "What the dickens is the matter, Constance?"

"Matter? Do you know what the time is? Do you know that everybody is waiting down there for you to make your speech?"

Lord Emsworth met her eye sternly.

"I do not," he said. "And I don't care. I'm not going to make my dashed speech. If you want a speech, let the vicar make it. Or make it yourself. Speech! I never heard such dashed nonsense in my life." He turned to Gladys. "Now, my dear," he said, "if you will just give me time to get out of these infernal clothes and this ghastly collar and put on something human, we'll go down to the village and have a chat with Ern."

Bertie Changes His Mind

It has happened so frequently in the past few years that young fellows starting in my profession have come to me for a word of advice, that I have found it convenient now to condense my system into a brief formula. "Resource and Tact"—that is my motto. Tact, of course, has always been with me a *sine qua non;* while as for resource, I think I may say that I have usually contrived to show a certain modicum of what I might call *finesse* in handling those little *contretemps* which inevitably arise from time to time in the daily life of a gentleman's personal gentleman. I am reminded, by way of an instance, of the Episode of the School for Young Ladies near Brighton—an affair which, I think, may be said to have commenced one evening at the moment when I brought Mr. Wooster his whisky and siphon and he addressed me with such remarkable petulance.

Not a little moody Mr. Wooster had been for some days—far from his usual bright self. This I had attributed to the natural reaction from a slight attack of influenza from which he had been suffering; and, of course, took no notice, merely performing my duties as usual, until on the evening of which I speak he exhibited this remarkable petulance when I brought him his whisky and siphon.

"Oh, dash it, Jeeves!" he said, manifestly overwrought. "I wish at least you'd put it on another table for a change."

"Sir?" I said.

"Every night, dash it all," proceeded Mr. Wooster morosely, "you come in at exactly the same old time with the same old tray and put in on the same old table. I'm fed up, I tell you. It's the bally monotony of it that makes it all seem so frightfully bally."

I confess that his words filled me with a certain apprehension. I had heard gentlemen in whose employment I have been speak in very much the same way before, and it had almost invariably meant that they were contemplating matrimony. It disturbed me, therefore, I am free to admit, when Mr. Wooster addressed me in this fashion. I had no desire to sever a connection so pleasant in every respect as his and mine had been, and my experience is that when the wife comes in at the front door the valet of bachelor days goes out the back.

"It's not your fault, of course," went on Mr. Wooster, regaining a certain degree of composure. "I'm not blaming you. But, by Jove, I mean, you must acknowledge—I mean to say, I've been thinking pretty deeply these last few days, Jeeves, and I've come to the conclusion mine is an empty life. I'm lonely, Jeeves."

"You have a great many friends, sir."

"What's the good of friends?"

"Emerson," I reminded him, "says a friend may well be reckoned the masterpiece of Nature, sir."

"Well, you can tell Emerson from me next time you see him that he's an ass."

"Very good, sir."

"What I want—Jeeves, have you ever seen that play called I-forget-its-dashed-name?"

"No, sir."

"It's on at the What-d'you-call-it. I went last night. The hero's a chap who's buzzing along, you know, quite merry and bright, and suddenly a kid turns up and says she's his daughter. Left over from act one, you know—absolutely the first he'd heard of it. Well, of course, there's a bit of a fuss and they say to him, 'What-ho?' and he says, 'Well, what about it?' and they say, 'Well, *what* about it?' and he says, 'Oh, all right, then, if that's the way you feel!' and he takes the kid and goes off with her out into the world together, you know. Well what I'm driving at, Jeeves, is that I envied that chappie. Most awfully jolly little girl, you know, clinging to him trustingly and what-not. Something to look after, if you know what I mean. Jeeves, I wish I had a daughter. I wonder what the procedure is?"

"Marriage is, I believe, considered the preliminary step, sir."

"No, I mean about adopting a kid. You can adopt kids, you know, Jeeves. But what I want to know is how you start about it."

"The process, I should imagine, would be highly complicated and labourious, sir. It would cut into your spare time."

"Well, I'll tell you what I could do, then. My sister will be back from India next week with her three little girls. I'll give up this flat and take a house and have them all to live with me. By Jove, Jeeves, I think that's rather a scheme, what? Prattle of childish voices, eh? Little feet pattering hither and thither, yes?"

I concealed my perturbation, but the effort to preserve my *sang-froid* tested my powers to the utmost. The course of action outlined by Mr. Wooster meant the finish of our cosy bachelor establishment if it came into being a practical proposition; and no doubt some men in my place would at this juncture have voiced their disapproval. I avoided this blunder.

"If you will pardon my saying so, sir," I suggested, "I think you are not quite yourself after your influenza. If I might express the opinion, what you require is a few days by the sea. Brighton is very handy, sir."

"Are you suggesting that I'm talking through my hat?"

"By no means, sir. I merely advocate a short stay at Brighton as a physical recuperative."

Mr. Wooster considered.

"Well, I'm not sure you're not right," he said at length. "I *am* feeling more or less of an onion. You might shove a few things in a suit-case and drive me down in the car to-morrow."

"Very good, sir."

"And when we get back I'll be in the pink and ready to tackle this pattering-feet wheeze."

"Exactly, sir."

Well, it was a respite, and I welcomed it. But I began to see that a crisis had arisen which would require adroit handling. Rarely had I observed Mr. Wooster more set on a thing. Indeed, I could recall no such exhibition of determination on his part since the time when he had insisted, against my frank disapproval, on wearing purple socks. However, I had coped successfully with that outbreak, and I was by no means unsanguine that I should eventually be able to bring the present affair to a happy issue. Employers are like horses. They require managing. Some gentlemen's personal gentlemen have the knack of managing them, some have not. I, I am happy to say, have no cause for complaint.

For myself, I found our stay at Brighton highly enjoyable, and should have been willing to extend it; but Mr. Wooster, still restless, wearied of the place by the end of two days, and on the third afternoon he instructed me to pick up and bring the car round to the hotel. We started back along the London road at about five of a fine summer's day, and had travelled perhaps two miles when

I perceived in the road before us a young lady, gesticulating with no little animation. I applied the brake and brought the vehicle to a stand-still.

"What," enquired Mr. Wooster, waking from a reverie, "is the big thought at the back of this, Jeeves?"

"I observed a young lady endeavouring to attract our attention with signals a little way down the road, sir," I explained. "She is now making her way towards us."

Mr. Wooster peered.

"I see her. I expect she wants a lift, Jeeves."

"That was the interpretation which I placed upon her actions, sir."

"A jolly-looking kid," said Mr. Wooster. "I wonder what she's doing, biffing about the high road."

"She has the air to me, sir, of one who has been absenting herself without leave from her school, sir."

"Hallo-allo-allo!" said Mr. Wooster, as the child reached us. "Do you want a lift?"

"Oh, I say, can you?" said the child, with marked pleasure.

"Where do you want to go?"

"There's a turning to the left about a mile farther on. If you'll put me down there, I'll walk the rest of the way. I say, thanks awfully. I've got a nail in my shoe."

She climbed in at the back. A red-haired young person with a snub nose and an extremely large grin. Her age, I should imagine, would be about twelve. She let down one of the spare seats, and knelt on it to facilitate coversation.

"I'm going to get into a frightful row," she began. "Miss Tomlinson will be perfectly furious."

"No, really?" said Mr. Wooster.

"It's a half-holiday, you know, and I sneaked away to Brighton, because I wanted to go on the pier and put pennies in the slot-machines. I thought I could get back in time so that nobody would notice I'd gone, but I got this nail in my shoe, and now there'll be a fearful row. Oh, well," she said, with a philosophy which, I confess, I admired, "it can't be helped. What's your car? A Sunbeam, isn't it? We've got a Wolseley at home."

Mr. Wooster was visibly perturbed. As I have indicated, he was at this time in a highly malleable frame of mind, tender-hearted to a degree where the young of the female sex was concerned. Her sad case touched him deeply.

"Oh, I say, this is rather rotten," he observed. "Isn't there anything to be done? I say, Jeeves, don't you think something could be done?"

"It was not my place to make the suggestion, sir," I replied, "but as you yourself have brought the matter up, I fancy the trouble is susceptible of adjustment. I think it would be a legitimate subterfuge were you to inform the young lady's school-mistress that you are an old friend of the young lady's father. In this case you could inform Miss Tomlinson that you had been passing the school and had seen the young lady at the gate and taken her for a drive. Miss Tomlinson's chagrin would no doubt in these circumstances be sensibly diminished if not altogether dispersed."

"Well, you *are* a sportsman!" observed the young person, with considerable enthusiasm. And she proceeded to kiss me—in connection with which I have only to say that I was sorry she had just been devouring some sticky species of sweetmeat.

"Jeeves, you've hit it!" said Mr. Wooster. "A sound, even fruity, scheme. I say, I suppose I'd better know your name and all that, if I'm a friend of your father's."

"My name's Peggy Mainwaring, thanks awfully," said the young person. "And my father's Professor Mainwaring. He's written a lot of books. You'll be expected to know that."

"Author of the well-known series of philosophical treatises, sir," I ventured to interject. "They have a great vogue, though, if the young lady will pardon my saying so, many of the Professor's opinions strike me personally as somewhat empirical. Shall I drive on to the school, sir?"

"Yes, carry on. I say, Jeeves, it's a rummy thing. Do you know, I've never been inside a girls' school in my life."

"Indeed, sir?"

"Ought to be a dashed interesting experience, Jeeves, what?"

"I fancy that you may find it so, sir." I said.

We drove on a matter of half a mile down a lane, and, directed by the young person, I turned in at the gates of a house of imposing dimensions, bringing the car to a halt at the front door. Mr. Wooster and the child entered, and presently a parlourmaid came out.

"You're to take the car round to the stables, please," she said.

"Ah!" I said. "Then everything is satisfactory, eh? Where has Mr. Wooster gone?"

"Miss Peggy has taken him off to meet her friends. And cook says she hopes you'll step round to the kitchen later and have a cup of tea."

"Inform her that I shall be delighted. Before I take the car to the stables, would it be possible for me to have a word with Miss Tomlinson?"

A moment later I was following her into the drawing-room.

Handsome but strong-minded—that was how I summed up Miss Tomlinson at first glance. In some ways she recalled to my mind Mr. Wooster's Aunt Agatha. She had the same penetrating gaze and that indefinable air of being reluctant to stand any nonsense.

"I fear I am possibly taking a liberty, madam," I began, "but I am hoping that you will allow me to say a word with respect to my employer. I fancy I am correct in supposing that Mr. Wooster did not tell you a great deal about himself?"

"He told me nothing about himself, except that he was a friend of Professor Mainwaring."

"He did not inform you, then, that he was *the* Mr. Wooster?"

"*The* Mr. Wooster?"

"Bertram Wooster, madam."

I will say for Mr. Wooster that, mentally negligible though no doubt he is, he has a name that suggests almost infinite possibilities. He sounds, if I may elucidate my meaning, like Someone—especially if you have just been informed that he is an intimate friend of so eminent a man as Professor Mainwaring. You might not, no doubt, be able to say off-hand whether he was Bertram Wooster the novelist, or Bertram Wooster the founder of a new school of thought; but you would have an uneasy feeling that you were exposing your ignorance if you did not give the impression of familiarity with the name. Miss Tomlinson, as I had rather foreseen, nodded brightly.

"Oh, *Bertram* Wooster!" she said.

"He is an extremely retiring gentleman, madam, and would be the last to suggest it himself, but, knowing him as I do, I am sure that he will take it as a graceful compliment if you were to ask him to address the young ladies. He is an excellent extempore speaker."

"A very good idea." said Miss Tomlinson decidedly. "I

am very much obliged to you for suggesting it. I will certainly ask him to talk to the girls."

"And should he make a pretence—through modesty—of not wishing—"

"I shall insist."

"Thank you, madam. I am obliged. You will not mention my share in the matter? Mr. Wooster might think that I had exceeded my duties."

I drove around to the stables and halted the car in the yard. As I got out, I looked at it somewhat intently. It was a good car, and appeared to be in excellent condition, but somehow I seemed to feel that something was going to go wrong with it—something serious—something that would not be able to be put right again for at least a couple of hours.

One gets these presentiments.

It may have been some half-hour later that Mr. Wooster came into the stable-yard as I was leaning against the car enjoying a quiet cigarette.

"No, don't chuck it away, Jeeves," he said, as I withdrew the cigarette from my mouth. "As a matter of fact, I've come to touch you for a smoke. Got one to spare?"

"Only gaspers, I fear, sir."

"They'll do," responded Mr. Wooster, with no little eagerness. I observed that his manner was a trifle fatigued and his eye somewhat wild. "It's a rummy thing, Jeeves, I seem to have lost my cigarette-case. Can't find it anywhere."

"I am sorry to hear that, sir. It is not in the car."

"No? Must have dropped it somewhere, then." He drew at his gasper with relish. "Jolly creatures, small girls, Jeeves," he remarked, after a pause.

"Extremely so, sir."

"Of course, I can imagine some fellows finding them a bit exhausting in—er—"

"*En masse*, sir?"

"That's the word. A bit exhausting *en masse*."

"I must confess, sir, that that is how they used to strike me. In my younger days, at the outset of my career, sir, I was at one time page-boy in a school for young ladies."

"No, really? I never knew that before. I say, Jeeves—er—did the—er—dear little souls *giggle* much in your day?"

"Practically without cessation, sir."

"Makes a fellow feel a bit of an ass, what? I shouldn't wonder if they usedn't to stare at you from time to time, too, eh?"

"At the school where I was employed, sir, the young ladies had a regular game which they were accustomed to play when a male visitor arrived. They would stare fixedly at him and giggle, and there was a small prize for the one who made him blush first."

"Oh, no, I say, Jeeves, not really?"

"Yes, sir. They derived great enjoyment from the pastime."

"I'd no idea small girls were such demons."

"More deadly than the male, sir."

Mr. Wooster passed a handkerchief over his brow.

"Well, we're going to have tea in a few minutes, Jeeves. I expect I shall feel better after tea."

"We will hope so, sir."

But I was by no means sanguine.

I had an agreeable tea in the kitchen. The buttered toast was good and the maids nice girls, though with little conversation. The parlourmaid, who joined us towards the end of the meal, after performing her duties in the school dining-room, reported that Mr. Wooster was sticking it pluckily, but seemed feverish. I went back to the stable-yard, and I was just giving the car another look over when the young Mainwaring child appeared.

"Oh, I say," she said, "will you give this to Mr. Wooster when you see him?" She held out Mr. Wooster's cigarette-case. "He must have dropped it somewhere. I say," she proceeded, "it's an awful lark. He's going to give a lecture to the school."

"Indeed, miss?"

"We love it when there are lectures. We sit and stare at the poor dears, and try to make them dry up. There was a man last term who got hiccoughs. Do you think Mr. Wooster will get hiccoughs?"

"We can but hope for the best, miss."

"It would be such a lark, wouldn't it?"

"Highly enjoyable, miss."

"Well, I must be getting back. I want to get a front seat."

And she scampered off. An engaging child. Full of spirits.

She had hardly gone when there was an agitated noise, and round the corner came Mr. Wooster. Perturbed. Deeply so.

"Jeeves!"

"Sir?"

"Start the car!"

"Sir?"

"I'm off!"

"Sir?"

Mr. Wooster danced a few steps.

"Don't stand there saying 'sir?' I tell you I'm off. Bally off! There's not a moment to waste. The situation's desperate. Dash it, Jeeves, do you know what's happened? The Tomlinson female has just sprung it on me that I'm expected to make a speech to the girls! Got to stand up there in front of the whole dashed collection and talk! I can just see myself! Get that car going, Jeeves, dash it all. A little speed, a little speed!"

"Impossible, I fear, sir. The car is out of order."

Mr. Wooster gaped at me. Very glassily he gaped.

"Out of order!"

"Yes, sir. Something is wrong. Trivial, perhaps, but possibly a matter of some little time to repair." Mr. Wooster, being one of those easygoing young gentlemen who will drive a car but never take the trouble to study its mechanism, I felt justified in becoming technical. "I think it is the differential gear, sir. Either that or the exhaust."

I am fond of Mr. Wooster, and I admit I came very near to melting as I looked at his face. He was staring at me in a sort of dumb despair that would have touched anybody.

"Then I'm sunk! Or—" a slight gleam of hope flickered across his drawn features—"do you think I could sneak out and leg it across country, Jeeves?"

"Too late, I fear, sir." I indicated with a slight gesture the approaching figure of Miss Tomlinson, who was advancing with a serene determination in his immediate rear.

"Ah, there you are, Mr. Wooster."

He smiled a sickly smile.

"Yes—er—here I am!"

"We are all waiting for you in the large schoolroom."

"But, I say, look here," said Mr. Wooster, "I—I don't know a bit what to talk about."

"Why, anything, Mr. Wooster. Anything that comes into your head. Be bright," said Miss Tomlinson. "Bright and amusing."

"Oh, bright and amusing?"

"Possibly tell them a few entertaining stories. But, at the

same time, do not neglect the graver note. Remember that my girls are on the threshold of life, and will be eager to hear something brave and helpful and stimulating—something which they can remember in after years. But, of course, you know the sort of thing, Mr. Wooster. Come. The young people are waiting."

I have spoken earlier of resource and the part it plays in the life of a gentleman's personal gentleman. It is a quality peculiarly necessary if one is to share in scenes not primarily designed for one's co-operation. So much that is interesting in life goes on apart behind closed doors that your gentleman's gentleman, if he is not to remain hopelessly behind the march of events, should exercise his wits in order to enable himself to be—if not a spectator—at least an auditor when there is anything of interest toward. I deprecate as vulgar and undignified the practice of listening at keyholes, but without lowering myself to that, I have generally contrived to find a way.

In the present case it was simple. The large schoolroom was situated on the ground floor, with commodious French windows, which, as the weather was clement, remained open throughout the proceedings. By stationing myself behind a pillar on the porch or verandah which adjoined the room, I was enabled to see and hear all. It was an experience which I should be sorry to have missed. Mr. Wooster, I may say at once, indubitably excelled himself.

Mr. Wooster is a young gentleman with practically every desirable quality except one. I do not mean brains, for in an employer brains are not desirable. The quality to which I allude is hard to define, but perhaps I might call it the gift of dealing with the Unusual Situation. In the presence of the Unusual, Mr. Wooster is too prone to smile weakly and allow his eyes to protrude. He lacks Presence. I have often wished that I had the power to bestow upon him some of the *savoir-faire* of a former employer of mine, Mr. Montague-Todd, the well-known financier, now in the second year of his sentence. I have known men call upon Mr. Todd with the express intention of horse-whipping him and go away half an hour later laughing heartily and smoking one of his cigars. To Mr. Todd it would have been child's play to speak a few impromptu words to a schoolroom full of young ladies; in fact, before he had finished, he would probably have induced them to invest all their pocket-money in one of his numerous companies; but to Mr. Wooster it was plainly an ordeal of the worst description. He gave one look at the young ladies, who were all staring at him in an extremely unwinking manner, then blinked and started to pick feebly at his coat-sleeve. His aspect reminded me of that of a bashful young man who, persuaded against his better judgment to go on the platform and assist a conjurer in his entertainment, suddenly discovers that rabbits and hard-boiled eggs are being taken out of the top of his head.

The proceedings opened with a short but graceful speech of introduction from Miss Tomlinson.

"Girls," said Miss Tomlinson, "some of you have already met Mr. Wooster—Mr. *Bertram* Wooster, and you all, I hope, know him by reputation." Here, I regret to say, Mr. Wooster gave a hideous, gurgling laugh and, catching Miss Tomlinson's eye, turned a bright scarlet. Miss Tomlinson resumed: "He has very kindly consented to say a few words to you before he leaves, and I am sure that you will all give him your very earnest attention. Now, please."

She gave a spacious gesture with her right hand as she said the last two words, and Mr. Wooster, apparently under the impression that they were addressed to him, cleared his throat and began to speak. But it appeared that her remark was directed to the young ladies, and was in the nature of a cue or signal, for she had no sooner spoken them than the whole school rose to its feet in a body and burst into a species of chant, of which I am glad to say I can remember the words, though the tune eludes me. The words ran as follows:—

> *Many greetings to you!*
> *Many greetings to you!*
> *Many greetings, dear stranger,*
> *Many greetings,*
> *Many greetings,*
> *Many greetings to you!*
> *Many greetings to you!*
> *To you!"*

Considerable latitude of choice was given to the singers in the matter of key, and there was little of what I might call co-operative effort. Each child went on till she had reached the end, then stopped and waited for the stragglers to come up. It was an unusual performance, and I, personally, found it extremely exhilarating. It seemed to smite Mr. Wooster, however, like a blow. He recoiled a couple of steps and flung up an arm defensively. Then the uproar died away, and an air of expectancy fell upon the room. Miss Tomlinson directed a brightly authoritative gaze upon Mr. Wooster, and he blinked, gulped once or twice, and tottered forward.

"Well, you know—" he said.

Then it seemed to strike him that his opening lacked the proper formal dignity.

"Ladies—"

A silvery peal of laughter from the front row stopped him again.

"Girls!" said Miss Tomlinson. She spoke in a low, soft voice, but the effect was immediate. Perfect stillness instantly descended upon all present. I am bound to say that, brief as my acquaintance with Miss Tomlinson had been, I could recall few women I had admired more. She had grip.

I fancy that Miss Tomlinson had gauged Mr. Wooster's oratorical capabilities pretty correctly by this time, and had come to the conclusion that little in the way of stirring address was to be expected from him.

"Perhaps," she said, "as it is getting late, and he has not very much time to spare, Mr. Wooster will just give you some little word of advice which may be helpful to you in after-life, and then we will sing the school song and disperse to our evening lessons."

She looked at Mr. Wooster. He passed a finger round the inside of his collar.

"Advice? After-life? What? Well, I don't know—"

"Just some brief word of counsel, Mr. Wooster," said Miss Tomlinson firmly.

"Oh, well—Well, yes—Well—" It was painful to see Mr. Wooster's brain endeavouring to work. "Well, I'll tell you something that's often done *me* a bit of good, and it's a thing not many people know. My old Uncle Henry gave me the tip when I first came to London. 'Never forget, my boy,' he said, 'that, if you stand outside Romano's in the Strand, you can see the clock on the wall of the Law Courts down in Fleet Street. Most people who don't know don't believe it's possible, because there are a couple of churches in the middle of the road, and you would think they would be in the way. But you can, and it's worth knowing. You can win a lot of money betting on it with fellows who haven't found it out.' And, by Jove, he was perfectly right, and it's a thing to remember. Many a quid have I—"

Miss Tomlinson gave a hard, dry cough, and he stopped in the middle of a sentence.

"Perhaps it will be better, Mr. Wooster," she said, in a cold, even voice, "if you were to tell my girls some little story. What you say is, no doubt, extemely interesting, but perhaps a little—"

"Oh, ah, yes," said Mr. Wooster. "Story? Story?" He appeared completely distraught, poor young gentleman. "I wonder if you've heard the one about the stockbroker and the chorus-girl?"

"We will now sing the school song," said Miss Tomlinson, rising like an iceberg.

I decided not to remain for the singing of the school song. It seemed probable to me that Mr. Wooster would shortly be requiring the car, so I made my way back to the stable-yard, to be in readiness.

I had not long to wait. In a very few moments he appeared, tottering. Mr. Wooster's is not one of those inscrutable faces which it is impossible to read. On the contrary, it is a limpid pool in which is mirrored each passing emotion. I could read it now like a book, and his first words were very much on the lines I had anticipated.

"Jeeves," he said hoarsely, "is that damned car mended yet?"

"Just this moment, sir. I have been working on it assiduously."

"Then, for heaven's sake, let's go!"

"But I understood that you were to address the young ladies, sir."

"Oh, I've done that!" responded Mr. Wooster, blinking twice with extraordinary rapidity. "Yes, I've done that."

"It was a success, I hope, sir?"

"Oh, yes. Oh, yes. Most extraordinarily successful. Went like a breeze. But—er—I think I may as well be going. No use outstaying one's welcome, what?"

"Assuredly not, sir."

I had climbed into my seat and was about to start the engine, when voices made themselves heard; and at the first sound of them Mr. Wooster sprang with almost incredible nimbleness into the tonneau, and when I glanced round he was on the floor covering himself with a rug. The last I saw of him was a pleading eye.

"Have you seen Mr. Wooster, my man?"

Miss Tomlinson had entered the stable-yard, accompanied by a lady of, I should say, judging from her accent, French origin.

"No, madam."

The French lady uttered some exclamation in her native tongue.

"Is anything wrong, madam?" I enquired.

Miss Tomlinson in normal mood was, I should be disposed to imagine, a lady who would not readily confide her troubles to the ear of a gentleman's gentleman, however sympathetic his aspect. That she did so now was sufficient indication of the depth to which she was stirred.

"Yes, there is! Mademoiselle has just found several of the girls smoking cigarettes in the shrubbery. When questioned, they stated that Mr. Wooster had given them the horrid things." She turned. "He must be in the garden somewhere, or in the house. I think the man is out of his senses. Come, mademoiselle!"

It must have been about a minute later that Mr. Wooster poked his head out of the rug like a tortoise.

"Jeeves!"

"Sir?"

"Get a move on! Start her up! Get going and *keep* going!"

I applied my foot to the self-starter.

"It would perhaps be safest to drive carefully until we are out of the school grounds, sir," I said. "I might run over one of the young ladies, sir."

"Well, what's the objection to that?" demanded Mr. Wooster with extraordinary bitterness.

"Or even Miss Tomlinson, sir."

"Don't!" said Mr. Wooster wistfully. "You make my mouth water!"

"Jeeves," said Mr. Wooster, when I brought him his whisky and siphon one night about a week later, "this is dashed jolly."

"Sir?"

"Jolly. Cosy and pleasant, you know. I mean, looking at the clock and wondering if you're going to be late with the good old drinks, and then you coming in with the tray always exactly on time, never a minute late, and shoving it down on the table and biffing off, and the next night coming in and shoving it down and biffing off, and the next night—I mean, gives you a sort of safe, restful feeling. Soothing! That's the word. Soothing!"

"Yes, sir. Oh, by the way, sir—"

"Well?"

"Have you succeeded in finding a suitable house yet, sir?"

"House? What do you mean, house?"

"I understood, sir, that it was your intention to give up the flat and take a house of sufficient size to enable you to have your sister, Mrs. Scholfield, and her three young ladies to live with you."

Mr. Wooster shuddered strongly.

"That's off, Jeeves," he said.
"Very good, sir," I replied.